Blaise Pascal's *Pensées*

Printed in the United States of America

ISBN:9781631741296

INTRODUCTION

It might seem that about Blaise Pascal, and about the two works on which his fame is founded, everything that there is to say had been said. The details of his life are as fully known as we can expect to know them; his mathematical and physical discoveries have been treated many times; his religious sentiment and his theological views have been discussed again and again; and his prose style has been analysed by French critics down to the finest particular. But Pascal is one of those writers who will be and who must be studied afresh by men in every generation. It is not he who changes, but we who change. It is not our knowledge of him that increases, but our world that alters and our attitudes towards it. The history of human opinions of Pascal and of men of his stature is a part of the history of humanity. That indicates his permanent importance.

The facts of Pascal's life, so far as they are necessary for this brief introduction to the Pensées, are as follows. He was born at Clermont, in Auvergne, in 1623. His family were people of substance of the upper middle class. His father was a government official, who was able to leave, when he died, a sufficient patrimony to his one son and his two daughters. In 1631 the father moved to Paris, and a few years later took up another government post at Rouen. Wherever he lived, the elder Pascal seems to have mingled with some of the best society, and with men of eminence in science and the arts. Blaise was educated entirely by his father at home. He was exceedingly precocious, indeed excessively precocious, for his application to studies in childhood and adolescence impaired his health, and is held responsible for his death at thirty-nine. Prodigious, though not incredible stories are preserved, especially of his precocity in mathematics. His mind was active rather than accumulative; he showed from his earliest years that disposition to find things out for himself, which has characterised the infancy[Pg viii] of Clerk-Maxwell and other scientists. Of his later discoveries in physics there is no need for mention here; it must only be remembered that he counts as one of the greatest physicists and mathematicians of all time; and that his discoveries were made during the years when most scientists are still apprentices.

The elder Pascal, Étienne, was a sincere Christian. About 1646 he fell in with some representatives of the religious revival within the Church which has become known as Jansenism—after Jansenius,

Bishop of Ypres, whose theological work is taken as the origin of the movement. This period is usually spoken of as the moment of Pascal's "first conversion." The word "conversion," however, is too forcible to be applied at this point to Blaise Pascal himself. The family had always been devout, and the younger Pascal, though absorbed in his scientific work, never seems to have been afflicted with infidelity. His attention was then directed, certainly, to religious and theological matters; but the term "conversion" can only be applied to his sisters —the elder, already Madame Périer, and particularly the younger, Jacqueline, who at that time conceived a vocation for the religious life. Pascal himself was by no means disposed to renounce the world. After the death of the father in 1650 Jacqueline, a young woman of remarkable strength and beauty of character, wished to take her vows as a sister of Port-Royal, and for some time her wish remained unfulfilled owing to the opposition of her brother. His objection was on the purely worldly ground that she wished to make over her patrimony to the Order; whereas while she lived with him, their combined resources made it possible for him to live more nearly on a scale of expense congenial to his tastes. He liked, in fact, not only to mix with the best society, but to keep a coach and horses—six horses is the number at one time attributed to his carriage. Though he had no legal power to prevent his sister from disposing of her property as she elected, the amiable Jacqueline shrank from doing so without her brother's willing approval. The Mother Superior, Mère Angélique—herself an eminent personage in the history of this religious movement—finally persuaded the young novice to enter the order without the satisfaction of bringing her patrimony with her; but Jacqueline remained so distressed by this situation that her brother finally relented.

So far as is known, the worldly life enjoyed by Pascal during[Pg ix] this period can hardly be qualified as "dissipation," and certainly not as "debauchery." Even gambling may have appealed to him chiefly as affording a study of mathematical probabilities. He appears to have led such a life as any cultivated intellectual man of good position and independent means might lead and consider himself a model of probity and virtue. Not even a love-affair is laid at his door, though he is said to have contemplated marriage. But Jansenism, as represented by the religious society of Port-Royal, was morally a Puritan movement within the Church, and its standards of conduct were at least as severe as those of any Puritanism in England or America. The period of fashionable society, in Pascal's life, is however, of great importance in his development. It enlarged his knowledge of men and refined his tastes; he became a man of the world and never lost what he had learnt; and when he turned his thoughts wholly towards religion, his worldly knowledge was a part of his composition which is essential to the value of his work.

Pascal's interest in society did not distract him from scientific research; nor did this period occupy much space in what is a very short and crowded life. Partly his natural dissatisfaction with such a life, once he had learned all it had to teach him, partly the influence of his saintly sister Jacqueline, partly increasing suffering as his health declined, directed him more and more out of the world and to thoughts of eternity. And in 1654 occurs what is called his "second conversion," but which might be called his conversion simply.

He made a note of his mystical experience, which he kept always about him, and which was found, after his death, sewn into the coat which he was wearing. The experience occurred on 23 November, 1654, and there is no reason to doubt its genuineness unless we choose to deny all mystical experience. Now, Pascal was not a mystic, and his works are not to be classified amongst mystical writings; but what can only be called mystical experience happens to many men who do not become mystics. The work which he undertook soon after, the Lettres écrites à un provincial, is a masterpiece of religious controversy at the opposite pole from mysticism. We know quite well that he was at the time when he received his illumination from God in extremely poor health; but it is a commonplace that some forms of illness are extremely favourable, not only to religious illumination, but to artistic[Pg x] and literary composition. A piece of writing meditated, apparently without progress, for months or years, may suddenly take shape and word; and in this state long passages may be produced which require little or no retouch. I have no good word to say for the cultivation of automatic writing as the model of literary composition; I doubt whether these moments can be cultivated by the writer; but he to whom this happens assuredly has the sensation of being a vehicle rather than a maker. No masterpiece can be produced whole by such means; but neither does even the higher form of religious inspiration suffice for the religious life; even the most exalted mystic must return to the world, and use his reason to employ the results of his experience in daily life. You may call it communion with the Divine, or you may call it a temporary crystallisation of the mind. Until science can teach us to reproduce such phenomena at will, science cannot claim to have explained them; and they can be judged only by their fruits.

From that time until his death, Pascal was closely associated with the society of Port-Royal which his sister Jacqueline, who predeceased him, had joined as a religieuse; the society was then fighting for its life against the Jesuits. Five propositions, judged by a committee of cardinals and theologians at Rome to be heretical, were found to be put forward in the work of Jansenius; and the society of Port-Royal, the representative of Jansenism among devotional communities, suffered a blow from which it never revived. It is not the place here to review the bitter controversy and conflict; the best account, from the point of view of a critic of genius who took no side, who was neither Jansenist nor Jesuit, Christian nor infidel, is that in the great book of Sainte-Beuve, Port-Royal. And in this book the parts devoted to Pascal himself are among the most brilliant pages of criticism that Sainte-Beuve ever wrote. It is sufficient to notice that the next occupation of Pascal, after his conversion, was to write these eighteen "Letters," which as prose are of capital importance in the foundation of French classical style, and which as polemic are surpassed by none, not by Demosthenes, or Cicero, or Swift. They have the limitation of all polemic and forensic: they persuade, they seduce, they are unfair. But it is also unfair to assert that, in these Letters to a Provincial, Pascal was attacking the Society of Jesus in itself. He was[Pg xi] attacking rather a particular school of casuistry which relaxed the requirements of the Confessional; a school which certainly flourished amongst the Society of Jesus at that time, and of which the Spaniards Escobar and Molina are the most eminent authorities. He undoubtedly abused the art of quotation, as a polemical writer can hardly help but do; but there were abuses for him to abuse; and he did the job thoroughly. His Letters must not be called theology. Academic theology was not a department in which Pascal was versed; when necessary, the fathers of Port-Royal came to his aid. The Letters are the work of one of the finest mathematical minds of any time, and of a man of the world who addressed, not theologians, but the world in general—all of the cultivated and many of the less cultivated of the French laity; and with this public they made an astonishing success.

During this time Pascal never wholly abandoned his scientific interests. Though in his religious writings he composed slowly and painfully, and revised often, in matters of mathematics his mind seemed to move with consummate natural ease and grace. Discoveries and inventions sprang from his brain without effort; among the minor devices of this later period, the first omnibus service in Paris is said to owe its origin to his inventiveness. But rapidly failing health, and absorption in the great work he had in mind, left him little time and energy during the last two years of his life.

The plan of what we call the Pensées formed itself about 1660. The completed book was to have been a carefully constructed defence of Christianity, a true Apology and a kind of Grammar of Assent, setting forth the reasons which will convince the intellect. As I have indicated before, Pascal was not a theologian, and on dogmatic theology had recourse to his spiritual advisers. Nor was he indeed a systematic philosopher. He was a man with an immense genius for science, and at the same time a natural psychologist and moralist. As he was a great literary artist, his book would have been also his own spiritual autobiography; his style, free from all diminishing idiosyncrasies, was yet very personal. Above all, he was a man of strong passions; and his intellectual passion for truth was reinforced by his passionate dissatisfaction with human life unless a spiritual explanation could be found.[Pg xii]

We must regard the Pensées as merely the first notes for a work which he left far from completion; we have, in Sainte-Beuve's words, a tower of which the stones have been laid on each other, but not cemented, and the structure unfinished. In early years his memory had been amazingly retentive of anything that he wished to remember; and had it not been impaired by increasing illness and pain, he probably would not have been obliged to set down these notes at all. But taking the book as it is left to us, we still find that it occupies a unique place in the history of French literature and in the history of religious meditation.

To understand the method which Pascal employs, the reader must be prepared to follow the process of the mind of the intelligent believer. The Christian thinker—and I mean the man who is trying consciously and conscientiously to explain to himself the sequence which culminated in faith, rather than the public apologist—proceeds by rejection and elimination. He finds the world to be so and so; he finds its character inexplicable by any non-religious theory; among religions he finds Christianity, and Catholic Christianity, to account most satisfactorily for the world and especially for the moral world within; and thus, by what Newman calls "powerful and concurrent" reasons, he finds himself inexorably committed to the dogma of the Incarnation. To the unbeliever, this method seems disingenuous and perverse; for the unbeliever is, as a rule, not so greatly troubled to explain the world to himself, nor so greatly distressed by its disorder; nor is he generally concerned (in modern terms) to "preserve values." He does not consider that if certain emotional states, certain developments of character, and what in the highest sense can be called "saintliness" are inherently and by inspection known to be good, then the satisfactory explanation of the world must be an explanation which will admit the "reality" of these values. Nor does he consider such reasoning admissible; he would, so to speak, trim his values according to his cloth, because to him such values are of no great value. The unbeliever starts from the other end, and as likely as not with the question: Is a case of human parthenogenesis credible? and this he would call going straight to the heart of the matter. Now Pascal's method is, on the whole, the method natural and right for the Christian; and the opposite method is that taken by Voltaire. It is worth[Pg xiii] while to remember that Voltaire, in his attempt to refute Pascal, has given once and for all the type of such refutation; and that later opponents of Pascal's Apology for the Christian Faith have contributed little beyond psychological irrelevancies. For Voltaire has presented, better than any one since, what is the unbelieving point of view; and in the end we must all choose for ourselves between one point of view and another.

I have said above that Pascal's method is "on the whole" that of the typical Christian apologist; and this reservation was directed at Pascal's belief in miracles, which plays a larger part in his construction than it would in that, at least, of the modern liberal Catholic. It would seem fantastic to accept Christianity because we first believe the Gospel miracles to be true, and it would seem impious to accept it primarily because we believe more recent miracles to be true; we accept the miracles, or some miracles, to be true because we believe the Gospel of Jesus Christ: we found our belief in the miracles on the Gospel, not our belief in the Gospel on the miracles. But it must be remembered that Pascal had been deeply impressed by a contemporary miracle, known as the miracle of the Holy Thorn: a thorn reputed to have been preserved from the Crown of Our Lord was pressed upon an ulcer which quickly healed. Sainte-Beuve, who as a medical man felt himself on solid ground, discusses fully the possible explanation of this apparent miracle. It is true that the miracle happened at Port-Royal, and that it arrived opportunely to revive the depressed spirits of the community in its political afflictions; and it is likely that Pascal was the more inclined to believe a miracle which was performed upon his beloved sister. In any case, it probably led him to assign a place to miracles, in his study of faith, which is not quite that which we should give to them ourselves.

Now the great adversary against whom Pascal set himself, from the time of his first conversations with M. de Saci at Port-Royal, was Montaigne. One cannot destroy Pascal, certainly; but of all authors Montaigne is one of the least destructible. You could as well dissipate a fog by flinging hand-grenades into it. For Montaigne is a fog, a gas, a fluid, insidious element. He does not reason, he insinuates, charms, and influences; or if he reasons, you must be prepared for his having some other design upon you than to convince you by[Pg xiv] his argument. It is hardly too much to say that Montaigne is the most essential author to know, if we would understand the course of French thought during the last three hundred years. In every way, the influence of Montaigne was repugnant to the men of Port-Royal. Pascal studied him with the intention of demolishing him. Yet, in the Pensées, at the very end of his life, we find passage after passage, and the slighter they are the more significant, almost "lifted" out of Montaigne, down to a figure of speech or a word. The parallels[A] are most often with the long essay of Montaigne called Apologie de Raymond Sébond—an astonishing piece of writing upon which Shakespeare also probably drew in Hamlet. Indeed, by the time a man knew Montaigne well enough to attack him, he would already be thoroughly infected by him.

It would, however, be grossly unfair to Pascal, to Montaigne, and indeed to French literature, to leave the matter at that. It is no diminution of Pascal, but only an aggrandisement of Montaigne. Had Montaigne been an ordinary life-sized sceptic, a small man like Anatole France, or even a greater man like Renan, or even like the greatest sceptic of all, Voltaire, this "influence" would be to the discredit of Pascal; but if Montaigne had been no more than Voltaire, he could not have affected Pascal at all. The picture of Montaigne which offers itself first to our eyes, that of the original and independent solitary "personality," absorbed in amused analysis of himself, is deceptive. Montaigne's is no limited Pyrrhonism, like that of Voltaire, Renan, or France. He exists, so to speak, on a plan of numerous concentric circles, the most apparent of which is the small inmost circle, a personal puckish scepticism which can be easily aped if not imitated. But what makes Montaigne a very great figure is that he succeeded, God knows how—for Montaigne very likely did not know that he had done it—it is not the sort of thing that men can observe about themselves, for it is essentially bigger than the individual's consciousness—he succeeded in giving[Pg xv] expression to the scepticism of every human being. For every man who thinks and lives by thought must have his own scepticism, that which stops at the question, that which ends in denial, or that which leads to faith and which is somehow integrated into the faith which transcends it. And Pascal, as the type of one kind of religious believer, which is highly passionate and ardent, but passionate only through a powerful and regulated intellect, is in the first sections of his unfinished Apology for Christianity facing unflinchingly the demon of doubt which is inseparable from the spirit of belief.

There is accordingly something quite different from an influence which would prove Pascal's weakness; there is a real affinity between his doubt and that of Montaigne; and through the common kinship with Montaigne Pascal is related to the noble and distinguished line of French moralists, from La Rochefoucauld down. In the honesty with which they face the données of the actual world this French tradition has a unique quality in European literature, and in the seventeenth century Hobbes is crude and uncivilised in comparison.

Pascal is a man of the world among ascetics, and an ascetic among men of the world; he had the knowledge of worldliness and the passion of asceticism, and in him the two are fused into an individual whole. The majority of mankind is lazy-minded, incurious, absorbed in vanities, and tepid in emotion, and is therefore incapable of either much doubt or much faith; and when the ordinary man calls himself a sceptic or an unbeliever, that is ordinarily a simple pose, cloaking a disinclination to think anything out to a conclusion. Pascal's disillusioned analysis of human bondage is sometimes interpreted to mean that Pascal was really and finally an unbeliever, who, in his despair, was incapable of enduring reality and enjoying the heroic satisfaction of the free man's worship of nothing. His despair, his disillusion, are, however, no illustration of personal weakness; they are perfectly objective, because they are essential moments in the progress of the intellectual soul; and for the type of Pascal they are the analogue of the drought, the dark night, which is an essential stage in the progress of the Christian mystic. A similar despair, when it is arrived at by a diseased character or an impure soul, may issue in the most disastrous consequences though with the most superb manifestations; and[Pg xvi] thus we get Gulliver's Travels; but in Pascal we find no such distortion; his despair is in itself more terrible than Swift's, because our heart tells us that it corresponds exactly to the facts and cannot be dismissed as mental disease; but it was also a despair which was a necessary prelude to, and element in, the joy of faith.

I do not wish to enter any further than necessary upon the question of the heterodoxy of Jansenism; and it is no concern of this essay, whether the Five Propositions condemned at Rome were really maintained by Jansenius in his book Augustinus; or whether we should deplore or approve the consequent decay (indeed with some persecution) of Port-Royal. It is impossible to discuss the matter without becoming involved as a controversialist either for or against Rome. But in a man of the type of Pascal—and the type always exists—there is, I think, an ingredient of what may be called Jansenism of temperament, without identifying it with the Jansenism of Jansenius and of other devout and sincere, but not immensely gifted doctors. [B] It is accordingly needful to state in brief what the dangerous doctrine of Jansenius was, without advancing too far into theological refinements. It is recognised in Christian theology—and indeed on a lower plane it is recognised by all men in affairs of daily life—that freewill or the natural effort and ability of the individual man, and also supernatural grace, a gift accorded we know not quite how, are both required, in co-operation, for salvation. Though numerous theologians have set their wits at the problem, it ends in a mystery which we can perceive but not finally decipher. At least, it is obvious that, like any doctrine, a slight excess or deviation to one side or the other will precipitate a heresy. The Pelagians, who were refuted by St. Augustine, emphasised the efficacy of human effort and belittled the importance of supernatural grace. The Calvinists emphasised the degradation of man through Original Sin, and considered mankind so corrupt that the will was of no avail; and thus fell into the doctrine of predestination. It was upon the doctrine of grace according to St. Augustine that the Jansenists relied; and the Augustinus of Jansenius was presented as a sound exposition of the Augustinian views.

[Pg xvii]Such heresies are never antiquated, because they forever assume new forms. For instance, the insistence upon good works and "service" which is preached from many quarters, or the simple faith that any one who lives a good and useful life need have no "morbid" anxieties about salvation, is a form of Pelagianism. On the other hand, one sometimes hears enounced the view that it will make no real difference if all the traditional religious sanctions for moral behaviour break down, because those who are born and bred to be nice people will always prefer to behave nicely, and those who are not will behave otherwise in any case: and this is surely a form of predestination—for the hazard of being born a nice person or not is as uncertain as the gift of grace.

It is likely that Pascal was attracted as much by the fruits of Jansenism in the life of Port-Royal as by the doctrine itself. This devout, ascetic, thoroughgoing society, striving heroically in the midst of a relaxed and easy-going Christianity, was formed to attract a nature so concentrated, so passionate, and so thoroughgoing as Pascal's. But the insistence upon the degraded and helpless state of man, in Jansenism, is something also to which we must be grateful, for to it we owe the magnificent analysis of human motives and occupations which was to have constituted the early part of his book. And apart from the Jansenism which is the work of a not very eminent bishop who wrote a Latin treatise which is now unread, there is also, so to speak, a Jansenism of the individual biography. A moment of Jansenism may naturally take place, and take place rightly, in the individual; particularly in the life of a man of great and intense intellectual powers, who cannot avoid seeing through human beings and observing the vanity of their thoughts and of their avocations, their dishonesty and self-deceptions, the insincerity of their emotions, their cowardice, the pettiness of their real ambitions. Actually, considering that Pascal died at the age of thirty-nine, one must be amazed at the balance and justice of his observations; much greater maturity is required for these qualities, than for any mathematical or scientific greatness. How easily his brooding on the misery of man without God might have encouraged in him the sin of spiritual pride, the concupiscence de l'esprit, and how fast a hold he has of humility!

And although Pascal brings to his work the same powers which he exerted in science, it is not as a scientist that he[Pg xviii] presents himself. He does not seem to say to the reader: I am one of the most distinguished scientists of the day; I understand many matters which will always be mysteries to you, and through science I have come to the Faith; you therefore who are not initiated into science ought to have faith if I have it. He is fully aware of the difference of subject-matter; and his famous distinction between the esprit de géométrie and the esprit de finesse is one to ponder over. It is the just combination of the scientist, the honnête homme, and the religious nature with a passionate craving for God, that makes Pascal unique. He succeeds where Descartes fails; for in Descartes the element of esprit de géométrie is excessive.[C] And in a few phrases about Descartes, in the present book, Pascal laid his finger on the place of weakness.

He who reads this book will observe at once its fragmentary nature; but only after some study will perceive that the fragmentariness lies in the expression more than in the thought. The "thoughts" cannot be detached from each other and quoted as if each were complete in itself. Le cœur a ses raisons que la raison ne connaît point: how often one has heard that quoted, and quoted often to the wrong purpose! For this is by no means an exaltation of the "heart" over the "head," a defence of unreason. The heart, in Pascal's terminology, is itself truly rational if it is truly the heart. For him, in theological matters, which seemed to him much larger, more difficult, and more important than scientific matters, the whole personality is involved.

We cannot quite understand any of the parts, fragmentary as they are, without some understanding of the whole. Capital, for instance, is his analysis of the three orders: the order of nature, the order of mind, and the order of charity. These three are discontinuous; the higher is not implicit in the lower as in an evolutionary doctrine it would be. [D] In this distinction Pascal offers much about which the modern world would do well to think. And indeed, because of his unique combination and balance of qualities, I know of no religious writer more pertinent to our time. The great mystics like[Pg xix] St. John of the Cross, are primarily for readers with a special determination of purpose; the devotional writers, such as St. François de Sales, are primarily for those who already feel consciously desirous of the love of God; the great theologians are for those interested in theology. But I can think of no Christian writer, not Newman even, more to be commended than Pascal to those who doubt, but who have the mind to conceive, and the sensibility to feel, the disorder, the futility, the meaninglessness, the mystery of life and suffering, and who can only find peace through a satisfaction of the whole being.

T. S. Eliot.

Notes

[A] Cf. the use of the simile of the couvreur. For comparing parallel passages, the edition of the Pensées by Henri Massis (A la cité des livres) is better than the two-volume edition of Jacques Chevalier (Gabalda). It seems just possible that in the latter edition, and also in his biographical study (Pascal; by Jacques Chevalier, English translation, published by Sheed & Ward), M. Chevalier is a little over-zealous to demonstrate the perfect orthodoxy of Pascal.

[B] The great man of Port-Royal was of course Saint-Cyran, but any one who is interested will certainly consult, first of all, the book of Sainte-Beuve mentioned.

[C] For a brilliant criticism of the errors of Descartes from a theological point of view the reader is referred to Three Reformers by Jacques Maritain (translation published by Sheed & Ward).

[D] An important modern theory of discontinuity, suggested partly by Pascal, is sketched in the collected fragments of Speculations by T. E. Hulme (Kegan Paul).

[Pg xxi]

NOTE

Passages erased by Pascal are enclosed in square brackets, thus []. Words, added or corrected by the editor of the text, are similarly denoted, but are in italics.

It has been seen fit to transfer Fragment 514 of the French edition to the Notes. All subsequent Fragments have accordingly been renumbered.

[Pg 1]

SECTION I

THOUGHTS ON MIND AND ON STYLE

1

The difference between the mathematical and the intuitive mind.[1] —In the one the principles are palpable, but removed from ordinary use; so that for want of habit it is difficult to turn one's mind in that direction: but if one turns it thither ever so little, one sees the principles fully, and one must have a quite inaccurate mind who reasons wrongly from principles so plain that it is almost impossible they should escape notice.

But in the intuitive mind the principles are found in common use, and are before the eyes of everybody. One has only to look, and no effort is necessary; it is only a question of good eyesight, but it must be good, for the principles are so subtle and so numerous, that it is almost impossible but that some escape notice. Now the omission of one principle leads to error; thus one must have very clear sight to see all the principles, and in the next place an accurate mind not to draw false deductions from known principles.

All mathematicians would then be intuitive if they had clear sight, for they do not reason incorrectly from principles known to them; and intuitive minds would be mathematical if they could turn their eyes to the principles of mathematics to which they are unused.

The reason, therefore, that some intuitive minds are not mathematical is that they cannot at all turn their attention to the principles of mathematics. But the reason that mathematicians are not intuitive is that they do not see what is before them, and that, accustomed to the exact and plain principles of mathematics, and not reasoning till they have well inspected and arranged their principles, they are lost in matters of intuition where the principles do not allow of such arrangement. They are scarcely seen; they are felt rather than seen; there is the greatest difficulty in making them felt by those[Pg 2] who do not of themselves perceive them. These principles are so fine and so numerous that a very delicate and very clear sense is needed to perceive them, and to judge rightly and justly when they are perceived, without for the most part being able to demonstrate them in order as in mathematics; because the principles are not known to us in the same way, and because it would be an endless matter to undertake it. We must see the matter at once, at one glance, and not by a process of reasoning, at least to a certain degree. And thus it is rare that mathematicians are intuitive, and that men of intuition are mathematicians, because mathematicians wish to treat matters of intuition mathematically, and make themselves ridiculous, wishing to begin with definitions and then with axioms, which is not the way to proceed in this kind of reasoning. Not that the mind does not do so, but it does it tacitly, naturally, and without technical rules; for the expression of it is beyond all men, and only a few can feel it.

Intuitive minds, on the contrary, being thus accustomed to judge at a single glance, are so astonished when they are presented with propositions of which they understand nothing, and the way to which is through definitions and axioms so sterile, and which they are not accustomed to see thus in detail, that they are repelled and disheartened.

But dull minds are never either intuitive or mathematical.

Mathematicians who are only mathematicians have exact minds, provided all things are explained to them by means of definitions and axioms; otherwise they are inaccurate and insufferable, for they are only right when the principles are quite clear.

And men of intuition who are only intuitive cannot have the patience to reach to first principles of things speculative and conceptual, which they have never seen in the world, and which are altogether out of the common.

2

There are different kinds of right understanding;[2] some have right understanding in a certain order of things, and not in others, where they go astray. Some draw conclusions well from a few premises, and this displays an acute judgment.

Others draw conclusions well where there are many premises.

For example, the former easily learn hydrostatics, where the[Pg 3] premises are few, but the conclusions are so fine that only the greatest acuteness can reach them.

And in spite of that these persons would perhaps not be great mathematicians, because mathematics contain a great number of premises, and there is perhaps a kind of intellect that can search with ease a few premises to the bottom, and cannot in the least penetrate those matters in which there are many premises.

There are then two kinds of intellect: the one able to penetrate acutely and deeply into the conclusions of given premises, and this is the precise intellect; the other able to comprehend a great number of premises without confusing them, and this is the mathematical intellect. The one has force and exactness, the other comprehension. Now the one quality can exist without the other; the intellect can be strong and narrow, and can also be comprehensive and weak.

3

Those who are accustomed to judge by feeling do not understand the process of reasoning, for they would understand at first sight, and are not used to seek for principles. And others, on the contrary, who are accustomed to reason from principles, do not at all understand matters of feeling, seeking principles, and being unable to see at a glance.

4

Mathematics, intuition.—True eloquence makes light of eloquence, true morality makes light of morality; that is to say, the morality of the judgment, which has no rules, makes light of the morality of the intellect.

For it is to judgment that perception belongs, as science belongs to intellect. Intuition is the part of judgment, mathematics of intellect.

To make light of philosophy is to be a true philosopher.

5

Those who judge of a work by rule[3] are in regard to others as those who have a watch are in regard to others. One says, "It is two hours ago"; the other says, "It is only three-quarters of an hour." I look at my watch, and say to the one, "You are weary," and to the other, "Time gallops with you"; for it[Pg 4] is only an hour and a half ago, and I laugh at those who tell me that time goes slowly with me, and that I judge by imagination. They do not know that I judge by my watch.[4]

6

Just as we harm the understanding, we harm the feelings also.

The understanding and the feelings are moulded by intercourse; the understanding and feelings are corrupted by intercourse. Thus good or bad society improves or corrupts them. It is, then, all-important to know how to choose in order to improve and not to corrupt them; and we cannot make this choice, if they be not already improved and not corrupted. Thus a circle is formed, and those are fortunate who escape it.

7

The greater intellect one has, the more originality one finds in men. Ordinary persons find no difference between men.

8

There are many people who listen to a sermon in the same way as they listen to vespers.

9

When we wish to correct with advantage, and to show another that he errs, we must notice from what side he views the matter, for on that side it is usually true, and admit that truth to him, but reveal to him the side on which it is false. He is satisfied with that, for he sees that he was not mistaken, and that he only failed to see all sides. Now, no one is offended at not seeing everything; but one does not like to be mistaken, and that perhaps arises from the fact that man naturally cannot see everything, and that naturally he cannot err in the side he looks at, since the perceptions of our senses are always true.

10

People are generally better persuaded by the reasons which they have themselves discovered than by those which have come into the mind of others.

11

All great amusements are dangerous to the Christian life; but among all those which the world has invented there is none[Pg 5] more to be feared than the theatre. It is a representation of the passions so natural and so delicate that it excites them and gives birth to them in our hearts, and, above all, to that of love, principally when it is represented as very chaste and virtuous. For the more innocent it appears to innocent souls, the more they are likely to be touched by it. Its violence pleases our self-love, which immediately forms a desire to produce the same effects which are seen so well represented; and, at the same time, we make ourselves a conscience founded on the propriety of the feelings which we see there, by which the fear of pure souls is removed, since they imagine that it cannot hurt their purity to love with a love which seems to them so reasonable.

So we depart from the theatre with our heart so filled with all the beauty and tenderness of love, the soul and the mind so persuaded of its innocence, that we are quite ready to receive its first impressions, or rather to seek an opportunity of awakening them in the heart of another, in order that we may receive the same pleasures and the same sacrifices which we have seen so well represented in the theatre.

12

Scaramouch,[5] who only thinks of one thing.

The doctor,[6] who speaks for a quarter of an hour after he has said everything, so full is he of the desire of talking.

13

One likes to see the error, the passion of Cleobuline,[7] because she is unconscious of it. She would be displeasing, if she were not deceived.

14

When a natural discourse paints a passion or an effect, one feels within oneself the truth of what one reads, which was there before, although one did not know it. Hence one is inclined to love him who makes us feel it, for he has not shown us his own riches, but ours. And thus this benefit renders him pleasing to us, besides that such community of intellect as we have with him necessarily inclines the heart to love.

15

Eloquence, which persuades by sweetness, not by authority; as a tyrant, not as a king.[Pg 6]

16

Eloquence is an art of saying things in such a way—(1) that those to whom we speak may listen to them without pain and with pleasure; (2) that they feel themselves interested, so that self-love leads them more willingly to reflection upon it.

It consists, then, in a correspondence which we seek to establish between the head and the heart of those to whom we speak on the one hand, and, on the other, between the thoughts and the expressions which we employ. This assumes that we have studied well the heart of man so as to know all its powers, and then to find the just proportions of the discourse which we wish to adapt to them. We must put ourselves in the place of those who are to hear us, and make trial on our own heart of the turn which we give to our discourse in order to see whether one is made for the other, and whether we can assure ourselves that the hearer will be, as it were, forced to surrender. We ought to restrict ourselves, so far as possible, to the simple and natural, and not to magnify that which is little, or belittle that which is great. It is not enough that a thing be beautiful; it must be suitable to the subject, and there must be in it nothing of excess or defect.

17

Rivers are roads which move,[8] and which carry us whither we desire to go.

18

When we do not know the truth of a thing, it is of advantage that there should exist a common error which determines the mind of man, as, for example, the moon, to which is attributed the change of seasons, the progress of diseases, etc. For the chief malady of man is restless curiosity about things which he cannot understand; and it is not so bad for him to be in error as to be curious to no purpose.

The manner in which Epictetus, Montaigne, and Salomon de Tultie[9] wrote, is the most usual, the most suggestive, the most remembered, and the oftenest quoted; because it is entirely composed of thoughts born from the common talk of life. As when we speak of the common error which exists among men that the moon is the cause of everything, we never fail to say that Salomon de Tultie says that when we do not know the[Pg 7] truth of a thing, it is of advantage that there should exist a common error, etc.; which is the thought above.

19

The last thing one settles in writing a book is what one should put in first.

20

Order.—Why should I undertake to divide my virtues into four rather than into six? Why should I rather establish virtue in four, in two, in one? Why into Abstine et sustine[10] rather than into "Follow Nature,"[11] or, "Conduct your private affairs without injustice," as Plato,[12] or anything else? But there, you will say, everything is contained in one word. Yes, but it is useless without explanation, and when we come to explain it, as soon as we unfold this maxim which contains all the rest, they emerge in that first confusion which you desired to avoid. So, when they are all included in one, they are hidden and useless, as in a chest, and never appear save in their natural confusion. Nature has established them all without including one in the other.

21

Nature has made all her truths independent of one another. Our art makes one dependent on the other. But this is not natural. Each keeps its own place.

22

Let no one say that I have said nothing new; the arrangement of the subject is new. When we play tennis, we both play with the same ball, but one of us places it better.

I had as soon it said that I used words employed before. And in the same way if the same thoughts in a different arrangement do not form a different discourse, no more do the same words in their different arrangement form different thoughts!

23

Words differently arranged have a different meaning, and meanings differently arranged have different effects.

24

Language.—We should not turn the mind from one thing to another, except for relaxation, and that when it is necessary[Pg 8] and the time suitable, and not otherwise. For he that relaxes out of season wearies, and he who wearies us out of season makes us languid, since we turn quite away. So much does our perverse lust like to do the contrary of what those wish to obtain from us without giving us pleasure, the coin for which we will do whatever is wanted.

25

Eloquence.—It requires the pleasant and the real; but the pleasant must itself be drawn from the true.

26

Eloquence is a painting of thought; and thus those who, after having painted it, add something more, make a picture instead of a portrait.

27

Miscellaneous. Language.—Those who make antitheses by forcing words are like those who make false windows for symmetry. Their rule is not to speak accurately, but to make apt figures of speech.

28

Symmetry is what we see at a glance; based on the fact that there is no reason for any difference, and based also on the face of man; whence it happens that symmetry is only wanted in breadth, not in height or depth.

29

When we see a natural style, we are astonished and delighted; for we expected to see an author, and we find a man. Whereas those who have good taste, and who seeing a book expect to find a man, are quite surprised to find an author. Plus poetice quam humane locutus es. Those honour Nature well, who teach that she can speak on everything, even on theology.

30

We only consult the ear because the heart is wanting. The rule is uprightness.

Beauty of omission, of judgment.[Pg 9]

31

All the false beauties which we blame in Cicero have their admirers, and in great number.

32

There is a certain standard of grace and beauty which consists in a certain relation between our nature, such as it is, weak or strong, and the thing which pleases us.

Whatever is formed according to this standard pleases us, be it house, song, discourse, verse, prose, woman, birds, rivers, trees, rooms, dress, etc. Whatever is not made according to this standard displeases those who have good taste.

And as there is a perfect relation between a song and a house which are made after a good model, because they are like this good model, though each after its kind; even so there is a perfect relation between things made after a bad model. Not that the bad model is unique, for there are many; but each bad sonnet, for example, on whatever false model it is formed, is just like a woman dressed after that model.

Nothing makes us understand better the ridiculousness of a false sonnet than to consider nature and the standard, and then to imagine a woman or a house made according to that standard.

33

Poetical beauty.—As we speak of poetical beauty, so ought we to speak of mathematical beauty and medical beauty. But we do not do so; and the reason is that we know well what is the object of mathematics, and that it consists in proofs, and what is the object of medicine, and that it consists in healing. But we do not know in what grace consists, which is the object of poetry. We do not know the natural model which we ought to imitate; and through lack of this knowledge, we have coined fantastic terms, "The golden age," "The wonder of our times," "Fatal," etc., and call this jargon poetical beauty.[13]

But whoever imagines a woman after this model, which consists in saying little things in big words, will see a pretty girl adorned with mirrors and chains, at whom he will smile; because we know better wherein consists the charm of woman than the charm of verse. But those who are ignorant would admire her in this dress, and there are many villages in which she would be taken for the queen; hence we call sonnets made after this model "Village Queens."[Pg 10]

34

No one passes in the world as skilled in verse unless he has put up the sign of a poet, a mathematician, etc. But educated people do not want a sign, and draw little distinction between the trade of a poet and that of an embroiderer.

People of education are not called poets or mathematicians, etc.; but they are all these, and judges of all these. No one guesses what they are. When they come into society, they talk on matters about which the rest are talking. We do not observe in them one quality rather than another, save when they have to make use of it. But then we remember it, for it is characteristic of such persons that we do not say of them that they are fine speakers, when it is not a question of oratory, and that we say of them that they are fine speakers, when it is such a question.

It is therefore false praise to give a man when we say of him, on his entry, that he is a very clever poet; and it is a bad sign when a man is not asked to give his judgment on some verses.

35

We should not be able to say of a man, "He is a mathematician," or "a preacher," or "eloquent"; but that he is "a gentleman." That universal quality alone pleases me. It is a bad sign when, on seeing a person, you remember his book. I would prefer you to see no quality till you meet it and have occasion to use it (Ne quid nimis[14]), for fear some one quality prevail and designate the man. Let none think him a fine speaker, unless oratory be in question, and then let them think it.

36

Man is full of wants: he loves only those who can satisfy them all. "This one is a good mathematician," one will say. But I have nothing to do with mathematics; he would take me for a proposition. "That one is a good soldier." He would take me for a besieged town. I need, then, an upright man who can accommodate himself generally to all my wants.

37

[Since we cannot be universal and know all that is to be known of everything, we ought to know a little about everything. For it is far better to know something about everything[Pg 11] than to know all about one thing. This universality is the best. If we can have both, still better; but if we must choose, we ought to choose the former. And the world feels this and does so; for the world is often a good judge.]

38

A poet and not an honest man.

39

If lightning fell on low places, etc., poets, and those who can only reason about things of that kind, would lack proofs.

40

If we wished to prove the examples which we take to prove other things, we should have to take those other things to be examples; for, as we always believe the difficulty is in what we wish to prove, we find the examples clearer and a help to demonstration.

Thus when we wish to demonstrate a general theorem, we must give the rule as applied to a particular case; but if we wish to demonstrate a particular case, we must begin with the general rule. For we always find the thing obscure which we wish to prove, and that clear which we use for the proof; for, when a thing is put forward to be proved, we first fill ourselves with the imagination that it is therefore obscure, and on the contrary that what is to prove it is clear, and so we understand it easily.

41

Epigrams of Martial.—Man loves malice, but not against one-eyed men nor the unfortunate, but against the fortunate and proud. People are mistaken in thinking otherwise.

For lust is the source of all our actions, and humanity, etc. We must please those who have humane and tender feelings. That epigram about two one-eyed people is worthless,[15] for it does not console them, and only gives a point to the author's glory. All that is only for the sake of the author is worthless. Ambitiosa recident ornamenta.[16]

42

To call a king "Prince" is pleasing, because it diminishes his rank.[Pg 12]

43

Certain authors, speaking of their works, say, "My book," "My commentary," "My history," etc. They resemble middle-class people who have a house of their own, and always have "My house" on their tongue. They would do better to say, "Our book," "Our commentary," "Our history," etc., because there is in them usually more of other people's than their own.

44

Do you wish people to believe good of you? Don't speak.

45

Languages are ciphers, wherein letters are not changed into letters, but words into words, so that an unknown language is decipherable.

46

A maker of witticisms, a bad character.

47

There are some who speak well and write badly. For the place and the audience warm them, and draw from their minds more than they think of without that warmth.

48

When we find words repeated in a discourse, and, in trying to correct them, discover that they are so appropriate that we would spoil the discourse, we must leave them alone. This is the test; and our attempt is the work of envy, which is blind, and does not see that repetition is not in this place a fault; for there is no general rule.

49

To mask nature and disguise her. No more king, pope, bishop—but august monarch, etc.; not Paris—the capital of the kingdom. There are places in which we ought to call Paris, Paris, and others in which we ought to call it the capital of the kingdom.

50

The same meaning changes with the words which express it. Meanings receive their dignity from words instead of giving it to them. Examples should be sought....[Pg 13]

51

Sceptic, for obstinate.

52

No one calls another a Cartesian[17] but he who is one himself, a pedant but a pedant, a provincial but a provincial; and I would wager it was the printer who put it on the title of Letters to a Provincial.

53

A carriage upset or overturned, according to the meaning To spread abroad or upset, according to the meaning. (The argument by force of M. le Maître[18] over the friar.)

54

Miscellaneous.—A form of speech, "I should have liked to apply myself to that."

55

The aperitive virtue of a key, the attractive virtue of a hook.

56

To guess: "The part that I take in your trouble." The Cardinal[19] did not want to be guessed.

"My mind is disquieted." I am disquieted is better.

57

I always feel uncomfortable under such compliments as these: "I have given you a great deal of trouble," "I am afraid I am boring you," "I fear this is too long." We either carry our audience with us, or irritate them.

58

You are ungraceful: "Excuse me, pray." Without that excuse I would not have known there was anything amiss. "With reverence be it spoken...." The only thing bad is their excuse.

59

"To extinguish the torch of sedition"; too luxuriant. "The restlessness of his genius"; two superfluous grand words.

[Pg 14]

SECTION II

THE MISERY OF MAN WITHOUT GOD

60

First part: Misery of man without God.

Second part: Happiness of man with God.

Or, First part: That nature is corrupt. Proved by nature itself.

Second part: That there is a Redeemer. Proved by Scripture.

61

Order.—I might well have taken this discourse in an order like this: to show the vanity of all conditions of men, to show the vanity of ordinary lives, and then the vanity of philosophic lives, sceptics, stoics; but the order would not have been kept. I know a little what it is, and how few people understand it. No human science can keep it. Saint Thomas[20] did not keep it. Mathematics keep it, but they are useless on account of their depth.

62

Preface to the first part.—To speak of those who have treated of the knowledge of self; of the divisions of Charron,[21] which sadden and weary us; of the confusion of Montaigne;[22] that he was quite aware of his want of method, and shunned it by jumping from subject to subject; that he sought to be fashionable.

His foolish project of describing himself! And this not casually and against his maxims, since every one makes mistakes, but by his maxims themselves, and by first and chief design. For to say silly things by chance and weakness is a common misfortune; but to say them intentionally is intolerable, and to say such as that ...

63

Montaigne.—Montaigne's faults are great. Lewd words; this is bad, notwithstanding Mademoiselle de Gournay.[23] Credulous;[Pg 15] people without eyes.[24] Ignorant; squaring the circle,[25] a greater world.[26] His opinions on suicide, on death.[27] He suggests an indifference about salvation, without fear and without repentance.[28] As his book was not written with a religious purpose, he was not bound to mention religion; but it is always our duty not to turn men from it. One can excuse his rather free and licentious opinions on some relations of life (730,231)[29]; but one cannot excuse his thoroughly pagan views on death, for a man must renounce piety altogether, if he does not at least wish to die like a Christian. Now, through the whole of his book his only conception of death is a cowardly and effeminate one.

64

It is not in Montaigne, but in myself, that I find all that I see in him.

65

What good there is in Montaigne can only have been acquired with difficulty. The evil that is in him, I mean apart from his morality, could have been corrected in a moment, if he had been informed that he made too much of trifles and spoke too much of himself.

66

One must know oneself. If this does not serve to discover truth, it at least serves as a rule of life, and there is nothing better.

67

The vanity of the sciences.—Physical science will not console me for the ignorance of morality in the time of affliction. But the science of ethics will always console me for the ignorance of the physical sciences.

68

Men are never taught to be gentlemen, and are taught everything else; and they never plume themselves so much on the rest of their knowledge as on knowing how to be gentlemen. They only plume themselves on knowing the one thing they do not know.[Pg 16]

69

The infinites, the mean.—When we read too fast or too slowly, we understand nothing.

70

Nature ...—[Nature has set us so well in the centre, that if we change one side of the balance, we change the other also. I act. Τά ζῶα τρέχει This makes me believe that the springs in our brain are so adjusted that he who touches one touches also its contrary.]

71

Too much and too little wine. Give him none, he cannot find truth; give him too much, the same.

72

Man's disproportion.—[This is where our innate knowledge leads us. If it be not true, there is no truth in man; and if it be true, he finds therein great cause for humiliation, being compelled to abase himself in one way or another. And since he cannot exist without this knowledge, I wish that, before entering on deeper researches into nature, he would consider her both seriously and at leisure, that he would reflect upon himself also, and knowing what proportion there is ...] Let man then contemplate the whole of nature in her full and grand majesty, and turn his vision from the low objects which surround him. Let him gaze on that brilliant light, set like an eternal lamp to illumine the universe; let the earth appear to him a point in comparison with the vast circle described by the sun; and let him wonder at the fact that this vast circle is itself but a very fine point in comparison with that described by the stars in their revolution round the firmament. But if our view be arrested there, let our imagination pass beyond; it will sooner exhaust the power of conception than nature that of supplying material for conception. The whole visible world is only an imperceptible atom in the ample bosom of nature. No idea approaches it. We may enlarge our conceptions beyond all imaginable space; we only produce atoms in comparison with the reality of things. It is an infinite sphere, the centre of which is everywhere, the circumference nowhere.[30] In short it is the greatest sensible mark of the almighty power of God, that imagination loses itself in that thought.[Pg 17]

Returning to himself, let man consider what he is in comparison with all existence; let him regard himself as lost in this remote corner of nature; and from the little cell in which he finds himself lodged, I mean the universe, let him estimate at their true value the earth, kingdoms, cities, and himself. What is a man in the Infinite?

But to show him another prodigy equally astonishing, let him examine the most delicate things he knows. Let a mite be given him, with its minute body and parts incomparably more minute, limbs with their joints, veins in the limbs, blood in the veins, humours in the blood, drops in the humours, vapours in the drops. Dividing these last things again, let him exhaust his powers of conception, and let the last object at which he can arrive be now that of our discourse. Perhaps he will think that here is the smallest point in nature. I will let him see therein a new abyss. I will paint for him not only the visible universe, but all that he can conceive of nature's immensity in the womb of this abridged atom. Let him see therein an infinity of universes, each of which has its firmament, its planets, its earth, in the same proportion as in the visible world; in each earth animals, and in the last mites, in which he will find again all that the first had, finding still in these others the same thing without end and without cessation. Let him lose himself in wonders as amazing in their littleness as the others in their vastness. For who will not be astounded at the fact that our body, which a little while ago was imperceptible in the universe, itself imperceptible in the bosom of the whole, is now a colossus, a world, or rather a whole, in respect of the nothingness which we cannot reach? He who regards himself in this light will be afraid of himself, and observing himself sustained in the body given him by nature between those two abysses of the Infinite and Nothing, will tremble at the sight of these marvels; and I think that, as his curiosity changes into admiration, he will be more disposed to contemplate them in silence than to examine them with presumption.

For in fact what is man in nature? A Nothing in comparison with the Infinite, an All in comparison with the Nothing, a mean between nothing and everything. Since he is infinitely removed from comprehending the extremes, the end of things and their beginning are hopelessly hidden from him in an impenetrable secret, he is equally incapable of seeing the[Pg 18] Nothing from which he was made, and the Infinite in which he is swallowed up.

What will he do then, but perceive the appearance of the middle of things, in an eternal despair of knowing either their beginning or their end. All things proceed from the Nothing, and are borne towards the Infinite. Who will follow these marvellous processes? The Author of these wonders understands them. None other can do so.

Through failure to contemplate these Infinites, men have rashly rushed into the examination of nature, as though they bore some proportion to her. It is strange that they have wished to understand the beginnings of things, and thence to arrive at the knowledge of the whole, with a presumption as infinite as their object. For surely this design cannot be formed without presumption or without a capacity infinite like nature.

If we are well informed, we understand that, as nature has graven her image and that of her Author on all things, they almost all partake of her double infinity. Thus we see that all the sciences are infinite in the extent of their researches. For who doubts that geometry, for instance, has an infinite infinity of problems to solve? They are also infinite in the multitude and fineness of their premises; for it is clear that those which are put forward as ultimate are not self-supporting, but are based on others which, again having others for their support, do not permit of finality. But we represent some as ultimate for reason, in the same way as in regard to material objects we call that an indivisible point beyond which our senses can no longer perceive anything, although by its nature it is infinitely divisible.

Of these two Infinites of science, that of greatness is the most palpable, and hence a few persons have pretended to know all things. "I will speak of the whole,"[31] said Democritus.

But the infinitely little is the least obvious. Philosophers have much oftener claimed to have reached it, and it is here they have all stumbled. This has given rise to such common titles as First Principles, Principles of Philosophy,[32] and the like, as ostentatious in fact, though not in appearance, as that one which blinds us, De omni scibili.[33]

We naturally believe ourselves far more capable of reaching the centre of things than of embracing their circumference. The visible extent of the world visibly exceeds us; but as we[Pg 19] exceed little things, we think ourselves more capable of knowing them. And yet we need no less capacity for attaining the Nothing than the All. Infinite capacity is required for both, and it seems to me that whoever shall have understood the ultimate principles of being might also attain to the knowledge of the Infinite. The one depends on the other, and one leads to the other. These extremes meet and reunite by force of distance, and find each other in God, and in God alone.

Let us then take our compass; we are something, and we are not everything. The nature of our existence hides from us the knowledge of first beginnings which are born of the Nothing; and the littleness of our being conceals from us the sight of the Infinite.

Our intellect holds the same position in the world of thought as our body occupies in the expanse of nature.

Limited as we are in every way, this state which holds the mean between two extremes is present in all our impotence. Our senses perceive no extreme. Too much sound deafens us; too much light dazzles us; too great distance or proximity hinders our view. Too great length and too great brevity of discourse tend to obscurity; too much truth is paralysing (I know some who cannot understand that to take four from nothing leaves nothing). First principles are too self-evident for us; too much pleasure disagrees with us. Too many concords are annoying in music; too many benefits irritate us; we wish to have the wherewithal to over-pay our debts. Beneficia eo usque læta sunt dum videntur exsolvi posse; ubi multum antevenere, pro gratia odium redditur.[34] We feel neither extreme heat nor extreme cold. Excessive

from one place to another; and these are qualities which belong only to bodies.

Instead of receiving the ideas of these things in their purity, we colour them with our own qualities, and stamp with our composite being all the simple things which we contemplate.

Who would not think, seeing us compose all things of mind and body, but that this mixture would be quite intelligible to us? Yet it is the very thing we least understand. Man is to himself the most wonderful object in nature; for he cannot conceive what the body is, still less what the mind is, and least of all how a body should be united to a mind. This is the consummation of his difficulties, and yet it is his very being. Modus quo corporibus adhærent spiritus comprehendi ab hominibus non potest, et hoc tamen homo est.[35] Finally, to complete the proof of our weakness, I shall conclude with these two considerations....

73

[But perhaps this subject goes beyond the capacity of reason. Let us therefore examine her solutions to problems within her[Pg 22] powers. If there be anything to which her own interest must have made her apply herself most seriously, it is the inquiry into her own sovereign good. Let us see, then, wherein these strong and clear-sighted souls have placed it, and whether they agree.

One says that the sovereign good consists in virtue, another in pleasure, another in the knowledge of nature, another in truth, Felix qui potuit rerum cognoscere causas,[36] another in total ignorance, another in indolence, others in disregarding appearances, another in wondering at nothing, nihil admirari prope res una quæ possit facere et servare beatum,[37] and the true sceptics in their indifference, doubt, and perpetual suspense, and others, wiser, think to find a better definition. We are well satisfied.

To transpose after the laws to the following title.

We must see if this fine philosophy have gained nothing certain from so long and so intent study; perhaps at least the soul will know itself. Let us hear the rulers of the world on this subject. What have they thought of her substance? 394.[38] Have they been more fortunate in locating her? 395.[39] What have they found out about her origin, duration, and departure? 399.[40]

Is then the soul too noble a subject for their feeble lights? Let us then abase her to matter and see if she knows whereof is made the very body which she animates, and those others which she contemplates and moves at her will. What have those great dogmatists, who are ignorant of nothing, known of this matter? Harum sententiarum,[41] 393.

This would doubtless suffice, if reason were reasonable. She is reasonable enough to admit that she has been unable to find anything durable, but she does not yet despair of reaching it; she is as ardent as ever in this search, and is confident she has within her the necessary powers for this conquest. We must therefore conclude, and, after having examined her powers in their effects, observe them in themselves, and see if she has a nature and a grasp capable of laying hold of the truth.]

74

A letter On the Foolishness of Human Knowledge and Philosophy.

This letter before Diversion.

Felix qui potuit ... Nihil admirari.[42]

280 kinds of sovereign good in Montaigne.[Pg 23][43]

75

Part I, 1, 2, c. 1, section 4.[44]

[Probability.—It will not be difficult to put the case a stage lower, and make it appear ridiculous. To begin at the very beginning.] What is more absurd than to say that lifeless bodies have passions, fears, hatreds—that insensible bodies, lifeless and incapable of life, have passions which presuppose at least a sensitive soul to feel them, nay more, that the object of their dread is the void? What is there in the void that could make them afraid? Nothing is more shallow and ridiculous. This is not all; it is said that they have in themselves a source of movement to shun the void. Have they arms, legs, muscles, nerves?

76

To write against those who made too profound a study of science: Descartes.

77

I cannot forgive Descartes. In all his philosophy he would have been quite willing to dispense with God. But he had to make Him give a fillip to set the world in motion; beyond this, he has no further need of God.

78

Descartes useless and uncertain.

79

[Descartes.—We must say summarily: "This is made by figure and motion," for it is true. But to say what these are, and to compose the machine, is ridiculous. For it is useless, uncertain, and painful. And were it true, we do not think all philosophy is worth one hour of pain.]

80

How comes it that a cripple does not offend us, but that a fool does?[45] Because a cripple recognises that we walk straight, whereas a fool declares that it is we who are silly; if it were not so, we should feel pity and not anger.

Epictetus[46] asks still more strongly: "Why are we not angry if we are told that we have a headache, and why are we angry if we are told that we reason badly, or choose wrongly?" The[Pg 24] reason is that we are quite certain that we have not a headache, or are not lame, but we are not so sure that we make a true choice. So having assurance only because we see with our whole sight, it puts us into suspense and surprise when another with his whole sight sees the opposite, and still more so when a thousand others deride our choice. For we must prefer our own lights to those of so many others, and that is bold and difficult. There is never this contradiction in the feelings towards a cripple.

81

It is natural for the mind to believe, and for the will to love;[47] so that, for want of true objects, they must attach themselves to false.

82

Imagination.[48]—It is that deceitful part in man, that mistress of error and falsity, the more deceptive that she is not always so; for she would be an infallible rule of truth, if she were an infallible rule of falsehood. But being most generally false, she gives no sign of her nature, impressing the same character on the true and the false.

I do not speak of fools, I speak of the wisest men; and it is among them that the imagination has the great gift of persuasion. Reason protests in vain; it cannot set a true value on things.

This arrogant power, the enemy of reason, who likes to rule and dominate it, has established in man a second nature to show how all-powerful she is. She makes men happy and sad, healthy and sick, rich and poor; she compels reason to believe, doubt, and deny; she blunts the senses, or quickens them; she has her fools and sages; and nothing vexes us more than to see that she fills her devotees with a satisfaction far more full and entire than does reason. Those who have a lively imagination are a great deal more pleased with themselves than the wise can reasonably be. They look down upon men with haughtiness; they argue with boldness and confidence, others with fear and diffidence; and this gaiety of countenance often gives them the advantage in the opinion of the hearers, such favour have the imaginary wise in the eyes of judges of like nature. Imagination cannot make fools wise; but she can make them happy, to the envy of reason which can only make its friends miserable; the one covers them with glory, the other with shame.

What but this faculty of imagination dispenses reputation,[Pg 25] awards respect and veneration to persons, works, laws, and the great? How insufficient are all the riches of the earth without her consent!

Would you not say that this magistrate, whose venerable age commands the respect of a whole people, is governed by pure and lofty reason, and that he judges causes according to their true nature without considering those mere trifles which only affect the imagination of the weak? See him go to sermon, full of devout zeal, strengthening his reason with the ardour of his love. He is ready to listen with exemplary respect. Let the preacher appear, and let nature have given him a hoarse voice or a comical cast of countenance, or let his barber have given him a bad shave, or let by chance his dress be more dirtied than usual, then however great the truths he announces. I wager our senator loses his gravity.

If the greatest philosopher in the world find himself upon a plank wider than actually necessary, but hanging over a precipice, his imagination will prevail, though his reason convince him of his safety. [49] Many cannot bear the thought without a cold sweat. I will not state all its effects.

Every one knows that the sight of cats or rats, the crushing of a coal, etc. may unhinge the reason. The tone of voice affects the wisest, and changes the force of a discourse or a poem.

Love or hate alters the aspect of justice. How much greater confidence has an advocate, retained with a large fee, in the justice of his cause! How much better does his bold manner make his case appear to the judges, deceived as they are by appearances! How ludicrous is reason, blown with a breath in every direction!

I should have to enumerate almost every action of men who scarce waver save under her assaults. For reason has been obliged to yield, and the wisest reason takes as her own principles those which the imagination of man has everywhere rashly introduced. [He who would follow reason only would be deemed foolish by the generality of men. We must judge by the opinion of the majority of mankind. Because it has pleased them, we must work all day for pleasures seen to be imaginary; and after sleep has refreshed our tired reason, we must forthwith start up and rush after phantoms, and suffer the impressions of this mistress of the world. This is one of the sources of error, but it is not the only one.]

Our magistrates have known well this mystery. Their red[Pg 26] robes, the ermine in which they wrap themselves like furry cats,[50] the courts in which they administer justice, the fleurs-de-lis, and all such august apparel were necessary; if the physicians had not their cassocks and their mules, if the doctors had not their square caps and their robes four times too wide, they would never have duped the world, which cannot resist so original an appearance. If magistrates had true justice, and if physicians had the true art of healing, they would have no occasion for square caps; the majesty of these sciences would of itself be venerable enough. But having only imaginary knowledge, they must employ those silly tools that strike the imagination with which they have to deal; and thereby in fact they inspire respect. Soldiers alone are not disguised in this manner, because indeed their part is the most essential; they establish themselves by force, the others by show.

Therefore our kings seek out no disguises. They do not mask themselves in extraordinary costumes to appear such; but they are accompanied by guards and halberdiers. Those armed and red-faced puppets who have hands and power for them alone, those trumpets and drums which go before them, and those legions round about them, make the stoutest tremble. They have not dress only, they have might. A very refined reason is required to regard as an ordinary man the Grand Turk, in his superb seraglio, surrounded by forty thousand janissaries.

We cannot even see an advocate in his robe and with his cap on his head, without a favourable opinion of his ability. The imagination disposes of everything; it makes beauty, justice, and happiness, which is everything in the world. I should much like to see an Italian work, of which I only know the title, which alone is worth many books, Della opinione regina del mondo.[51] I approve of the book without knowing it, save the evil in it, if any. These are pretty much the effects of that deceptive faculty, which seems to have been expressly given us to lead us into necessary error. We have, however, many other sources of error.

Not only are old impressions capable of misleading us; the charms of novelty have the same power. Hence arise all the disputes of men, who taunt each other either with following the false impressions of childhood or with running rashly after the new. Who keeps the due mean? Let him appear and prove it. There is no principle, however natural to us from[Pg 27] infancy, which may not be made to pass for a false impression either of education or of sense.

"Because," say some, "you have believed from childhood that a box was empty when you saw nothing in it, you have believed in the possibility of a vacuum. This is an illusion of your senses, strengthened by custom, which science must correct." "Because," say others, "you have been taught at school that there is no vacuum, you have perverted your common sense which clearly comprehended it, and you must correct this by returning to your first state." Which has deceived you, your senses or your education?

We have another source of error in diseases.[52] They spoil the judgment and the senses; and if the more serious produce a sensible change, I do not doubt that slighter ills produce a proportionate impression.

Our own interest is again a marvellous instrument for nicely putting out our eyes. The justest man in the world is not allowed to be judge in his own cause; I know some who, in order not to fall into this self-love, have been perfectly unjust out of opposition. The sure way of losing a just cause has been to get it recommended to these men by their near relatives.

Justice and truth are two such subtle points, that our tools are too blunt to touch them accurately. If they reach the point, they either crush it, or lean all round, more on the false than on the true.

[Man is so happily formed that he has no ... good of the true, and several excellent of the false. Let us now see how much ... But the most powerful cause of error is the war existing between the senses and reason.]

83

We must thus begin the chapter on the deceptive powers. Man is only a subject full of error, natural and ineffaceable, without grace. Nothing shows him the truth. Everything deceives him. These two sources of truth, reason and the senses, besides being both wanting in sincerity, deceive each other in turn. The senses mislead the reason with false appearances, and receive from reason in their turn the same trickery which they apply to her; reason has her revenge. The passions of the soul trouble the senses, and make false impressions upon them. They rival each other in falsehood and deception.[Pg 28][53]

But besides those errors which arise accidentally and through lack of intelligence, with these heterogeneous faculties ...

84

The imagination enlarges little objects so as to fill our souls with a fantastic estimate; and, with rash insolence, it belittles the great to its own measure, as when talking of God.

85

Things which have most hold on us, as the concealment of our few possessions, are often a mere nothing. It is a nothing which our imagination magnifies into a mountain. Another turn of the imagination would make us discover this without difficulty.

86

[My fancy makes me hate a croaker, and one who pants when eating. Fancy has great weight. Shall we profit by it? Shall we yield to this weight because it is natural? No, but by resisting it ...]

87

Næ iste magno conatu magnas nugas dixerit.[54]

Quasi quidquam infelicius sit homini cui sua figmenta dominantur. [55] (Plin.)

88

Children who are frightened at the face they have blackened are but children. But how shall one who is so weak in his childhood become really strong when he grows older? We only change our fancies. All that is made perfect by progress perishes also by progress. All that has been weak can never become absolutely strong. We say in vain, "He has grown, he has changed"; he is also the same.

89

Custom is our nature. He who is accustomed to the faith believes in it, can no longer fear hell, and believes in nothing else. He who is accustomed to believe that the king is terrible ... etc. Who doubts then that our soul, being accustomed to see number, space, motion, believes that and nothing else?

90

Quod crebro videt non miratur, etiamsi cur fiat nescit; quod ante non viderit, id si evenerit, ostentum esse censet.[56] (Cic. 583.)[Pg 29]

91

Spongia solis.[57]—When we see the same effect always recur, we infer a natural necessity in it, as that there will be a to-morrow, etc. But nature often deceives us, and does not subject herself to her own rules.

92

What are our natural principles but principles of custom? In children they are those which they have received from the habits of their fathers, as hunting in animals. A different custom will cause different natural principles. This is seen in experience; and if there are some natural principles ineradicable by custom, there are also some customs opposed to nature, ineradicable by nature, or by a second custom. This depends on disposition.

93

Parents fear lest the natural love of their children may fade away. What kind of nature is that which is subject to decay? Custom is a second nature which destroys the former.[58] But what is nature? For is custom not natural? I am much afraid that nature is itself only a first custom, as custom is a second nature.

94

The nature of man is wholly natural, omne animal.[59]

There is nothing he may not make natural; there is nothing natural he may not lose.

95

Memory, joy, are intuitions; and even mathematical propositions become intuitions, for education produces natural intuitions, and natural intuitions are erased by education.

96

When we are accustomed to use bad reasons for proving natural effects, we are not willing to receive good reasons when they are discovered. An example may be given from the circulation of the blood as a reason why the vein swells below the ligature.

97

The most important affair in life is the choice of a calling; chance decides it. Custom makes men masons, soldiers,[Pg 30] slaters. "He is a good slater," says one, and, speaking of soldiers, remarks, "They are perfect fools." But others affirm, "There is nothing great but war, the rest of men are good for nothing." We choose our callings according as we hear this or that praised or despised in our childhood, for we naturally love truth and hate folly. These words move us; the only error is in their application. So great is the force of custom that out of those whom nature has only made men, are created all conditions of men. For some districts are full of masons, others of soldiers, etc. Certainly nature is not so uniform. It is custom then which does this, for it constrains nature. But sometimes nature gains the ascendancy, and preserves man's instinct, in spite of all custom, good or bad.

98

Bias leading to error.—It is a deplorable thing to see all men deliberating on means alone, and not on the end. Each thinks how he will acquit himself in his condition; but as for the choice of condition, or of country, chance gives them to us.

It is a pitiable thing to see so many Turks, heretics, and infidels follow the way of their fathers for the sole reason that each has been imbued with the prejudice that it is the best. And that fixes for each man his conditions of locksmith, soldier, etc.

Hence savages care nothing for Providence.[60]

99

There is an universal and essential difference between the actions of the will and all other actions.

The will is one of the chief factors in belief, not that it creates belief, but because things are true or false according to the aspect in which we look at them. The will, which prefers one aspect to another, turns away the mind from considering the qualities of all that it does not like to see; and thus the mind, moving in accord with the will, stops to consider the aspect which it likes, and so judges by what it sees.

100

Self-love.—The nature of self-love and of this human Ego is to love self only and consider self only. But what will man do? He cannot prevent this object that he loves from being full of faults and wants. He wants to be great, and he sees himself small. He wants to be happy, and he sees himself miserable.[Pg 31] He wants to be perfect, and he sees himself full of imperfections. He wants to be the object of love and esteem among men, and he sees that his faults merit only their hatred and contempt. This embarrassment in which he finds himself produces in him the most unrighteous and criminal passion that can be imagined; for he conceives a mortal enmity against that truth which reproves him, and which convinces him of his faults. He would annihilate it, but, unable to destroy it in its essence, he destroys it as far as possible in his own knowledge and in that of others; that is to say, he devotes all his attention to hiding his faults both from others and from himself, and he cannot endure either that others should point them out to him, or that they should see them.

Truly it is an evil to be full of faults; but it is a still greater evil to be full of them, and to be unwilling to recognise them, since that is to add the further fault of a voluntary illusion. We do not like others to deceive us; we do not think it fair that they should be held in higher esteem by us than they deserve; it is not then fair that we should deceive them, and should wish them to esteem us more highly than we deserve.

Thus, when they discover only the imperfections and vices which we really have, it is plain they do us no wrong, since it is not they who cause them; they rather do us good, since they help us to free ourselves from an evil, namely, the ignorance of these imperfections. We ought not to be angry at their knowing our faults and despising us; it is but right that they should know us for what we are, and should despise us, if we are contemptible.

Such are the feelings that would arise in a heart full of equity and justice. What must we say then of our own heart, when we see in it a wholly different disposition? For is it not true that we hate truth and those who tell it us, and that we like them to be deceived in our favour, and prefer to be esteemed by them as being other than what we are in fact? One proof of this makes me shudder. The Catholic religion does not bind us to confess our sins indiscriminately to everybody; it allows them to remain hidden from all other men save one, to whom she bids us reveal the innermost recesses of our heart, and show ourselves as we are. There is only this one man in the world whom she orders us to undeceive, and she binds him to an inviolable secrecy, which makes this knowledge to him as if it were not. Can we imagine anything more charitable and[Pg 32] pleasant? And yet the corruption of man is such that he finds even this law harsh; and it is one of the main reasons which has caused a great part of Europe to rebel against the Church.[61]

How unjust and unreasonable is the heart of man, which feels it disagreeable to be obliged to do in regard to one man what in some measure it were right to do to all men! For is it right that we should deceive men?

There are different degrees in this aversion to truth; but all may perhaps be said to have it in some degree, because it is inseparable from self-love. It is this false delicacy which makes those who are under the necessity of reproving others choose so many windings and middle courses to avoid offence. They must lessen our faults, appear to excuse them, intersperse praises and evidence of love and esteem. Despite all this, the medicine does not cease to be bitter to self-love. It takes as little as it can, always with disgust, and often with a secret spite against those who administer it.

Hence it happens that if any have some interest in being loved by us, they are averse to render us a service which they know to be disagreeable. They treat us as we wish to be treated. We hate the truth, and they hide it from us. We desire flattery, and they flatter us. We like to be deceived, and they deceive us.

So each degree of good fortune which raises us in the world removes us farther from truth, because we are most afraid of wounding those whose affection is most useful and whose dislike is most dangerous. A prince may be the byword of all Europe, and he alone will know nothing of it. I am not astonished. To tell the truth is useful to those to whom it is spoken, but disadvantageous to those who tell it, because it makes them disliked. Now those who live with princes love their own interests more than that of the prince whom they serve; and so they take care not to confer on him a benefit so as to injure themselves.

This evil is no doubt greater and more common among the higher classes; but the lower are not exempt from it, since there is always some advantage in making men love us. Human life is thus only a perpetual illusion; men deceive and flatter each other. No one speaks of us in our presence as he does of us in our absence. Human society is founded on mutual deceit; few friendships would endure if each knew what his friend said of him in his absence, although he then spoke in sincerity and without passion.[Pg 33]

Man is then only disguise, falsehood, and hypocrisy, both in himself and in regard to others. He does not wish any one to tell him the truth; he avoids telling it to others, and all these dispositions, so removed from justice and reason, have a natural root in his heart.

101

I set it down as a fact that if all men knew what each said of the other, there would not be four friends in the world. This is apparent from the quarrels which arise from the indiscreet tales told from time to time. [I say, further, all men would be ...]

102

Some vices only lay hold of us by means of others, and these, like branches, fall on removal of the trunk.

103

The example of Alexander's chastity[62] has not made so many continent as that of his drunkenness has made intemperate. It is not shameful not to be as virtuous as he, and it seems excusable to be no more vicious. We do not believe ourselves to be exactly sharing in the vices of the vulgar, when we see that we are sharing in those of great men; and yet we do not observe that in these matters they are ordinary men. We hold on to them by the same end by which they hold on to the rabble; for, however exalted they are, they are still united at some point to the lowest of men. They are not suspended in the air, quite removed from our society. No, no; if they are greater than we, it is because their heads are higher; but their feet are as low as ours. They are all on the same level, and rest on the same earth; and by that extremity they are as low as we are, as the meanest folk, as infants, and as the beasts.

104

When our passion leads us to do something, we forget our duty; for example, we like a book and read it, when we ought to be doing something else. Now, to remind ourselves of our duty, we must set ourselves a task we dislike; we then plead that we have something else to do, and by this means remember our duty.

105

How difficult it is to submit anything to the judgment of another, without prejudicing his judgment by the manner in[Pg 34] which we submit it! If we say, "I think it beautiful," "I think it obscure," or the like, we either entice the imagination into that view, or irritate it to the contrary. It is better to say nothing; and then the other judges according to what really is, that is to say, according as it then is, and according as the other circumstances, not of our making, have placed it. But we at least shall have added nothing, unless it be that silence also produces an effect, according to the turn and the interpretation which the other will be disposed to give it, or as he will guess it from gestures or countenance, or from the tone of the voice, if he is a physiognomist. So difficult is it not to upset a judgment from its natural place, or, rather, so rarely is it firm and stable!

106

By knowing each man's ruling passion, we are sure of pleasing him; and yet each has his fancies, opposed to his true good, in the very idea which he has of the good. It is a singularly puzzling fact.

107

Lustravit lampade terras.[63]—The weather and my mood have little connection. I have my foggy and my fine days within me; my prosperity or misfortune has little to do with the matter. I sometimes struggle against luck, the glory of mastering it makes me master it gaily; whereas I am sometimes surfeited in the midst of good fortune.

108

Although people may have no interest in what they are saying, we must not absolutely conclude from this that they are not lying; for there are some people who lie for the mere sake of lying.

109

When we are well we wonder what we would do if we were ill, but when we are ill we take medicine cheerfully; the illness persuades us to do so. We have no longer the passions and desires for amusements and promenades which health gave to us, but which are incompatible with the necessities of illness. Nature gives us, then, passions and desires suitable to our present state.[64] We are only troubled by the fears which we, and not nature, give ourselves, for they add to the state in which we are the passions of the state in which we are not.[Pg 35]

As nature makes us always unhappy in every state, our desires picture to us a happy state; because they add to the state in which we are the pleasures of the state in which we are not. And if we attained to these pleasures, we should not be happy after all; because we should have other desires natural to this new state.

We must particularise this general proposition....

110

The consciousness of the falsity of present pleasures, and the ignorance of the vanity of absent pleasures, cause inconstancy.

111

Inconstancy.—We think we are playing on ordinary organs when playing upon man. Men are organs, it is true, but, odd, changeable, variable [with pipes not arranged in proper order. Those who only know how to play on ordinary organs] will not produce harmonies on these. We must know where [the keys] are.

112

Inconstancy.—Things have different qualities, and the soul different inclinations; for nothing is simple which is presented to the soul, and the soul never presents itself simply to any object. Hence it comes that we weep and laugh at the same thing.

113

Inconstancy and oddity.—To live only by work, and to rule over the most powerful State in the world, are very opposite things. They are united in the person of the great Sultan of the Turks.

114

Variety is as abundant as all tones of the voice, all ways of walking, coughing, blowing the nose, sneezing. We distinguish vines by their fruit, and call them the Condrien, the Desargues, and such and such a stock. Is this all? Has a vine ever produced two bunches exactly the same, and has a bunch two grapes alike? etc.

I can never judge of the same thing exactly in the same way. I cannot judge of my work, while doing it. I must do as the artists, stand at a distance, but not too far. How far, then? Guess.[Pg 36]

115

Variety.—Theology is a science, but at the same time how many sciences? A man is a whole; but if we dissect him, will he be the head, the heart, the stomach, the veins, each vein, each portion of a vein, the blood, each humour in the blood?

A town, a country-place, is from afar a town and a country-place. But, as we draw near, there are houses, trees, tiles, leaves, grass, ants, limbs of ants, in infinity. All this is contained under the name of country-place.

116

Thoughts.—All is one, all is different. How many natures exist in man? How many vocations? And by what chance does each man ordinarily choose what he has heard praised? A well-turned heel.

117

The heel of a slipper.—"Ah! How well this is turned! Here is a clever workman! How brave is this soldier!" This is the source of our inclinations, and of the choice of conditions. "How much this man drinks! How little that one!" This makes people sober or drunk, soldiers, cowards, etc.

118

Chief talent, that which rules the rest.

119

Nature imitates herself. A seed sown in good ground brings forth fruit. A principle, instilled into a good mind, brings forth fruit. Numbers imitate space, which is of a different nature.

All is made and led by the same master, root, branches, and fruits; principles and consequences.

120

[Nature diversifies and imitates; art imitates and diversifies.]

121

Nature always begins the same things again, the years, the days, the hours; in like manner spaces and numbers follow each other from beginning to end. Thus is made a kind of infinity and eternity. Not that anything in all this is infinite and eternal, but these finite realities are infinitely multiplied. Thus[Pg 37] it seems to me to be only the number which multiplies them that is infinite.

122

Time heals griefs and quarrels, for we change and are no longer the same persons. Neither the offender nor the offended are any more themselves. It is like a nation which we have provoked, but meet again after two generations. They are still Frenchmen, but not the same.

123

He no longer loves the person whom he loved ten years ago. I quite believe it. She is no longer the same, nor is he. He was young, and she also; she is quite different. He would perhaps love her yet, if she were what she was then.

124

We view things not only from different sides, but with different eyes; we have no wish to find them alike.

125

Contraries.—Man is naturally credulous and incredulous, timid and rash.

126

Description of man: dependency, desire of independence, need.

127

Condition of man: inconstancy, weariness, unrest.

128

The weariness which is felt by us in leaving pursuits to which we are attached. A man dwells at home with pleasure; but if he sees a woman who charms him, or if he enjoys himself in play for five or six days, he is miserable if he returns to his former way of living. Nothing is more common than that.

129

Our nature consists in motion; complete rest is death.[65]

130

Restlessness.—If a soldier, or labourer, complain of the hardship of his lot, set him to do nothing.[Pg 38]

131

Weariness.[66]—Nothing is so insufferable to man as to be completely at rest, without passions, without business, without diversion, without study. He then feels his nothingness, his forlornness, his insufficiency, his dependence, his weakness, his emptiness. There will immediately arise from the depth of his heart weariness, gloom, sadness, fretfulness, vexation, despair.

132

Methinks Cæsar was too old to set about amusing himself with conquering the world.[67] Such sport was good for Augustus or Alexander. They were still young men, and thus difficult to restrain. But Cæsar should have been more mature.

133

Two faces which resemble each other, make us laugh, when together, by their resemblance, though neither of them by itself makes us laugh.

134

How useless is painting, which attracts admiration by the resemblance of things, the originals of which we do not admire!

135

The struggle alone pleases us, not the victory. We love to see animals fighting, not the victor infuriated over the vanquished. We would only see the victorious end; and, as soon as it comes, we are satiated. It is the same in play, and the same in the search for truth. In disputes we like to see the clash of opinions, but not at all to contemplate truth when found. To observe it with pleasure, we have to see it emerge out of strife. So in the passions, there is pleasure in seeing the collision of two contraries; but when one acquires the mastery, it becomes only brutality. We never seek things for themselves, but for the search. Likewise in plays, scenes which do not rouse the emotion of fear are worthless, so are extreme and hopeless misery, brutal lust, and extreme cruelty.

136

A mere trifle consoles us, for a mere trifle distresses us.[Pg 39][68]

137

Without examining every particular pursuit, it is enough to comprehend them under diversion.

138

Men naturally slaters and of all callings, save in their own rooms.

139

Diversion.—When I have occasionally set myself to consider the different distractions of men, the pains and perils to which they expose themselves at court or in war, whence arise so many quarrels, passions, bold and often bad ventures, etc., I have discovered that all the unhappiness of men arises from one single fact, that they cannot stay quietly in their own chamber. A man who has enough to live on, if he knew how to stay with pleasure at home, would not leave it to go to sea or to besiege a town. A commission in the army would not be bought so dearly, but that it is found insufferable not to budge from the town; and men only seek conversation and entering games, because they cannot remain with pleasure at home.

But on further consideration, when, after finding the cause of all our ills, I have sought to discover the reason of it, I have found that there is one very real reason, namely, the natural poverty of our feeble and mortal condition, so miserable that nothing can comfort us when we think of it closely.

Whatever condition we picture to ourselves, if we muster all the good things which it is possible to possess, royalty is the finest position in the world. Yet, when we imagine a king attended with every pleasure he can feel, if he be without diversion, and be left to consider and reflect on what he is, this feeble happiness will not sustain him; he will necessarily fall into forebodings of dangers, of revolutions which may happen, and, finally, of death and inevitable disease; so that if he be without what is called diversion, he is unhappy, and more unhappy than the least of his subjects who plays and diverts himself.

Hence it comes that play and the society of women, war, and high posts, are so sought after. Not that there is in fact any happiness in them, or that men imagine true bliss to consist in money won at play, or in the hare which they hunt; we would not take these as a gift. We do not seek that easy and peaceful[Pg 40] lot which permits us to think of our unhappy condition, nor the dangers of war, nor the labour of office, but the bustle which averts these thoughts of ours, and amuses us.

Reasons why we like the chase better than the quarry.

Hence it comes that men so much love noise and stir; hence it comes that the prison is so horrible a punishment; hence it comes that the pleasure of solitude is a thing incomprehensible. And it is in fact the greatest source of happiness in the condition of kings, that men try incessantly to divert them, and to procure for them all kinds of pleasures.

The king is surrounded by persons whose only thought is to divert the king, and to prevent his thinking of self. For he is unhappy, king though he be, if he think of himself.

This is all that men have been able to discover to make themselves happy. And those who philosophise on the matter, and who think men unreasonable for spending a whole day in chasing a hare which they would not have bought, scarce know our nature. The hare in itself would not screen us from the sight of death and calamities; but the chase which turns away our attention from these, does screen us.

The advice given to Pyrrhus to take the rest which he was about to seek with so much labour, was full of difficulties.[69]

[To bid a man live quietly is to bid him live happily. It is to advise him to be in a state perfectly happy, in which he can think at leisure without finding therein a cause of distress. This is to misunderstand nature.

As men who naturally understand their own condition avoid nothing so much as rest, so there is nothing they leave undone in seeking turmoil. Not that they have an instinctive knowledge of true happiness ...

So we are wrong in blaming them. Their error does not lie in seeking excitement, if they seek it only as a diversion; the evil is that they seek it as if the possession of the objects of their quest would make them really happy. In this respect it is right to call their quest a vain one. Hence in all this both the censurers and the censured do not understand man's true nature.]

And thus, when we take the exception against them, that what they seek with such fervour cannot satisfy them, if they replied—as they should do if they considered the matter thoroughly—that they sought in it only a violent and impetuous occupation which turned their thoughts from self, and that they therefore chose an attractive object to charm and ardently[Pg 41] attract them, they would leave their opponents without a reply. But they do not make this reply, because they do not know themselves.[70] They do not know that it is the chase, and not the quarry, which they seek.

Dancing: we must consider rightly where to place our feet.—A gentleman sincerely believes that hunting is great and royal sport; but a beater is not of this opinion.

They imagine that if they obtained such a post, they would then rest with pleasure, and are insensible of the insatiable nature of their desire. They think they are truly seeking quiet, and they are only seeking excitement.

They have a secret instinct which impels them to seek amusement and occupation abroad, and which arises from the sense of their constant unhappiness. They have another secret instinct, a remnant of the greatness of our original nature, which teaches them that happiness in reality consists only in rest, and not in stir. And of these two contrary instincts they form within themselves a confused idea, which hides itself from their view in the depths of their soul, inciting them to aim at rest through excitement, and always to fancy that the satisfaction which they have not will come to them, if, by surmounting whatever difficulties confront them, they can thereby open the door to rest.

Thus passes away all man's life. Men seek rest in a struggle against difficulties; and when they have conquered these, rest becomes insufferable. For we think either of the misfortunes we have or of those which threaten us. And even if we should see ourselves sufficiently sheltered on all sides, weariness of its own accord would not fail to arise from the depths of the heart wherein it has its natural roots, and to fill the mind with its poison.

Thus so wretched is man that he would weary even without any cause for weariness from the peculiar state of his disposition; and so frivolous is he, that, though full of a thousand reasons for weariness, the least thing, such as playing billiards or hitting a ball, is sufficient to amuse him.

But will you say what object has he in all this? The pleasure of bragging to-morrow among his friends that he has played better than another. So others sweat in their own rooms to show to the learned that they have solved a problem in algebra, which no one had hitherto been able to solve. Many more expose themselves to extreme perils, in my opinion as foolishly, in order to boast afterwards that they have captured a town.[Pg 42] Lastly, others wear themselves out in studying all these things, not in order to become wiser, but only in order to prove that they know them; and these are the most senseless of the band, since they are so knowingly, whereas one may suppose of the others, that if they knew it, they would no longer be foolish.

This man spends his life without weariness in playing every day for a small stake. Give him each morning the money he can win each day, on condition he does not play; you make him miserable. It will perhaps be said that he seeks the amusement of play and not the winnings. Make him then play for nothing; he will not become excited over it, and will feel bored. It is then not the amusement alone that he seeks; a languid and passionless amusement will weary him.

He must get excited over it, and deceive himself by the fancy that he will be happy to win what he would not have as a gift on condition of not playing; and he must make for himself an object of passion, and excite over it his desire, his anger, his fear, to obtain his imagined end, as children are frightened at the face they have blackened.

Whence comes it that this man, who lost his only son a few months ago, or who this morning was in such trouble through being distressed by lawsuits and quarrels, now no longer thinks of them? Do not wonder; he is quite taken up in looking out for the boar which his dogs have been hunting so hotly for the last six hours. He requires nothing more. However full of sadness a man may be, he is happy for the time, if you can prevail upon him to enter into some amusement; and however happy a man may be, he will soon be discontented and wretched, if he be not diverted and occupied by some passion or pursuit which prevents weariness from overcoming him. Without amusement there is no joy; with amusement there is no sadness. And this also constitutes the happiness of persons in high position, that they have a number of people to amuse them, and have the power to keep themselves in this state.

Consider this. What is it to be superintendent, chancellor, first president, but to be in a condition wherein from early morning a large number of people come from all quarters to see them, so as not to leave them an hour in the day in which they can think of themselves? And when they are in disgrace and sent back to their country houses, where they lack neither wealth nor servants to help them on occasion, they do not fail to be wretched and desolate, because no one prevents them from thinking of themselves.[Pg 43]

140

[How does it happen that this man, so distressed at the death of his wife and his only son, or who has some great lawsuit which annoys him, is not at this moment sad, and that he seems so free from all painful and disquieting thoughts? We need not wonder; for a ball has been served him, and he must return it to his companion. He is occupied in catching it in its fall from the roof, to win a game. How can he think of his own affairs, pray, when he has this other matter in hand? Here is a care worthy of occupying this great soul, and taking away from him every other thought of the mind. This man, born to know the universe, to judge all causes, to govern a whole state, is altogether occupied and taken up with the business of catching a hare. And if he does not lower himself to this, and wants always to be on the strain, he will be more foolish still, because he would raise himself above humanity; and after all he is only a man, that is to say capable of little and of much, of all and of nothing; he is neither angel nor brute, but man.]

141

Men spend their time in following a ball or a hare; it is the pleasure even of kings.

142

Diversion.—Is not the royal dignity sufficiently great in itself to make its possessor happy by the mere contemplation of what he is? Must he be diverted from this thought like ordinary folk? I see well that a man is made happy by diverting him from the view of his domestic sorrows so as to occupy all his thoughts with the care of dancing well. But will it be the same with a king, and will he be happier in the pursuit of these idle amusements than in the contemplation of his greatness? And what more satisfactory object could be presented to his mind? Would it not be a deprivation of his delight for him to occupy his soul with the thought of how to adjust his steps to the cadence of an air, or of how to throw a [ball] skilfully, instead of leaving it to enjoy quietly the contemplation of the majestic glory which encompasses him? Let us make the trial; let us leave a king all alone to reflect on himself quite at leisure, without any gratification of the senses, without any care in his mind, without society; and we will see that a king without[Pg 44] diversion is a man full of wretchedness. So this is carefully avoided, and near the persons of kings there never fail to be a great number of people who see to it that amusement follows business, and who watch all the time of their leisure to supply them with delights and games, so that there is no blank in it. In fact, kings are surrounded with persons who are wonderfully attentive in taking care that the king be not alone and in a state to think of himself, knowing well that he will be miserable, king though he be, if he meditate on self.

In all this I am not talking of Christian kings as Christians, but only as kings.

143

Diversion.—Men are entrusted from infancy with the care of their honour, their property, their friends, and even with the property and the honour of their friends. They are overwhelmed with business, with the study of languages, and with physical exercise;[71] and they are made to understand that they cannot be happy unless their health, their honour, their fortune and that of their friends be in good condition, and that a single thing wanting will make them unhappy. Thus they are given cares and business which make them bustle about from break of day.—It is, you will exclaim, a strange way to make them happy! What more could be done to make them miserable?—Indeed! what could be done? We should only have to relieve them from all these cares; for then they would see themselves: they would reflect on what they are, whence they came, whither they go, and thus we cannot employ and divert them too much. And this is why, after having given them so much business, we advise them, if they have some time for relaxation, to employ it in amusement, in play, and to be always fully occupied.

How hollow and full of ribaldry is the heart of man!

144

I spent a long time in the study of the abstract sciences, and was disheartened by the small number of fellow-students in them. When I commenced the study of man, I saw that these abstract sciences are not suited to man, and that I was wandering farther from my own state in examining them, than others in not knowing them. I pardoned their little knowledge; but I thought at least to find many companions in the study of man, and that it was the true study which is suited to him. I have[Pg 45] been deceived; still fewer study it than geometry. It is only from the want of knowing how to study this that we seek the other studies. But is it not that even here is not the knowledge which man should have, and that for the purpose of happiness it is better for him not to know himself?

145

[One thought alone occupies us; we cannot think of two things at the same time. This is lucky for us according to the world, not according to God.]

146

Man is obviously made to think. It is his whole dignity and his whole merit; and his whole duty is to think as he ought. Now, the order of thought is to begin with self, and with its Author and its end.

Now, of what does the world think? Never of this, but of dancing, playing the lute, singing, making verses, running at the ring, etc., fighting, making oneself king, without thinking what it is to be a king and what to be a man.

147

We do not content ourselves with the life we have in ourselves and in our own being; we desire to live an imaginary life in the mind of others, and for this purpose we endeavour to shine. We labour unceasingly to adorn and preserve this imaginary existence, and neglect the real. And if we possess calmness, or generosity, or truthfulness, we are eager to make it known, so as to attach these virtues to that imaginary existence. We would rather separate them from ourselves to join them to it; and we would willingly be cowards in order to acquire the reputation of being brave. A great proof of the nothingness of our being, not to be satisfied with the one without the other, and to renounce the one for the other! For he would be infamous who would not die to preserve his honour.

148

We are so presumptuous that we would wish to be known by all the world, even by people who shall come after, when we shall be no more; and we are so vain that the esteem of five or six neighbours delights and contents us.[Pg 46]

149

We do not trouble ourselves about being esteemed in the towns through which we pass. But if we are to remain a little while there, we are so concerned. How long is necessary? A time commensurate with our vain and paltry life.

150

Vanity is so anchored in the heart of man that a soldier, a soldier's servant, a cook, a porter brags, and wishes to have his admirers. Even philosophers wish for them. Those who write against it want to have the glory of having written well;[72] and those who read it desire the glory of having read it. I who write this have perhaps this desire, and perhaps those who will read it ...

151

Glory.—Admiration spoils all from infancy. Ah! How well said! Ah! How well done! How well-behaved he is! etc.

The children of Port-Royal, who do not receive this stimulus of envy and glory, fall into carelessness.

152

Pride.—Curiosity is only vanity. Most frequently we wish to know but to talk. Otherwise we would not take a sea voyage in order never to talk of it, and for the sole pleasure of seeing without hope of ever communicating it.

153

Of the desire of being esteemed by those with whom we are.—Pride takes such natural possession of us in the midst of our woes, errors, etc. We even lose our life with joy, provided people talk of it.

Vanity: play, hunting, visiting, false shame, a lasting name.

154

[I have no friends] to your advantage].

155

A true friend is so great an advantage, even for the greatest lords, in order that he may speak well of them, and back them in their absence, that they should do all to have one. But they should choose well; for, if they spend all their efforts in the interests of fools, it will be of no use, however well these may speak of them; and these will not even speak well of them if[Pg 47] they find themselves on the weakest side, for they have no influence; and thus they will speak ill of them in company.

156

Ferox gens, nullam esse vitam sine armis rati.[73]—They prefer death to peace; others prefer death to war.

Every opinion may be held preferable to life, the love of which is so strong and so natural.[74]

157

Contradiction: contempt for our existence, to die for nothing, hatred of our existence.

158

Pursuits.—The charm of fame is so great, that we like every object to which it is attached, even death.

159

Noble deeds are most estimable when hidden. When I see some of these in history (as p. 184)[75], they please me greatly. But after all they have not been quite hidden, since they have been known; and though people have done what they could to hide them, the little publication of them spoils all, for what was best in them was the wish to hide them.

160

Sneezing absorbs all the functions of the soul, as well as work does; but we do not draw therefrom the same conclusions against the greatness of man, because it is against his will. And although we bring it on ourselves, it is nevertheless against our will that we sneeze. It is not in view of the act itself; it is for another end. And thus it is not a proof of the weakness of man, and of his slavery under that action.

It is not disgraceful for man to yield to pain, and it is disgraceful to yield to pleasure. This is not because pain comes to us from without, and we ourselves seek pleasure; for it is possible to seek pain, and yield to it purposely, without this kind of baseness. Whence comes it, then, that reason thinks it honourable to succumb under stress of pain, and disgraceful to yield to the attack of pleasure? It is because pain does not tempt and attract us. It is we ourselves who choose it voluntarily, and will it to prevail over us. So that we are masters of[Pg 48] the situation; and in this man yields to himself. But in pleasure it is man who yields to pleasure. Now only mastery and sovereignty bring glory, and only slavery brings shame.

161

Vanity.—How wonderful it is that a thing so evident as the vanity of the world is so little known, that it is a strange and surprising thing to say that it is foolish to seek greatness!

162

He who will know fully the vanity of man has only to consider the causes and effects of love. The cause is a je ne sais quoi (Corneille),[76] and the effects are dreadful. This je ne sais quoi, so small an object that we cannot recognise it, agitates a whole country, princes, armies, the entire world.

Cleopatra's nose: had it been shorter, the whole aspect of the world would have been altered.

163

Vanity.—The cause and the effects of love: Cleopatra.

164

He who does not see the vanity of the world is himself very vain. Indeed who do not see it but youths who are absorbed in fame, diversion, and the thought of the future? But take away diversion, and you will see them dried up with weariness. They feel then their nothingness without knowing it; for it is indeed to be unhappy to be in insufferable sadness as soon as we are reduced to thinking of self, and have no diversion.

165

Thoughts.—In omnibus requiem quæsivi.[77] If our condition were truly happy, we would not need diversion from thinking of it in order to make ourselves happy.

166

Diversion.—Death is easier to bear without thinking of it, than is the thought of death without peril.

167

The miseries of human life have established all this: as men have seen this, they have taken up diversion.[Pg 49]

168

Diversion.—As men are not able to fight against death, misery, ignorance, they have taken it into their heads, in order to be happy, not to think of them at all.

169

Despite these miseries, man wishes to be happy, and only wishes to be happy, and cannot wish not to be so. But how will he set about it? To be happy he would have to make himself immortal; but, not being able to do so, it has occurred to him to prevent himself from thinking of death.

170

Diversion.—If man were happy, he would be the more so, the less he was diverted, like the Saints and God.—Yes; but is it not to be happy to have a faculty of being amused by diversion?—No; for that comes from elsewhere and from without, and thus is dependent, and therefore subject to be disturbed by a thousand accidents, which bring inevitable griefs.

171

Misery.—The only thing which consoles us for our miseries is diversion, and yet this it the greatest of our miseries. For it is this which principally hinders us from reflecting upon ourselves, and which makes us insensibly ruin ourselves. Without this we should be in a state of weariness, and this weariness would spur us to seek a more solid means of escaping from it. But diversion amuses us, and leads us unconsciously to death.

172

We do not rest satisfied with the present. We anticipate the future as too slow in coming, as if in order to hasten its course; or we recall the past, to stop its too rapid flight. So imprudent are we that we wander in the times which are not ours, and do not think of the only one which belongs to us; and so idle are we that we dream of those times which are no more, and thoughtlessly overlook that which alone exists. For the present is generally painful to us. We conceal it from our sight, because it troubles us; and if it be delightful to us, we regret to see it pass away. We try to sustain it by the future, and think of arranging matters which are not in our power, for a time which we have no certainty of reaching.[Pg 50]

Let each one examine his thoughts, and he will find them all occupied with the past and the future. We scarcely ever think of the present; and if we think of it, it is only to take light from it to arrange the future. The present is never our end. The past and the present are our means; the future alone is our end.[78] So we never live, but we hope to live; and, as we are always preparing to be happy, it is inevitable we should never be so.

173

They say that eclipses foretoken misfortune, because misfortunes are common, so that, as evil happens so often, they often foretell it; whereas if they said that they predict good fortune, they would often be wrong. They attribute good fortune only to rare conjunctions of the heavens; so they seldom fail in prediction.

174

Misery.—Solomon[79] and Job have best known and best spoken of the misery of man; the former the most fortunate, and the latter the most unfortunate of men; the former knowing the vanity of pleasures from experience, the latter the reality of evils.

175

We know ourselves so little, that many think they are about to die when they are well, and many think they are well when they are near death, unconscious of approaching fever,[80] or of the abscess ready to form itself.

176

Cromwell[81] was about to ravage all Christendom; the royal family was undone, and his own for ever established, save for a little grain of sand which formed in his ureter. Rome herself was trembling under him; but this small piece of gravel having formed there, he is dead, his family cast down, all is peaceful, and the king is restored.

177

[Three hosts.[82]] Would he who had possessed the friendship of the King of England, the King of Poland, and the Queen of Sweden, have believed he would lack a refuge and shelter in the world?

178

Macrobius:[83] on the innocents slain by Herod.[Pg 51]

179

When Augustus learnt that Herod's own son was amongst the infants under two years of age, whom he had caused to be slain, he said that it was better to be Herod's pig than his son.—Macrobius, Sat., book ii, chap. 4.

180

The great and the humble have the same misfortunes, the same griefs, the same passions;[84] but the one is at the top of the wheel, and the other near the centre, and so less disturbed by the same revolutions.

181

We are so unfortunate that we can only take pleasure in a thing on condition of being annoyed if it turn out ill, as a thousand things can do, and do every hour. He who should find the secret of rejoicing in the good, without troubling himself with its contrary evil, would have hit the mark. It is perpetual motion.

182

Those who have always good hope in the midst of misfortunes, and who are delighted with good luck, are suspected of being very pleased with the ill success of the affair, if they are not equally distressed by bad luck; and they are overjoyed to find these pretexts of hope, in order to show that they are concerned and to conceal by the joy which they feign to feel that which they have at seeing the failure of the matter.

183

We run carelessly to the precipice, after we have put something before us to prevent us seeing it.

[Pg 52]

SECTION III

OF THE NECESSITY OF THE WAGER

184

A letter to incite to the search after God.

And then to make people seek Him among the philosophers, sceptics, and dogmatists, who disquiet him who inquires of them.

185

The conduct of God, who disposes all things kindly, is to put religion into the mind by reason, and into the heart by grace. But to will to put it into the mind and heart by force and threats is not to put religion there, but terror, terorrem potius quam religionem.

186

Nisi terrerentur et non docerentur, improba quasi dominatio videretur (Aug., Ep. 48 or 49), Contra Mendacium ad Consentium.

187

Order.—Men despise religion; they hate it, and fear it is true. To remedy this, we must begin by showing that religion is not contrary to reason; that it is venerable, to inspire respect for it; then we must make it lovable, to make good men hope it is true; finally, we must prove it is true.

Venerable, because it has perfect knowledge of man; lovable, because it promises the true good.

188

In every dialogue and discourse, we must be able to say to those who take offence, "Of what do you complain?"

189

To begin by pitying unbelievers; they are wretched enough by their condition. We ought only to revile them where it is beneficial; but this does them harm.[Pg 53]

190

To pity atheists who seek, for are they not unhappy enough? To inveigh against those who make a boast of it.

191

And will this one scoff at the other? Who ought to scoff? And yet, the latter does not scoff at the other, but pities him.

192

To reproach Miton[85] with not being troubled, since God will reproach him.

193

Quid fiet hominibus qui minima contemnunt, majora non credunt?

194

... Let them at least learn what is the religion they attack, before attacking it. If this religion boasted of having a clear view of God, and of possessing it open and unveiled, it would be attacking it to say that we see nothing in the world which shows it with this clearness. But since, on the contrary, it says that men are in darkness and estranged from God, that He has hidden Himself from their knowledge, that this is in fact the name which He gives Himself in the Scriptures, Deus absconditus;[86] and finally, if it endeavours equally to establish these two things: that God has set up in the Church visible signs to make Himself known to those who should seek Him sincerely, and that He has nevertheless so disguised them that He will only be perceived by those who seek Him with all their heart; what advantage can they obtain, when, in the negligence with which they make profession of being in search of the truth, they cry out that nothing reveals it to them; and since that darkness in which they are, and with which they upbraid the Church, establishes only one of the things which she affirms, without touching the other, and, very far from destroying, proves her doctrine?

In order to attack it, they should have protested that they had made every effort to seek Him everywhere, and even in that which the Church proposes for their instruction, but without satisfaction. If they talked in this manner, they would in truth be attacking one of her pretensions. But I hope here to show that no reasonable person can speak thus, and I venture[Pg 54] even to say that no one has ever done so. We know well enough how those who are of this mind behave. They believe they have made great efforts for their instruction, when they have spent a few hours in reading some book of Scripture, and have questioned some priest on the truths of the faith. After that, they boast of having made vain search in books and among men. But, verily, I will tell them what I have often said, that this negligence is insufferable. We are not here concerned with the trifling interests of some stranger, that we should treat it in this fashion; the matter concerns ourselves and our all.

The immortality of the soul is a matter which is of so great consequence to us, and which touches us so profoundly, that we must have lost all feeling to be indifferent as to knowing what it is. All our actions and thoughts must take such different courses, according as there are or are not eternal joys to hope for, that it is impossible to take one step with sense and judgment, unless we regulate our course by our view of this point which ought to be our ultimate end.

Thus our first interest and our first duty is to enlighten ourselves on this subject, whereon depends all our conduct. Therefore among those who do not believe, I make a vast difference between those who strive with all their power to inform themselves, and those who live without troubling or thinking about it.

I can have only compassion for those who sincerely bewail their doubt, who regard it as the greatest of misfortunes, and who, sparing no effort to escape it, make of this inquiry their principal and most serious occupations.

But as for those who pass their life without thinking of this ultimate end of life, and who, for this sole reason that they do not find within themselves the lights which convince them of it, neglect to seek them elsewhere, and to examine thoroughly whether this opinion is one of those which people receive with credulous simplicity, or one of those which, although obscure in themselves, have nevertheless a solid and immovable foundation, I look upon them in a manner quite different.

This carelessness in a matter which concerns themselves, their eternity, their all, moves me more to anger than pity; it astonishes and shocks me; it is to me monstrous. I do not say this out of the pious zeal of a spiritual devotion. I expect, on the contrary, that we ought to have this feeling from principles of human interest and self-love; for this we need only see what the least enlightened persons see.[Pg 55]

We do not require great education of the mind to understand that here is no real and lasting satisfaction; that our pleasures are only vanity; that our evils are infinite; and, lastly, that death, which threatens us every moment, must infallibly place us within a few years under the dreadful necessity of being for ever either annihilated or unhappy.

There is nothing more real than this, nothing more terrible. Be we as heroic as we like, that is the end which awaits the noblest life in the world. Let us reflect on this, and then say whether it is not beyond doubt that there is no good in this life but in the hope of another; that we are happy only in proportion as we draw near it; and that, as there are no more woes for those who have complete assurance of eternity, so there is no more happiness for those who have no insight into it.

Surely then it is a great evil thus to be in doubt, but it is at least an indispensable duty to seek when we are in such doubt; and thus the doubter who does not seek is altogether completely unhappy and completely wrong. And if besides this he is easy and content, professes to be so, and indeed boasts of it; if it is this state itself which is the subject of his joy and vanity, I have no words to describe so silly a creature.

How can people hold these opinions? What joy can we find in the expectation of nothing but hopeless misery? What reason for boasting that we are in impenetrable darkness? And how can it happen that the following argument occurs to a reasonable man?

"I know not who put me into the world, nor what the world is, nor what I myself am. I am in terrible ignorance of everything. I know not what my body is, nor my senses, nor my soul, not even that part of me which thinks what I say, which reflects on all and on itself, and knows itself no more than the rest. I see those frightful spaces of the universe which surround me, and I find myself tied to one corner of this vast expanse, without knowing why I am put in this place rather than in another, nor why the short time which is given me to live is assigned to me at this point rather than at another of the whole eternity which was before me or which shall come after me. I see nothing but infinites on all sides, which surround me as an atom, and as a shadow which endures only for an instant and returns no more. All I know is that I must soon die, but what I know least is this very death which I cannot escape.

"As I know not whence I come, so I know not whither I go.[Pg 56] I know only that, in leaving this world, I fall for ever either into annihilation or into the hands of an angry God, without knowing to which of these two states I shall be for ever assigned. Such is my state, full of weakness and uncertainty. And from all this I conclude that I ought to spend all the days of my life without caring to inquire into what must happen to me. Perhaps I might find some solution to my doubts, but I will not take the trouble, nor take a step to seek it; and after treating with scorn those who are concerned with this care, I will go without foresight and without fear to try the great event, and let myself be led carelessly to death, uncertain of the eternity of my future state."

Who would desire to have for a friend a man who talks in this fashion? Who would choose him out from others to tell him of his affairs? Who would have recourse to him in affliction? And indeed to what use in life could one put him?

In truth, it is the glory of religion to have for enemies men so unreasonable: and their opposition to it is so little dangerous that it serves on the contrary to establish its truths. For the Christian faith goes mainly to establish these two facts, the corruption of nature, and redemption by Jesus Christ. Now I contend that if these men do not serve to prove the truth of the redemption by the holiness of their behaviour, they at least serve admirably to show the corruption of nature by sentiments so unnatural.

Nothing is so important to man as his own state, nothing is so formidable to him as eternity; and thus it is not natural that there should be men indifferent to the loss of their existence, and to the perils of everlasting suffering. They are quite different with regard to all other things. They are afraid of mere trifles; they foresee them; they feel them. And this same man who spends so many days and nights in rage and despair for the loss of office, or for some imaginary insult to his honour, is the very one who knows without anxiety and without emotion that he will lose all by death. It is a monstrous thing to see in the same heart and at the same time this sensibility to trifles and this strange insensibility to the greatest objects. It is an incomprehensible enchantment, and a supernatural slumber, which indicates as its cause an all-powerful force.

There must be a strange confusion in the nature of man, that he should boast of being in that state in which it seems incredible that a single individual should be. However, experience has[Pg 57] shown me so great a number of such persons that the fact would be surprising, if we did not know that the greater part of those who trouble themselves about the matter are disingenuous, and not in fact what they say. They are people who have heard it said that it is the fashion to be thus daring. It is what they call shaking off the yoke, and they try to imitate this. But it would not be difficult to make them understand how greatly they deceive themselves in thus seeking esteem. This is not the way to gain it, even I say among those men of the world who take a healthy view of things, and who know that the only way to succeed in this life is to make ourselves appear honourable, faithful, judicious, and capable of useful service to a friend; because naturally men love only what may be useful to them. Now, what do we gain by hearing it said of a man that he has now thrown off the yoke, that he does not believe there is a God who watches our actions, that he considers himself the sole master of his conduct, and that he thinks he is accountable for it only to himself? Does he think that he has thus brought us to have henceforth complete confidence in him, and to look to him for consolation, advice, and help in every need of life? Do they profess to have delighted us by telling us that they hold our soul to be only a little wind and smoke, especially by telling us this in a haughty and self-satisfied tone of voice? Is this a thing to say gaily? Is it not, on the contrary, a thing to say sadly, as the saddest thing in the world?

If they thought of it seriously, they would see that this is so bad a mistake, so contrary to good sense, so opposed to decency and so removed in every respect from that good breeding which they seek, that they would be more likely to correct than to pervert those who had an inclination to follow them. And indeed, make them give an account of their opinions, and of the reasons which they have for doubting religion, and they will say to you things so feeble and so petty, that they will persuade you of the contrary. The following is what a person one day said to such a one very appositely: "If you continue to talk in this manner, you will really make me religious." And he was right, for who would not have a horror of holding opinions in which he would have such contemptible persons as companions!

Thus those who only feign these opinions would be very unhappy, if they restrained their natural feelings in order to make themselves the most conceited of men. If, at the bottom of their heart, they are troubled at not having more light, let[Pg 58] them not disguise the fact; this avowal will not be shameful. The only shame is to have none. Nothing reveals more an extreme weakness of mind than not to know the misery of a godless man. Nothing is more indicative of a bad disposition of heart than not to desire the truth of eternal promises. Nothing is more dastardly than to act with bravado before

God. Let them then leave these impieties to those who are sufficiently ill-bred to be really capable of them. Let them at least be honest men, if they cannot be Christians. Finally, let them recognise that there are two kinds of people one can call reasonable; those who serve God with all their heart because they know Him, and those who seek Him with all their heart because they do not know Him.

But as for those who live without knowing Him and without seeking Him, they judge themselves so little worthy of their own care, that they are not worthy of the care of others; and it needs all the charity of the religion which they despise, not to despise them even to the point of leaving them to their folly. But because this religion obliges us always to regard them, so long as they are in this life, as capable of the grace which can enlighten them, and to believe that they may, in a little time, be more replenished with faith than we are, and that, on the other hand, we may fall into the blindness wherein they are, we must do for them what we would they should do for us if we were in their place, and call upon them to have pity upon themselves, and to take at least some steps in the endeavour to find light. Let them give to reading this some of the hours which they otherwise employ so uselessly; whatever aversion they may bring to the task, they will perhaps gain something, and at least will not lose much. But as for those who bring to the task perfect sincerity and a real desire to meet with truth, those I hope will be satisfied and convinced of the proofs of a religion so divine, which I have here collected, and in which I have followed somewhat after this order ...

195

Before entering into the proofs of the Christian religion, I find it necessary to point out the sinfulness of those men who live in indifference to the search for truth in a matter which is so important to them, and which touches them so nearly.

Of all their errors, this doubtless is the one which most convicts them of foolishness and blindness, and in which it is[Pg 59] easiest to confound them by the first glimmerings of common sense, and by natural feelings.

For it is not to be doubted that the duration of this life is but a moment; that the state of death is eternal, whatever may be its nature; and that thus all our actions and thoughts must take such different directions according to the state of that eternity, that it is impossible to take one step with sense and judgment, unless we regulate our course by the truth of that point which ought to be our ultimate end.

There is nothing clearer than this; and thus, according to the principles of reason, the conduct of men is wholly unreasonable, if they do not take another course.

On this point, therefore, we condemn those who live without thought of the ultimate end of life, who let themselves be guided by their own inclinations and their own pleasures without reflection and without concern, and, as if they could annihilate eternity by turning away their thought from it, think only of making themselves happy for the moment.

Yet this eternity exists, and death, which must open into it, and threatens them every hour, must in a little time infallibly put them under the dreadful necessity of being either annihilated or unhappy for ever, without knowing which of these eternities is for ever prepared for them.

This is a doubt of terrible consequence. They are in peril of eternal woe; and thereupon, as if the matter were not worth the trouble, they neglect to inquire whether this is one of those opinions which people receive with too credulous a facility, or one of those which, obscure in themselves, have a very firm, though hidden, foundation. Thus they know not whether there be truth or falsity in the matter, nor whether there be strength or weakness in the proofs. They have them before their eyes; they refuse to look at them; and in that ignorance they choose all that is necessary to fall into this misfortune if it exists, to await death to make trial of it, yet to be very content in this state, to make profession of it, and indeed to boast of it. Can we think seriously on the importance of this subject without being horrified at conduct so extravagant?

This resting in ignorance is a monstrous thing, and they who pass their life in it must be made to feel its extravagance and stupidity, by having it shown to them, so that they may be confounded by the sight of their folly. For this is how men reason, when they choose to live in such ignorance of what they[Pg 60] are, and without seeking enlightenment. "I know not," they say ...

196

Men lack heart; they would not make a friend of it.

197

To be insensible to the extent of despising interesting things, and to become insensible to the point which interests us most.

198

The sensibility of man to trifles, and his insensibility to great things, indicates a strange inversion.

199

Let us imagine a number of men in chains, and all condemned to death, where some are killed each day in the sight of the others, and those who remain see their own fate in that of their fellows, and wait their turn, looking at each other sorrowfully and without hope. It is an image of the condition of men.

200

A man in a dungeon, ignorant whether his sentence be pronounced, and having only one hour to learn it, but this hour enough, if he know that it is pronounced, to obtain its repeal, would act unnaturally in spending that hour, not in ascertaining his sentence, but in playing piquet. So it is against nature that man, etc. It is making heavy the hand of God.

Thus not only the zeal of those who seek Him proves God, but also the blindness of those who seek Him not.

201

All the objections of this one and that one only go against themselves, and not against religion. All that infidels say ...

202

[From those who are in despair at being without faith, we see that God does not enlighten them; but as to the rest, we see there is a God who makes them blind.]

203

Fascinatio nugacitatis.[87]—That passion may not harm us, let us act as if we had only eight hours to live.[Pg 61]

204

If we ought to devote eight hours of life, we ought to devote a hundred years.

205

When I consider the short duration of my life, swallowed up in the eternity before and after, the little space which I fill, and even can see, engulfed in the infinite immensity of spaces of which I am ignorant, and which know me not, I am frightened, and am astonished at being here rather than there; for there is no reason why here rather than there, why now rather than then. Who has put me here? By whose order and direction have this place and time been allotted to me? Memoria hospitis unius diei prætereuntis.[88]

206

The eternal silence of these infinite spaces frightens me.

207

How many kingdoms know us not!

208

Why is my knowledge limited? Why my stature? Why my life to one hundred years rather than to a thousand? What reason has nature had for giving me such, and for choosing this number rather than another in the infinity of those from which there is no more reason to choose one than another, trying nothing else?

209

Art thou less a slave by being loved and favoured by thy master? Thou art indeed well off, slave. Thy master favours thee; he will soon beat thee.

210

The last act is tragic, however happy all the rest of the play is; at the last a little earth is thrown upon our head, and that is the end for ever.

211

We are fools to depend upon the society of our fellow-men. Wretched as we are, powerless as we are, they will not aid us;[Pg 62] we shall die alone. We should therefore act as if we were alone, and in that case should we build fine houses, etc.? We should seek the truth without hesitation; and, if we refuse it, we show that we value the esteem of men more than the search for truth.

212

Instability.[89]—It is a horrible thing to feel all that we possess slipping away.

213

Between us and heaven or hell there is only life, which is the frailest thing in the world.

214

Injustice.—That presumption should be joined to meanness is extreme injustice.

215

To fear death without danger, and not in danger, for one must be a man.

216

Sudden death alone is feared; hence confessors stay with lords.

217

An heir finds the title-deeds of his house. Will he say, "Perhaps they are forged?" and neglect to examine them?

218

Dungeon.—I approve of not examining the opinion of Copernicus; but this...! It concerns all our life to know whether the soul be mortal or immortal.

219

It is certain that the mortality or immortality of the soul must make an entire difference to morality. And yet philosophers have constructed their ethics independently of this: they discuss to pass an hour.

Plato, to incline to Christianity.

220

The fallacy of philosophers who have not discussed the immortality of the soul. The fallacy of their dilemma in Montaigne.[Pg 63]

221

Atheists ought to say what is perfectly evident; now it is not perfectly evident that the soul is material.

222

Atheists.—What reason have they for saying that we cannot rise from the dead? What is more difficult, to be born or to rise again; that what has never been should be, or that what has been should be again? Is it more difficult to come into existence than to return to it? Habit makes the one appear easy to us; want of habit makes the other impossible. A popular way of thinking!

Why cannot a virgin bear a child? Does a hen not lay eggs without a cock? What distinguishes these outwardly from others? And who has told us that the hen may not form the germ as well as the cock?

223

What have they to say against the resurrection, and against the child-bearing of the Virgin? Which is the more difficult, to produce a man or an animal, or to reproduce it? And if they had never seen any species of animals, could they have conjectured whether they were produced without connection with each other?

224

How I hate these follies of not believing in the Eucharist, etc.! If the Gospel be true, if Jesus Christ be God, what difficulty is there?

225

Atheism shows strength of mind, but only to a certain degree.

226

Infidels, who profess to follow reason, ought to be exceedingly strong in reason. What say they then? "Do we not see," say they, "that the brutes live and die like men, and Turks like Christians? They have their ceremonies, their prophets, their doctors, their saints, their monks, like us," etc. (Is this contrary to Scripture? Does it not say all this?)

If you care but little to know the truth, here is enough of it to leave you in repose. But if you desire with all your heart[Pg 64] to know it, it is not enough; look at it in detail. This would be sufficient for a question in philosophy; but not here, where it concerns your all. And yet, after a trifling reflection of this kind, we go to amuse ourselves, etc. Let us inquire of this same religion whether it does not give a reason for this obscurity; perhaps it will teach it to us.

227

Order by dialogues.—What ought I to do? I see only darkness everywhere. Shall I believe I am nothing? Shall I believe I am God?

"All things change and succeed each other." You are mistaken; there is ...

228

Objection of atheists: "But we have no light."

229

This is what I see and what troubles me. I look on all sides, and I see only darkness everywhere. Nature presents to me nothing which is not matter of doubt and concern. If I saw nothing there which revealed a Divinity, I would come to a negative conclusion; if I saw everywhere the signs of a Creator, I would remain peacefully in faith. But, seeing too much to deny and too little to be sure, I am in a state to be pitied; wherefore I have a hundred time wished that if a God maintains nature, she should testify to Him unequivocally, and that, if the signs she gives are deceptive, she should suppress them altogether; that she should say everything or nothing, that I might see which cause I ought to follow. Whereas in my present state, ignorant of what I am or of what I ought to do, I know neither my condition nor my duty. My heart inclines wholly to know where is the true good, in order to follow it; nothing would be too dear to me for eternity.

I envy those whom I see living in the faith with such carelessness, and who make such a bad use of a gift of which it seems to me I would make such a different use.

230

It is incomprehensible that God should exist, and it is incomprehensible that He should not exist; that the soul should be joined to the body, and that we should have no soul; that the[Pg 65] world should be created, and that it should not be created, etc.; that original sin should be, and that it should not be.

231

Do you believe it to be impossible that God is infinite, without parts? —Yes. I wish therefore to show you an infinite and indivisible thing.

It is a point moving everywhere with an infinite velocity; for it is one in all places, and is all totality in every place.

Let this effect of nature, which previously seemed to you impossible, make you know that there may be others of which you are still ignorant. Do not draw this conclusion from your experiment, that there remains nothing for you to know; but rather that there remains an infinity for you to know.

232

Infinite movement, the point which fills everything, the moment of rest; infinite without quantity, indivisible and infinite.

233

Infinite—nothing.—Our soul is cast into a body, where it finds number, time, dimension. Thereupon it reasons, and calls this nature, necessity, and can believe nothing else.

Unity joined to infinity adds nothing to it, no more than one foot to an infinite measure. The finite is annihilated in the presence of the infinite, and becomes a pure nothing. So our spirit before God, so our justice before divine justice. There is not so great a disproportion between our justice and that of God, as between unity and infinity.

The justice of God must be vast like His compassion. Now justice to the outcast is less vast, and ought less to offend our feelings than mercy towards the elect.

We know that there is an infinite, and are ignorant of its nature. As we know it to be false that numbers are finite, it is therefore true that there is an infinity in number. But we do not know what it is. It is false that it is even, it is false that it is odd; for the addition of a unit can make no change in its nature. Yet it is a number, and every number is odd or even (this is certainly true of every finite number). So we may well know that there is a God without knowing what He is. Is there not one substantial truth, seeing there are so many things which are not the truth itself?[Pg 66]

We know then the existence and nature of the finite, because we also are finite and have extension. We know the existence of the infinite, and are ignorant of its nature, because it has extension like us, but not limits like us. But we know neither the existence nor the nature of God, because He has neither extension nor limits.

But by faith we know His existence; in glory we shall know His nature. Now, I have already shown that we may well know the existence of a thing, without knowing its nature.

Let us now speak according to natural lights.

If there is a God, He is infinitely incomprehensible, since, having neither parts nor limits, He has no affinity to us. We are then incapable of knowing either what He is or if He is. This being so, who will dare to undertake the decision of the question? Not we, who have no affinity to Him.

Who then will blame Christians for not being able to give a reason for their belief, since they profess a religion for which they cannot give a reason? They declare, in expounding it to the world, that it is a foolishness, stultitiam;[90] and then you complain that they do not prove it! If they proved it, they would not keep their word; it is in lacking proofs, that they are not lacking in sense. "Yes, but although this excuses those who offer it as such, and takes away from them the blame of putting it forward without reason, it does not excuse those who receive it." Let us then examine this point, and say, "God is, or He is not." But to which side shall we incline? Reason can decide nothing here. There is an infinite chaos which separated us. A game is being played at the extremity of this infinite distance where heads or tails will turn up. What will you wager? According to reason, you can do neither the one thing nor the other; according to reason, you can defend neither of the propositions.

Do not then reprove for error those who have made a choice; for you know nothing about it. "No, but I blame them for having made, not this choice, but a choice; for again both he who chooses heads and he who chooses tails are equally at fault, they are both in the wrong. The true course is not to wager at all."

Yes; but you must wager. It is not optional. You are embarked. Which will you choose then? Let us see. Since you must choose, let us see which interests you least. You have two things to lose, the true and the good; and two things to stake,[Pg 67] your reason and your will, your knowledge and your happiness; and your nature has two things to shun, error and misery. Your reason is no more shocked in choosing one rather than the other, since you must of necessity choose. This is one point settled. But your happiness? Let us weigh the gain and the loss in wagering that God is. Let us estimate these two chances. If you gain, you gain all; if you lose, you lose nothing. Wager, then, without hesitation that He is.—"That is very fine. Yes, I must wager; but I may perhaps wager too much."—Let us see. Since there is an equal risk of gain and of loss, if you had only to gain two lives, instead of one, you might still wager. But if there were three lives to gain, you would have to play (since you are under the necessity of playing), and you would be imprudent, when you are forced to play, not to chance your life to gain three at a game where there is an equal risk of loss and gain. But there is an eternity of life and happiness. And this being so, if there were an infinity of chances, of which one only would be for you, you would still be right in wagering one to win two, and you would act stupidly, being obliged to play, by refusing to stake one life against three at a game in which out of an infinity of chances there is one for you, if there were an infinity of an infinitely happy life to gain. But there is here an infinity of an infinitely happy life to gain, a chance of gain against a finite number of chances of loss, and what you stake is finite. It is all divided; wherever the infinite is and there is not an infinity of chances of loss against that of gain, there is no time to hesitate, you must give all. And thus, when one is forced to play, he must renounce reason to preserve his life, rather than risk it for infinite gain, as likely to happen as the loss of nothingness.

For it is no use to say it is uncertain if we will gain, and it is certain that we risk, and that the infinite distance between the certainty of what is staked and the uncertainty of what will be gained, equals the finite good which is certainly staked against the uncertain infinite. It is not so, as every player stakes a certainty to gain an uncertainty, and yet he stakes a finite certainty to gain a finite uncertainty, without transgressing against reason. There is not an infinite distance between the certainty staked and the uncertainty of the gain; that is untrue. In truth, there is an infinity between the certainty of gain and the certainty of loss. But the uncertainty of the gain is proportioned to the certainty of the stake according to the[Pg 68] proportion of the chances of gain and loss. Hence it comes that, if there are as many risks on one side as on the other, the course is to play even; and then the certainty of the stake is equal to the uncertainty of the gain, so far is it from fact that there is an infinite distance between them. And so our proposition is of infinite force, when there is the finite to stake in a game where there are equal risks of gain and of loss, and the infinite to gain. This is demonstrable; and if men are capable of any truths, this is one.

"I confess it, I admit it. But, still, is there no means of seeing the faces of the cards?"—Yes, Scripture and the rest, etc. "Yes, but I have my hands tied and my mouth closed; I am forced to wager, and am not free. I am not released, and am so made that I cannot believe. What, then, would you have me do?"

True. But at least learn your inability to believe, since reason brings you to this, and yet you cannot believe. Endeavour then to convince yourself, not by increase of proofs of God, but by the abatement of your passions. You would like to attain faith, and do not know the way; you would like to cure yourself of unbelief, and ask the remedy for it. Learn of those who have been bound like you, and who now stake all their possessions. These are people who know the way which you would follow, and who are cured of an ill of which you would be cured. Follow the way by which they began; by acting as if they believed, taking the holy water, having masses said, etc. Even this will naturally make you believe, and deaden your acuteness.—"But this is what I am afraid of."—And why? What have you to lose?

But to show you that this leads you there, it is this which will lessen the passions, which are your stumbling-blocks.

The end of this discourse.—Now, what harm will befall you in taking this side? You will be faithful, honest, humble, grateful, generous, a sincere friend, truthful. Certainly you will not have those poisonous pleasures, glory and luxury; but will you not have others? I will tell you that you will thereby gain in this life, and that, at each step you take on this road, you will see so great certainty of gain, so much nothingness in what you risk, that you will at last recognise that you have wagered for something certain and infinite, for which you have given nothing.

"Ah! This discourse transports me, charms me," etc.

If this discourse pleases you and seems impressive, know[Pg 69] that it is made by a man who has knelt, both before and after it, in prayer to that Being, infinite and without parts, before whom he lays all he has, for you also to lay before Him all you have for your own good and for His glory, that so strength may be given to lowliness.

234

If we must not act save on a certainty, we ought not to act on religion, for it is not certain. But how many things we do on an uncertainty, sea voyages, battles! I say then we must do nothing at all, for nothing is certain, and that there is more certainty in religion than there is as to whether we may see to-morrow; for it is not certain that we may see to-morrow, and it is certainly possible that we may not see it. We cannot say as much about religion. It is not certain that it is; but who will venture to say that it is certainly possible that it is not? Now when we work for to-morrow, and so on an uncertainty, we act reasonably; for we ought to work for an uncertainty according to the doctrine of chance which was demonstrated above.

Saint Augustine has seen that we work for an uncertainty, on sea, in battle, etc. But he has not seen the doctrine of chance which proves that we should do so. Montaigne has seen that we are shocked at a fool, and that habit is all-powerful; but he has not seen the reason of this effect.

All these persons have seen the effects, but they have not seen the causes. They are, in comparison with those who have discovered the causes, as those who have only eyes are in comparison with those who have intellect. For the effects are perceptible by sense, and the causes are visible only to the intellect. And although these effects are seen by the mind, this mind is, in comparison with the mind which sees the causes, as the bodily senses are in comparison with the intellect.

235

Rem viderunt, causam non viderunt.

236

According to the doctrine of chance, you ought to put yourself to the trouble of searching for the truth; for if you die without worshipping the True Cause, you are lost.—"But," say you, "if He had wished me to worship Him, He would have left me[Pg 70] signs of His will."—

He has done so; but you neglect them. Seek them, therefore; it is well worth it.

237

Chances.—We must live differently in the world, according to these different assumptions: (1) that we could always remain in it; (2) that it is certain that we shall not remain here long, and uncertain if we shall remain here one hour. This last assumption is our condition.

238

What do you then promise me, in addition to certain troubles, but ten years of self-love (for ten years is the chance), to try hard to please without success?

239

Objection.—Those who hope for salvation are so far happy; but they have as a counterpoise the fear of hell.

Reply.—Who has most reason to fear hell: he who is in ignorance whether there is a hell, and who is certain of damnation if there is; or he who certainly believes there is a hell, and hopes to be saved if there is?

240

"I would soon have renounced pleasure," say they, "had I faith." For my part I tell you, "You would soon have faith, if you renounced pleasure." Now, it is for you to begin. If I could, I would give you faith. I cannot do so, nor therefore test the truth of what you say. But you can well renounce pleasure, and test whether what I say is true.

241

Order.—I would have far more fear of being mistaken, and of finding that the Christian religion was true, than of not being mistaken in believing it true.[Pg 71]

SECTION IV

OF THE MEANS OF BELIEF

242

Preface to the second part.—To speak of those who have treated of this matter.

I admire the boldness with which these persons undertake to speak of God. In addressing their argument to infidels, their first chapter is to prove Divinity from the works of nature.[91] I should not be astonished at their enterprise, if they were addressing their argument to the faithful; for it is certain that those who have the living faith in their heart see at once that all existence is none other than the work of the God whom they adore. But for those in whom this light is extinguished, and in whom we purpose to rekindle it, persons destitute of faith and grace, who, seeking with all their light whatever they see in nature that can bring them to this knowledge, find only obscurity and darkness; to tell them that they have only to look at the smallest things which surround them, and they will see God openly, to give them, as a complete proof of this great and important matter, the course of the moon and planets, and to claim to have concluded the proof with such an argument, is to give them ground for believing that the proofs of our religion are very weak. And I see by reason and experience that nothing is more calculated to arouse their contempt.

It is not after this manner that Scripture speaks, which has a better knowledge of the things that are of God. It says, on the contrary, that God is a hidden God, and that, since the corruption of nature, He has left men in a darkness from which they can escape only through Jesus Christ, without whom all communion with God is cut off. Nemo novit Patrem, nisi Filius, et cui voluerit Filius revelare.[92]

This is what Scripture points out to us, when it says in so many places that those who seek God find Him.[93] It is not of that light, "like the noonday sun," that this is said. We do[Pg 72] not say that those who seek the noonday sun, or water in the sea, shall find them; and hence the evidence of God must not be of this nature. So it tells us elsewhere: Vere tu es Deus absconditus.[94]

243

It is an astounding fact that no canonical writer has ever made use of nature to prove God. They all strive to make us believe in Him. David, Solomon, etc., have never said, "There is no void, therefore there is a God." They must have had more knowledge than the most learned people who came after them, and who have all made use of this argument. This is worthy of attention.

244

"Why! Do you not say yourself that the heavens and birds prove God?" No. "And does your religion not say so?" No. For although it is true in a sense for some souls to whom God gives this light, yet it is false with respect to the majority of men.

245

There are three sources of belief: reason, custom, inspiration. The Christian religion, which alone has reason, does not acknowledge as her true children those who believe without inspiration. It is not that she excludes reason and custom. On the contrary, the mind must be opened to proofs, must be confirmed by custom, and offer itself in humbleness to inspirations, which alone can produce a true and saving effect. Ne evacuetur crux Christi.[95]

246

Order.—After the letter That we ought to seek God, to write the letter On removing obstacles; which is the discourse on "the machine,"[96] on preparing the machine, on seeking by reason.

247

Order.—A letter of exhortation to a friend to induce him to seek. And he will reply, "But what is the use of seeking? Nothing is seen." Then to reply to him, "Do not despair." And he will answer that he would be glad to find some light, but that, according to this very religion, if he believed in it, it will be of no use to him, and that therefore he prefers not to seek. And to answer to that: The machine. [Pg 73]

248

A letter which indicates the use of proofs by the machine.— Faith is different from proof; the one is human, the other is a gift of God. Justus ex fide vivit.[97] It is this faith that God Himself puts into the heart, of which the proof is often the instrument, fides ex auditu;[98] but this faith is in the heart, and makes us not say scio, but credo.

249

It is superstition to put one's hope in formalities; but it is pride to be unwilling to submit to them.

250

The external must be joined to the internal to obtain anything from God, that is to say, we must kneel, pray with the lips, etc., in order that proud man, who would not submit himself to God, may be now subject to the creature.[99] To expect help from these externals is superstition; to refuse to join them to the internal is pride.

251

Other religions, as the pagan, are more popular, for they consist in externals. But they are not for educated people. A purely intellectual religion would be more suited to the learned, but it would be of no use to the common people. The Christian religion alone is adapted to all, being composed of externals and internals. It raises the common people to the internal, and humbles the proud to the external; it is not perfect without the two, for the people must understand the spirit of the letter, and the learned must submit their spirit to the letter.

252

For we must not misunderstand ourselves; we are as much automatic as intellectual; and hence it comes that the instrument by which conviction is attained is not demonstrated alone. How few things are demonstrated? Proofs only convince the mind. Custom is the source of our strongest and most believed proofs. It bends the automaton, which persuades the mind without its thinking about the matter. Who has demonstrated that there will be a to-morrow, and that we shall die? And what is more believed? It is, then, custom which persuades us of it; it is[Pg 74] custom that makes so many men

Christians; custom that makes them Turks, heathens, artisans, soldiers, etc. (Faith in baptism is more received among Christians than among Turks.) Finally, we must have recourse to it when once the mind has seen where the truth is, in order to quench our thirst, and steep ourselves in that belief, which escapes us at every hour; for always to have proofs ready is too much trouble. We must get an easier belief, which is that of custom, which, without violence, without art, without argument, makes us believe things, and inclines all our powers to this belief, so that out soul falls naturally into it. It is not enough to believe only by force of conviction, when the automaton is inclined to believe the contrary. Both our parts must be made to believe, the mind by reasons which it is sufficient to have seen once in a lifetime, and the automaton by custom, and by not allowing it to incline to the contrary. Inclina cor meum, Deus.[100]

The reason acts slowly, with so many examinations, and on so many principles, which must be always present, that at every hour it falls asleep, or wanders, through want of having all its principles present. Feeling does not act thus; it acts in a moment, and is always ready to act. We must then put our faith in feeling; otherwise it will be always vacillating.

253

Two extremes: to exclude reason, to admit reason only.

254

It is not a rare thing to have to reprove the world for too much docility. It is a natural vice like credulity, and as pernicious. Superstition.

255

Piety is different from superstition.

To carry piety as far as superstition is to destroy it.

The heretics reproach us for this superstitious submission. This is to do what they reproach us for ...

Infidelity, not to believe in the Eucharist, because it is not seen.

Superstition to believe propositions. Faith, etc.

256

I say there are few true Christians, even as regards faith. There are many who believe but from superstition. There are[Pg 75] many who do not believe solely from wickedness. Few are between the two.

In this I do not include those who are of truly pious character, nor all those who believe from a feeling in their heart.

257

There are only three kinds of persons; those who serve God, having found Him; others who are occupied in seeking Him, not having found Him; while the remainder live without seeking Him, and without having found Him. The first are reasonable and happy, the last are foolish and unhappy; those between are unhappy and reasonable.

258

Unusquisque sibi Deum fingit.[101]

Disgust.

259

Ordinary people have the power of not thinking of that about which they do not wish to think. "Do not meditate on the passages about the Messiah," said the Jew to his son. Thus our people often act. Thus are false religions preserved, and even the true one, in regard to many persons.

But there are some who have not the power of thus preventing thought, and who think so much the more as they are forbidden. These undo false religions, and even the true one, if they do not find solid arguments.

260

They hide themselves in the press, and call numbers to their rescue. Tumult.

Authority.—So far from making it a rule to believe a thing because you have heard it, you ought to believe nothing without putting yourself into the position as if you had never heard it.

It is your own assent to yourself, and the constant voice of your own reason, and not of others, that should make you believe.

Belief is so important! A hundred contradictions might be true. If antiquity were the rule of belief, men of ancient time would then be without rule. If general consent, if men had perished?

False humanity, pride.

Lift the curtain. You try in vain; if you must either believe,[Pg 76] or deny, or doubt. Shall we then have no rule? We judge that animals do well what they do. Is there no rule whereby to judge men?

To deny, to believe, and to doubt well, are to a man what the race is to a horse.

Punishment of those who sin, error.

261

Those who do not love the truth take as a pretext that it is disputed, and that a multitude deny it. And so their error arises only from this, that they do not love either truth or charity. Thus they are without excuse.

262

Superstition and lust. Scruples, evil desires. Evil fear; fear, not such as comes from a belief in God, but such as comes from a doubt whether He exists or not. True fear comes from faith; false fear comes from doubt. True fear is joined to hope, because it is born of faith, and because men hope in the God in whom they believe. False fear is joined to despair, because men fear the God in whom they have no belief. The former fear to lose Him; the latter fear to find Him.

263

"A miracle," says one, "would strengthen my faith." He says so when he does not see one. Reasons, seen from afar, appear to limit our view; but when they are reached, we begin to see beyond. Nothing stops the nimbleness of our mind. There is no rule, say we, which has not some exceptions, no truth so general which has not some aspect in which it fails. It is sufficient that it be not absolutely universal to give us a pretext for applying the exceptions to the present subject, and for saying, "This is not always true; there are therefore cases where it is not so." It only remains to show that this is one of them; and that is why we are very awkward or unlucky, if we do not find one some day.

264

We do not weary of eating and sleeping every day, for hunger and sleepiness recur. Without that we should weary of them. So, without the hunger for spiritual things, we weary of them. Hunger after righteousness, the eighth beatitude.[Pg 77][102]

265

Faith indeed tells what the senses do not tell, but not the contrary of what they see. It is above them and not contrary to them.

266

How many stars have telescopes revealed to us which did not exist for our philosophers of old! We freely attack Holy Scripture on the great number of stars, saying, "There are only one thousand and twenty-eight,[103] we know it." There is grass on the earth, we see it—from the moon we would not see it—and on the grass are leaves, and in these leaves are small animals; but after that no more.—O presumptuous man!—The compounds are composed of elements, and the elements not.—O presumptuous man! Here is a fine reflection.—We must not say that there is anything which we do not see.—We must then talk like others, but not think like them.

267

The last proceeding of reason is to recognise that there is an infinity of things which are beyond it. It is but feeble if it does not see so far as to know this. But if natural things are beyond it, what will be said of supernatural?

268

Submission.—We must know where to doubt, where to feel certain, where to submit. He who does not do so, understands not the force of reason. There are some who offend against these three rules, either by affirming everything as demonstrative, from want of knowing what demonstration is; or by doubting everything, from want of knowing where to submit; or by submitting in everything, from want of knowing where they must judge.

269

Submission is the use of reason in which consists true Christianity.

270

St. Augustine.[104]—Reason would never submit, if it did not judge that there are some occasions on which it ought to submit. It is then right for it to submit, when it judges that it ought to submit.[Pg 78]

271

Wisdom sends us to childhood. Nisi efficiamini sicut parvuli.[105]

272

There is nothing so conformable to reason as this disavowal of reason.

273

If we submit everything to reason, our religion will have no mysterious and supernatural element. If we offend the principles of reason, our religion will be absurd and ridiculous.

274

All our reasoning reduces itself to yielding to feeling.

But fancy is like, though contrary to feeling, so that we cannot distinguish between these contraries. One person says that my feeling is fancy, another that his fancy is feeling. We should have a rule. Reason offers itself; but it is pliable in every sense; and thus there is no rule.

275

Men often take their imagination for their heart; and they believe they are converted as soon as they think of being converted.

276

M. de Roannez said: "Reasons come to me afterwards, but at first a thing pleases or shocks me without my knowing the reason, and yet it shocks me for that reason which I only discover afterwards." But I believe, not that it shocked him for the reasons which were found afterwards, but that these reasons were only found because it shocks him.

277

The heart has its reasons, which reason does not know. We feel it in a thousand things. I say that the heart naturally loves the Universal Being, and also itself naturally, according as it gives itself to them; and it hardens itself against one or the other at its will. You have rejected the one, and kept the other. Is it by reason that you love yourself?

278

It is the heart which experiences God, and not the reason. This, then, is faith: God felt by the heart, not by the reason.[Pg 79]

279

Faith is a gift of God; do not believe that we said it was a gift of reasoning. Other religions do not say this of their faith. They only gave reasoning in order to arrive at it, and yet it does not bring them to it.

280

The knowledge of God is very far from the love of Him.

281

Heart, instinct, principles.

282

We know truth, not only by the reason, but also by the heart, and it is in this last way that we know first principles; and reason, which has no part in it, tries in vain to impugn them. The sceptics, who have only this for their object, labour to no purpose. We know that we do not dream, and however impossible it is for us to prove it by reason, this inability demonstrates only the weakness of our reason, but not, as they affirm, the uncertainty of all our knowledge. For the knowledge of first principles, as space, time, motion, number, is as sure as any of those which we get from reasoning. And reason must trust these intuitions of the heart, and must base them on every argument. (We have intuitive knowledge of the tri-dimensional nature of space, and of the infinity of number, and reason then shows that there are no two square numbers one of which is double of the other. Principles are intuited, propositions are inferred, all with certainty, though in different ways.) And it is as useless and absurd for reason to demand from the heart proofs of her first principles, before admitting them, as it would be for the heart to demand from reason an intuition of all demonstrated propositions before accepting them.

This inability ought, then, to serve only to humble reason, which would judge all, but not to impugn our certainty, as if only reason were capable of instructing us. Would to God, on the contrary, that we had never need of it, and that we knew everything by instinct and intuition! But nature has refused us this boon. On the contrary, she has given us but very little knowledge of this kind; and all the rest can be acquired only by reasoning.[Pg 80]

Therefore, those to whom God has imparted religion by intuition are very fortunate, and justly convinced. But to those who do not have it, we can give it only by reasoning, waiting for God to give them spiritual insight, without which faith is only human, and useless for salvation.

283

Order.—Against the objection that Scripture has no order.

The heart has its own order; the intellect has its own, which is by principle and demonstration. The heart has another. We do not prove that we ought to be loved by enumerating in order the causes of love; that would be ridiculous.

Jesus Christ and Saint Paul employ the rule of love, not of intellect; for they would warm, not instruct. It is the same with Saint Augustine. This order consists chiefly in digressions on each point to indicate the end, and keep it always in sight.

284

Do not wonder to see simple people believe without reasoning. God imparts to them love of Him and hatred of self. He inclines their heart to believe. Men will never believe with a saving and real faith, unless God inclines their heart; and they will believe as soon as He inclines it. And this is what David knew well, when he said: Inclina cor meum, Deus, in ...[106]

285

Religion is suited to all kinds of minds. Some pay attention only to its establishment,[107] and this religion is such that its very establishment suffices to prove its truth. Others trace it even to the apostles. The more learned go back to the beginning of the world. The angels see it better still, and from a more distant time.

286

Those who believe without having read the Testaments, do so because they have an inward disposition entirely holy, and all that they hear of our religion conforms to it. They feel that a God has made them; they desire only to love God; they desire to hate themselves only. They feel that they have no strength in themselves; that they are incapable of coming to God; and that if God does not come to them, they can have no communion with Him. And they hear our religion say that men must love[Pg 81] God only, and hate self only; but that all being corrupt and unworthy of God, God made Himself man to unite Himself to us. No more is required to persuade men who have this disposition in their heart, and who have this knowledge of their duty and of their inefficiency.

287

Those whom we see to be Christians without the knowledge of the prophets and evidences, nevertheless judge of their religion as well as those who have that knowledge. They judge of it by the heart, as others judge of it by the intellect. God Himself inclines them to believe, and thus they are most effectively convinced.

I confess indeed that one of those Christians who believe without proofs will not perhaps be capable of convincing an infidel who will say the same of himself. But those who know the proofs of religion will prove without difficulty that such a believer is truly inspired by God, though he cannot prove it himself.

For God having said in His prophecies (which are undoubtedly prophecies), that in the reign of Jesus Christ He would spread His spirit abroad among nations, and that the youths and maidens and children of the Church would prophesy;[108] it is certain that the Spirit of God is in these, and not in the others.

288

Instead of complaining that God had hidden Himself, you will give Him thanks for having revealed so much of Himself; and you will also give Him thanks for not having revealed Himself to haughty sages, unworthy to know so holy a God.

Two kinds of persons know Him: those who have a humble heart, and who love lowliness, whatever kind of intellect they may have, high or low; and those who have sufficient understanding to see the truth, whatever opposition they may have to it.

289

Proof.—1. The Christian religion, by its establishment, having established itself so strongly, so gently, whilst contrary to nature.—2. The sanctity, the dignity, and the humility of a Christian soul.—3. The miracles of Holy Scripture.—4. Jesus Christ in particular.—5. The apostles in particular.—6. Moses[Pg 82] and the prophets in particular.—7. The Jewish people.—8. The prophecies.—9. Perpetuity; no religion has perpetuity.— 10. The doctrine which gives a reason for everything.—11. The sanctity of this law.—12. By the course of the world.

Surely, after considering what is life and what is religion, we should not refuse to obey the inclination to follow it, if it comes into our heart; and it is certain that there is no ground for laughing at those who follow it.

290

Proofs of religion.—Morality, Doctrine, Miracles, Prophecies, Types.

[Pg 83]

SECTION V

JUSTICE AND THE REASON OF EFFECTS

291

In the letter On Injustice can come the ridiculousness of the law that the elder gets all. "My friend, you were born on this side of the mountain, it is therefore just that your elder brother gets everything."

"Why do you kill me?"

292

He lives on the other side of the water.

293

"Why do you kill me? What! do you not live on the other side of the water? If you lived on this side, my friend, I should be an assassin, and it would be unjust to slay you in this manner. But since you live on the other side, I am a hero, and it is just."

294

On what shall man found the order of the world which he would govern?[109] Shall it be on the caprice of each individual? What confusion! Shall it be on justice? Man is ignorant of it.

Certainly had he known it, he would not have established this maxim, the most general of all that obtain among men, that each should follow the custom of his own country. The glory of true equity would have brought all nations under subjection, and legislators would not have taken as their model the fancies and caprice of Persians and Germans instead of this unchanging justice. We should have seen it set up in all the States on earth and in all times; whereas we see neither justice nor injustice which does not change its nature with change in climate. Three degrees of latitude reverse all jurisprudence; a meridian decides the truth. Fundamental laws change after a few years of possession; right has its epochs; the entry of Saturn into the Lion[Pg 84] marks to us the origin of such and such a crime. A strange justice that is bounded by a river! Truth on this side of the Pyrenees, error on the other side.

Men admit that justice does not consist in these customs, but that it resides in natural laws, common to every country. They would certainly maintain it obstinately, if reckless chance which has distributed human laws had encountered even one which was universal; but the farce is that the caprice of men has so many vagaries that there is no such law.

Theft, incest, infanticide, parricide, have all had a place among virtuous actions. Can anything be more ridiculous than that a man should have the right to kill me because he lives on the other side of the water, and because his ruler has a quarrel with mine, though I have none with him?

Doubtless there are natural laws; but good reason once corrupted has corrupted all. Nihil amplius nostrum est;[110] quod nostrum dicimus, artis est. Ex senatus—consultis et plebiscitis crimina exercentur.[111] Ut olim vitiis, sic nunc legibus laboramus.[112]

The result of this confusion is that one affirms the essence of justice to be the authority of the legislator; another, the interest of the sovereign;[113] another, present custom,[114] and this is the most sure. Nothing, according to reason alone, is just in itself; all changes with time. Custom creates the whole of equity, for the simple reason that it is accepted. It is the mystical foundation of its authority;[115] whoever carries it back to first principles destroys it. Nothing is so faulty as those laws which correct faults. He who obeys them because they are just, obeys a justice which is imaginary, and not the essence of law; it is quite self-contained, it is law and nothing more. He who will examine its motive will find it so feeble and so trifling that if he be not accustomed to contemplate the wonders of human imagination, he will marvel that one century has gained for it so much pomp and reverence. The art of opposition and of revolution is to unsettle established customs, sounding them even to their source, to point out their want of authority and justice. We must, it is said, get back to the natural and fundamental laws of the State, which an unjust custom has abolished. It is a game certain to result in the loss of all; nothing will be just on the balance. Yet people readily lend their ear to such arguments. They shake off the yoke as soon as they recognise it; and the great profit by their ruin, and by that of these curious investigators of accepted customs. But from a contrary mistake[Pg 85] men sometimes think they can justly do everything which is not without an example. That is why the wisest of legislators[116] said that it was necessary to deceive men for their own good; and another, a good politician, Cum veritatem qua liberetur ignoret, expedit quod fallatur.[117] We must not see the fact of usurpation; law was once introduced without reason, and has become reasonable. We must make it regarded as authoritative, eternal, and conceal its origin, if we do not wish that it should soon come to an end.

295

Mine, thine.—"This dog is mine," said those poor children; "that is my place in the sun." Here is the beginning and the image of the usurpation of all the earth.

296

When the question for consideration is whether we ought to make war, and kill so many men—condemn so many Spaniards to death—only one man is judge, and he is an interested party. There should be a third, who is disinterested.

297

Veri juris.[118]—We have it no more; if we had it, we should take conformity to the customs of a country as the rule of justice. It is here that, not finding justice, we have found force, etc.

298

Justice, might.—It is right that what is just should be obeyed; it is necessary that what is strongest should be obeyed. Justice without might is helpless; might without justice is tyrannical. Justice without might is gainsaid, because there are always offenders; might without justice is condemned. We must then combine justice and might, and for this end make what is just strong, or what is strong just.

Justice is subject to dispute; might is easily recognised and is not disputed. So we cannot give might to justice, because might has gainsaid justice, and has declared that it is she herself who is just. And thus being unable to make what is just strong, we have made what is strong just.

299

The only universal rules are the laws of the country in ordinary affairs, and of the majority in others. Whence comes this?[Pg 86] From the might which is in them. Hence it comes that kings, who have power of a different kind, do not follow the majority of their ministers.

No doubt equality of goods is just; but, being unable to cause might to obey justice, men have made it just to obey might. Unable to strengthen justice, they have justified might; so that the just and the strong should unite, and there should be peace, which is the sovereign good.

300

"When a strong man armed keepeth his goods, his goods are in peace."[119]

301

Why do we follow the majority? It is because they have more reason? No, because they have more power.

Why do we follow the ancient laws and opinions? Is it because they are more sound? No, but because they are unique, and remove from us the root of difference.

302

... It is the effect of might, not of custom. For those who are capable of originality are few; the greater number will only follow, and refuse glory to those inventors who seek it by their inventions. And if these are obstinate in their wish to obtain glory, and despise those who do not invent, the latter will call them ridiculous names, and would beat them with a stick. Let no one then boast of his subtlety, or let him keep his complacency to himself.

303

Might is the sovereign of the world, and not opinion.—But opinion makes use of might.—It is might that makes opinion. Gentleness is beautiful in our opinion. Why? Because he who will dance on a rope will be alone,[120] and I will gather a stronger mob of people who will say that it is unbecoming.

304

The cords which bind the respect of men to each other are in general cords of necessity; for there must be different degrees, all men wishing to rule, and not all being able to do so, but some being able.[Pg 87]

Let us then imagine we see society in the process of formation. Men will doubtless fight till the stronger party overcomes the weaker, and a dominant party is established. But when this is once determined, the masters, who do not desire the continuation of strife, then decree that the power which is in their hands shall be transmitted as they please. Some place it in election by the people, others in hereditary succession, etc.

And this is the point where imagination begins to play its part. Till now power makes fact; now power is sustained by imagination in a certain party, in France in the nobility, in Switzerland in the burgesses, etc.

These cords which bind the respect of men to such and such an individual are therefore the cords of imagination.

305

The Swiss are offended by being called gentlemen, and prove themselves true plebeians in order to be thought worthy of great office.

306

As duchies, kingships, and magistracies are real and necessary, because might rules all, they exist everywhere and always. But since only caprice makes such and such a one a ruler, the principle is not constant, but subject to variation, etc.

307

The chancellor is grave, and clothed with ornaments, for his position is unreal. Not so the king, he has power, and has nothing to do with the imagination. Judges, physicians, etc. appeal only to the imagination.

308

The habit of seeing kings accompanied by guards, drums, officers, and all the paraphernalia which mechanically inspire respect and awe, makes their countenance, when sometimes seen alone without these accompaniments, impress respect and awe on their subjects; because we cannot separate in thought their persons from the surroundings with which we see them usually joined. And the world, which knows not that this effect is the result of habit, believes that it arises by a natural force, whence come these words, "The character of Divinity is stamped on his countenance," etc.[Pg 88]

309

Justice.—As custom determines what is agreeable, so also does it determine justice.

310

King and tyrant.—I, too, will keep my thoughts secret.

I will take care on every journey.

Greatness of establishment, respect for establishment.

The pleasure of the great is the power to make people happy.

The property of riches is to be given liberally.

The property of each thing must be sought. The property of power is to protect.

When force attacks humbug, when a private soldier takes the square cap off a first president, and throws it out of the window.

311

The government founded on opinion and imagination reigns for some time, and this government is pleasant and voluntary; that founded on might lasts for ever. Thus opinion is the queen of the world, but might is its tyrant.

312

Justice is what is established; and thus all our established laws will necessarily be regarded as just without examination, since they are established.

313

Sound opinions of the people.—Civil wars are the greatest of evils. [121] They are inevitable, if we wish to reward desert; for all will say they are deserving. The evil we have to fear from a fool who succeeds by right of birth, is neither so great nor so sure.

314

God has created all for Himself. He has bestowed upon Himself the power of pain and pleasure.

You can apply it to God, or to yourself. If to God, the Gospel is the rule. If to yourself, you will take the place of God. As God is surrounded by persons full of charity, who ask of Him the blessings of charity that are in His power, so ... Recognise then and learn that you are only a king of lust, and take the ways of lust.[Pg 89]

315

The reason of effects.—It is wonderful that men would not have me honour a man clothed in brocade, and followed by seven or eight lackeys! Why! He will have me thrashed, if I do not salute him. This custom is a force. It is the same with a horse in fine trappings in comparison with another! Montaigne[122] is a fool not to see what difference there is, to wonder at our finding any, and to ask the reason. "Indeed," says he, "how comes it," etc....

316

Sound opinions of the people.—To be spruce is not altogether foolish, for it proves that a great number of people work for one. It shows by one's hair, that one has a valet, a perfumer, etc., by one's band, thread, lace, ... etc. Now it is not merely superficial nor merely outward show to have many arms at command. The more arms one has, the more powerful one is. To be spruce is to show one's power.

317

Deference means, "Put yourself to inconvenience." This is apparently silly, but is quite right. For it is to say, "I would indeed put myself to inconvenience if you required it, since indeed I do so when it is of no service to you." Deference further serves to distinguish the great. Now if deference was displayed by sitting in an arm-chair, we should show deference to everybody, and so no distinction would be made; but, being put to inconvenience, we distinguish very well.

318

He has four lackeys.

319

How rightly do we distinguish men by external appearances rather than by internal qualities! Which of us two shall have precedence? Who will give place to the other? The least clever. But I am as clever as he. We should have to fight over this. He has four lackeys, and I have only one. This can be seen; we have only to count. It falls to me to yield, and I am a fool if I contest the matter. By this means we are at peace, which is the greatest of boons.[Pg 90]

320

The most unreasonable things in the world become most reasonable, because of the unruliness of men. What is less reasonable than to choose the eldest son of a queen to rule a State? We do not choose as captain of a ship the passenger who is of the best family.

This law would be absurd and unjust; but because men are so themselves, and always will be so, it becomes reasonable and just. For whom will men choose, as the most virtuous and able? We at once come to blows, as each claims to be the most virtuous and able. Let us then attach this quality to something indisputable. This is the king's eldest son. That is clear, and there is no dispute. Reason can do no better, for civil war is the greatest of evils.

321

Children are astonished to see their comrades respected.

322

To be of noble birth is a great advantage. In eighteen years it places a man within the select circle, known and respected, as another would have merited in fifty years. It is a gain of thirty years without trouble.

323

What is the Ego?

Suppose a man puts himself at a window to see those who pass by. If I pass by, can I say that he placed himself there to see me? No; for he does not think of me in particular. But does he who loves someone on account of beauty really love that person? No; for the small-pox, which will kill beauty without killing the person, will cause him to love her no more.

And if one loves me for my judgment, memory, he does not love me, for I can lose these qualities without losing myself. Where, then, is this Ego, if it be neither in the body nor in the soul? And how love the body or the soul, except for these qualities which do not constitute me, since they are perishable? For it is impossible and would be unjust to love the soul of a person in the abstract, and whatever qualities might be therein. We never, then, love a person, but only qualities.

Let us, then, jeer no more at those who are honoured on account of rank and office; for we love a person only on account of borrowed qualities.[Pg 91]

324

The people have very sound opinions, for example:

1. In having preferred diversion and hunting to poetry. The half-learned laugh at it, and glory in being above the folly of the world; but the people are right for a reason which these do not fathom.

2. In having distinguished men by external marks, as birth or wealth. The world again exults in showing how unreasonable this is; but it is very reasonable. Savages laugh at an infant king.[123]

3. In being offended at a blow, on in desiring glory so much. But it is very desirable on account of the other essential goods which are joined to it; and a man who has received a blow, without resenting it, is overwhelmed with taunts and indignities.

4. In working for the uncertain; in sailing on the sea; in walking over a plank.

325

Montaigne is wrong. Custom should be followed only because it is custom, and not because it is reasonable or just. But people follow it for this sole reason, that they think it just. Otherwise they would follow it no longer, although it were the custom; for they will only submit to reason or justice. Custom without this would pass for tyranny; but the sovereignty of reason and justice is no more tyrannical than that of desire. They are principles natural to man.

It would therefore be right to obey laws and customs, because they are laws; but we should know that there is neither truth nor justice to introduce into them, that we know nothing of these, and so must follow what is accepted. By this means we would never depart from them. But people cannot accept this doctrine; and, as they believe that truth can be found, and that it exists in law and custom, they believe them, and take their antiquity as a proof of their truth, and not simply of their authority apart from truth. Thus they obey laws, but they are liable to revolt when these are proved to be valueless; and this can be shown of all, looked at from a certain aspect.

326

Injustice.—It is dangerous to tell the people that the laws are unjust; for they obey them only because they think them just.[Pg 92] Therefore it is necessary to tell them at the same time that they must obey them because they are laws, just as they must obey superiors, not because they are just, but because they are superiors. In this way all sedition is prevented, if this can be made intelligible, and it be understood what is the proper definition of justice.

327

The world is a good judge of things, for it is in natural ignorance, which is man's true state.[124] The sciences have two extremes which meet. The first is the pure natural ignorance in which all men find themselves at birth. The other extreme is that reached by great intellects, who, having run through all that men can know, find they know nothing, and come back again to that same ignorance from which they set out; but this is a learned ignorance which is conscious of itself. Those between the two, who have departed from natural ignorance and not been able to reach the other, have some smattering of this vain knowledge, and pretend to be wise. These trouble the world, and are bad judges of everything. The people and the wise constitute the world; these despise it, and are despised. They judge badly of everything, and the world judges rightly of them.

328

The reason of effects.—Continual alternation of pro and con.

We have then shown that man is foolish, by the estimation he makes of things which are not essential; and all these opinions are destroyed. We have next shown that all these opinions are very sound, and that thus, since all these vanities are well founded, the people are not so foolish as is said. And so we have destroyed the opinion which destroyed that of the people.

But we must now destroy this last proposition, and show that it remains always true that the people are foolish, though their opinions are sound; because they do not perceive the truth where it is, and, as they place it where it is not, their opinions are always very false and very unsound.

329

The reason of effects.—The weakness of man is the reason why so many things are considered fine, as to be good at playing the lute. It is only an evil because of our weakness.[Pg 93]

330

The power of kings is founded on the reason and on the folly of the people, and specially on their folly. The greatest and most important thing in the world has weakness for its foundation, and this foundation is wonderfully sure; for there is nothing more sure than this, that the people will be weak. What is based on sound reason is very ill founded, as the estimate of wisdom.

331

We can only think of Plato and Aristotle in grand academic robes. They were honest men, like others, laughing with their friends, and when they diverted themselves with writing their Laws and the Politics, they did it as an amusement. That part of their life was the least philosophic and the least serious; the most philosophic was to live simply and quietly. If they wrote on politics, it was as if laying down rules for a lunatic asylum; and if they presented the appearance of speaking of a great matter, it was because they knew that the madmen, to whom they spoke, thought they were kings and emperors. They entered into their principles in order to make their madness as little harmful as possible.

332

Tyranny consists in the desire of universal power beyond its scope.

There are different assemblies of the strong, the fair, the sensible, the pious, in which each man rules at home, not elsewhere. And sometimes they meet, and the strong and the fair foolishly fight as to who shall be master, for their mastery is of different kinds. They do not understand one another, and their fault is the desire to rule everywhere. Nothing can effect this, not even might, which is of no use in the kingdom of the wise, and is only mistress of external actions.

Tyranny— ... So these expressions are false and tyrannical: "I am fair, therefore I must be feared. I am strong, therefore I must be loved. I am ..."

Tyranny is the wish to have in one way what can only be had in another. We render different duties to different merits; the duty of love to the pleasant; the duty of fear to the strong; the duty of belief to the learned.[Pg 94]

We must render these duties; it is unjust to refuse them, and unjust to ask others. And so it is false and tyrannical to say, "He is not strong, therefore I will not esteem him; he is not able, therefore I will not fear him."

333

Have you never seen people who, in order to complain of the little fuss you make about them, parade before you the example of great men who esteem them? In answer I reply to them, "Show me the merit whereby you have charmed these persons, and I also will esteem you."

334

The reason of effects.—Lust and force are the source of all our actions; lust causes voluntary actions, force involuntary ones.

335

The reason of effects.—It is then true to say that all the world is under a delusion; for, although the opinions of the people are sound, they are not so as conceived by them, since they think the truth to be where it is not. Truth is indeed in their opinions, but not at the point where they imagine it. [Thus] it is true that we must honour noblemen, but not because noble birth is real superiority, etc.

336

The reason of effects.—We must keep our thought secret, and judge everything by it, while talking like the people.

337

The reason of effects.—Degrees. The people honour persons of high birth. The semi-learned despise them, saying that birth is not a personal, but a chance superiority. The learned honour them, not for popular reasons, but for secret reasons. Devout persons, who have more zeal than knowledge, despise them, in spite of that consideration which makes them honoured by the learned, because they judge them by a new light which piety gives them. But perfect Christians honour them by another and higher light. So arise a succession of opinions for and against, according to the light one has. [Pg 95]

338

True Christians nevertheless comply with folly, not because they respect folly, but the command of God, who for the punishment of men has made them subject to these follies. Omnis creatura subjecta est vanitati.[125] Liberabitur.[126] Thus Saint Thomas[127] explains the passage in Saint James on giving place to the rich, that if they do it not in the sight of God, they depart from the command of religion.

[Pg 96]

SECTION VI

THE PHILOSOPHERS

339

I can well conceive a man without hands, feet, head (for it is only experience which teaches us that the head is more necessary than feet). But I cannot conceive man without thought; he would be a stone or a brute.

340

The arithmetical machine produces effects which approach nearer to thought than all the actions of animals. But it does nothing which would enable us to attribute will to it, as to the animals.

341

The account of the pike and frog of Liancourt.[128] They do it always, and never otherwise, nor any other thing showing mind.

342

If an animal did by mind what it does by instinct, and if it spoke by mind what it speaks by instinct, in hunting, and in warning its mates that the prey is found or lost; it would indeed also speak in regard to those things which affect it closer, as example, "Gnaw me this cord which is wounding me, and which I cannot reach."

343

The beak of the parrot, which it wipes, although it is clean.

344

Instinct and reason, marks of two natures.

345

Reason commands us far more imperiously than a master; for in disobeying the one we are unfortunate, and in disobeying the other we are fools.[Pg 97]

346

Thought constitutes the greatness of man.

347

Man is but a reed, the most feeble thing in nature; but he is a thinking reed. The entire universe need not arm itself to crush him. A vapour, a drop of water suffices to kill him. But, if the universe were to crush him, man would still be more noble than that which killed him, because he knows that he dies and the advantage which the universe has over him; the universe knows nothing of this.

All our dignity consists, then, in thought. By it we must elevate ourselves, and not by space and time which we cannot fill. Let us endeavour, then, to think well; this is the principle of morality.

348

A thinking reed.—It is not from space that I must seek my dignity, but from the government of my thought. I shall have no more if I possess worlds. By space the universe encompasses and swallows me up like an atom; by thought I comprehend the world.

349

Immateriality of the soul.—Philosophers[129] who have mastered their passions. What matter could do that?

350

The Stoics.—They conclude that what has been done once can be done always, and that since the desire of glory imparts some power to those whom it possesses, others can do likewise. There are feverish movements which health cannot imitate.

Epictetus[130] concludes that since there are consistent Christians, every man can easily be so.

351

Those great spiritual efforts, which the soul sometimes assays, are things on which it does not lay hold.[131] It only leaps to them, not as upon a throne, for ever, but merely for an instant.

352

The strength of a man's virtue must not be measured by his efforts, but by his ordinary life.[Pg 98]

353

I do not admire the excess of a virtue as of valour, except I see at the same time the excess of the opposite virtue, as in Epaminondas,[132] who had the greatest valour and the greatest kindness. For otherwise it is not to rise, it is to fall. We do not display greatness by going to one extreme, but in touching both at once, and filling all the intervening space. But perhaps this is only a sudden movement of the soul from one to the other extreme, and in fact it is ever at one point only, as in the case of a firebrand. Be it so, but at least this indicates agility if not expanse of soul.

354

Man's nature is not always to advance; it has its advances and retreats.

Fever has its cold and hot fits; and the cold proves as well as the hot the greatness of the fire of fever.

The discoveries of men from age to age turn out the same. The kindness and the malice of the world in general are the same. Plerumque gratæ principibus vices.[133]

355

Continuous eloquence wearies.

Princes and kings sometimes play. They are not always on their thrones. They weary there. Grandeur must be abandoned to be appreciated. Continuity in everything is unpleasant. Cold is agreeable, that we may get warm.

Nature acts by progress, itus et reditus. It goes and returns, then advances further, then twice as much backwards, then more forward than ever, etc.

The tide of the sea behaves in the same manner; and so apparently does the sun in its course.

356

The nourishment of the body is little by little. Fullness of nourishment and smallness of substance.

357

When we would pursue virtues to their extremes on either side, vices present themselves, which insinuate themselves insensibly there, in their insensible journey towards the infinitely little:[Pg 99] and vices present themselves in a crowd towards the infinitely great, so that we lose ourselves in them, and no longer see virtues. We find fault with perfection itself.

358

Man is neither angel nor brute, and the unfortunate thing is that he who would act the angel acts the brute.[134]

359

We do not sustain ourselves in virtue by our own strength, but by the balancing of two opposed vices, just as we remain upright amidst two contrary gales. Remove one of the vices, and we fall into the other.

360

What the Stoics propose is so difficult and foolish!

The Stoics lay down that all those who are not at the high degree of wisdom are equally foolish and vicious, as those who are two inches under water.

361

The sovereign good. Dispute about the sovereign good.—Ut sis contentus temetipso et ex te nascentibus bonis.[135] There is a contradiction, for in the end they advise suicide. Oh! What a happy life, from which we are to free ourselves as from the plague!

362

Ex senatus-consultis et plebiscitis ...

To ask like passages.

363

Ex senatus-consultis et plebiscitis scelera exercentur. Sen. 588.[136]

Nihil tam absurde dici potest quod non dicatur ab aliquo philosophorum. Divin.[137]

Quibusdam destinatis sententiis consecrati quæ non probant coguntur defendere. Cic.[138]

Ut omnium rerum sic litterarum quoque intemperantia laboramus. Senec.[139]

Id maxime quemque decet, quod est cujusque suum maxime.[140]

Hos natura modos primum dedit.[141] Georg.

Paucis opus est litteris ad bonam mentem.[Pg 100][142]

Si quando turpe non sit, tamen non est non turpe quum id a multitudine laudetur.

Mihi sic usus est, tibi ut opus est facto, fac.[143] Ter.

364

Rarum est enim ut satis se quisque vereatur.[144]

Tot circa unum caput tumultuantes deos.[145]

Nihil turpius quam cognitioni assertionem præcurrere. Cic.[146]

Nec me pudet, ut istos, fateri nescire quid nesciam.[147]

Melius non incipient.[148]

365

Thought.—All the dignity of man consists in thought. Thought is therefore by its nature a wonderful and incomparable thing. It must have strange defects to be contemptible. But it has such, so that nothing is more ridiculous. How great it is in its nature! How vile it is in its defects!

But what is this thought? How foolish it is!

366

The mind of this sovereign judge of the world is not so independent that it is not liable to be disturbed by the first din about it. The noise of a cannon is not necessary to hinder its thoughts; it needs only the creaking of a weathercock or a pulley. Do not wonder if at present it does not reason well; a fly is buzzing in its ears; that is enough to render it incapable of good judgment. If you wish it to be able to reach the truth, chase away that animal which holds its reason in check and disturbs that powerful intellect which rules towns and kingdoms. Here is a comical god! O ridicolosissimo eroe!

367

The power of flies; they win battles,[149] hinder our soul from acting, eat our body.

368

When it is said that heat is only the motions of certain molecules, and light the conatus recedendi which we feel,[150] it astonishes us. What! Is pleasure only the ballet of our spirits? We have conceived so different an idea of it! And these sensations seem so removed from those others which we say are the same as those with which we compare them! The sensation[Pg 101] from the fire, that warmth which affects us in a manner wholly different from touch, the reception of sound and light, all this appears to us mysterious, and yet it is material like the blow of a stone. It is true that the smallness of the spirits which enter into the pores touches other nerves, but there are always some nerves touched.

369

Memory is necessary for all the operations of reason.

370

[Chance gives rise to thoughts, and chance removes them; no art can keep or acquire them.

A thought has escaped me. I wanted to write it down. I write instead, that it has escaped me.]

371

[When I was small, I hugged my book; and because it sometimes happened to me to ... in believing I hugged it, I doubted....]

372

In writing down my thought, it sometimes escapes me; but this makes me remember my weakness, that I constantly forget. This is as instructive to me as my forgotten thought; for I strive only to know my nothingness.

373

Scepticism.—I shall here write my thoughts without order, and not perhaps in unintentional confusion; that is true order, which will always indicate my object by its very disorder. I should do too much honour to my subject, if I treated it with order, since I want to show that it is incapable of it.

374

What astonishes me most is to see that all the world is not astonished at its own weakness. Men act seriously, and each follows his own mode of life, not because it is in fact good to follow since it is the custom, but as if each man knew certainly where reason and justice are. They find themselves continually deceived, and by a comical humility think it is their own fault, and not that of the art which they claim always to possess. But[Pg 102] it is well there are so many such people in the world, who are not sceptics for the glory of scepticism, in order to show that man is quite capable of the most extravagant opinions, since he is capable of believing that he is not in a state of natural and inevitable weakness, but, on the contrary, of natural wisdom. Nothing fortifies scepticism more than that there are some who are not sceptics; if all were so, they would be wrong.

375

[I have passed a great part of my life believing that there was justice, and in this I was not mistaken; for there is justice according as God has willed to reveal it to us. But I did not take it so, and this is where I made a mistake; for I believed that our justice was essentially just, and that I had that whereby to know and judge of it. But I have so often found my right judgment at fault, that at last I have come to distrust myself, and then others. I have seen changes in all nations and men, and thus after many changes of judgment regarding true justice, I have recognised that our nature was but in continual change, and I have not changed since; and if I changed, I would confirm my opinion.

The sceptic Arcesilaus,[151] who became a dogmatist.]

376

This sect derives more strength from its enemies than from its friends; for the weakness of man is far more evident in those who know it not than in those who know it.

377

Discourses on humility are a source of pride in the vain, and of humility in the humble. So those on scepticism cause believers to affirm. Few men speak humbly of humility, chastely of chastity, few doubtingly of scepticism. We are only falsehood, duplicity, contradiction; we both conceal and disguise ourselves from ourselves.

378

Scepticism.—Excess, like defect of intellect, is accused of madness. Nothing is good but mediocrity. The majority has settled that, and finds fault with him who escapes it at whichever end. I will not oppose it. I quite consent to put myself[Pg 103] there, and refuse to be at the lower end, not because it is low, but because it is an end; for I would likewise refuse to be placed at the top. To leave the mean is to abandon humanity. The greatness of the human soul consists in knowing how to preserve the mean. So far from greatness consisting in leaving it, it consists in not leaving it.

379

It is not good to have too much liberty. It is not good to have all one wants.

380

All good maxims are in the world. We only need to apply them. For instance, we do not doubt that we ought to risk our lives in defence of the public good; but for religion, no.

It is true there must be inequality among men; but if this be conceded, the door is opened not only to the highest power, but to the highest tyranny.

We must relax our minds a little; but this opens the door to the greatest debauchery. Let us mark the limits. There are no limits in things. Laws would put them there, and the mind cannot suffer it.

381

When we are too young, we do not judge well; so, also, when we are too old. If we do not think enough, or if we think too much on any matter, we get obstinate and infatuated about it. If one considers one's work immediately after having done it, one is entirely prepossessed in its favour; by delaying too long, one can no longer enter into the spirit of it. So with pictures seen from too far or too near; there is but one exact point which is the true place wherefrom to look at them: the rest are too near, too far, too high, or too low. Perspective determines that point in the art of painting. But who shall determine it in truth and morality?

382

When all is equally agitated, nothing appears to be agitated, as in a ship. When all tend to debauchery, none appears to do so. He who stops draws attention to the excess of others, like a fixed point.[Pg 104]

383

The licentious tell men of orderly lives that they stray from nature's path, while they themselves follow it; as people in a ship think those move who are on the shore. On all sides the language is similar. We must have a fixed point in order to judge. The harbour decides for those who are in a ship; but where shall we find a harbour in morality?

384

Contradiction is a bad sign of truth; several things which are certain are contradicted; several things which are false pass without contradiction. Contradiction is not a sign of falsity, nor the want of contradiction a sign of truth.

385

Scepticism.—Each thing here is partly true and partly false. Essential truth is not so; it is altogether pure and altogether true. This mixture dishonours and annihilates it. Nothing is purely true, and thus nothing is true, meaning by that pure truth. You will say it is true that homicide is wrong. Yes; for we know well the wrong and the false. But what will you say is good? Chastity? I say no; for the world would come to an end. Marriage? No; continence is better. Not to kill? No; for lawlessness would be horrible, and the wicked would kill all the good. To kill? No; for that destroys nature. We possess truth and goodness only in part, and mingled with falsehood and evil.

386

If we dreamt the same thing every night, it would affect us as much as the objects we see every day. And if an artisan were sure to dream every night for twelve hours' duration that he was a king, I believe he would be almost as happy as a king, who should dream every night for twelve hours on end that he was an artisan.

If we were to dream every night that we were pursued by enemies, and harassed by these painful phantoms, or that we passed every day in different occupations, as in making a voyage, we should suffer almost as much as if it were real, and should fear to sleep, as we fear to wake when we dread in fact to enter[Pg 105] on such mishaps. And, indeed, it would cause pretty nearly the same discomforts as the reality.

But since dreams are all different, and each single one is diversified, what is seen in them affects us much less than what we see when awake, because of its continuity, which is not, however, so continuous and level as not to change too; but it changes less abruptly, except rarely, as when we travel, and then we say, "It seems to me I am dreaming." For life is a dream a little less inconstant.

387

[It may be that there are true demonstrations; but this is not certain. Thus, this proves nothing else but that it is not certain that all is uncertain, to the glory of scepticism.]

388

Good sense.—They are compelled to say, "You are not acting in good faith; we are not asleep," etc. How I love to see this proud reason humiliated and suppliant! For this is not the language of a man whose right is disputed, and who defends it with the power of armed hands. He is not foolish enough to declare that men are not acting in good faith, but he punishes this bad faith with force.

389

Ecclesiastes[152] shows that man without God is in total ignorance and inevitable misery. For it is wretched to have the wish, but not the power. Now he would be happy and assured of some truth, and yet he can neither know, nor desire not to know. He cannot even doubt.

390

My God! How foolish this talk is! "Would God have made the world to damn it? Would He ask so much from persons so weak?" etc. Scepticism is the cure for this evil, and will take down this vanity.

391

Conversation.—Great words: Religion, I deny it.

Conversation.—Scepticism helps religion.[Pg 106]

392

Against Scepticism.—[... It is, then, a strange fact that we cannot define these things without obscuring them, while we speak of them with all assurance.] We assume that all conceive of them in the same way; but we assume it quite gratuitously, for we have no proof of it. I see, in truth, that the same words are applied on the same occasions, and that every time two men see a body change its place, they both express their view of this same fact by the same word, both saying that it has moved; and from this conformity of application we derive a strong conviction of a conformity of ideas. But this is not absolutely or finally convincing, though there is enough to support a bet on the affirmative, since we know that we often draw the same conclusions from different premisses.

This is enough, at least, to obscure the matter; not that it completely extinguishes the natural light which assures us of these things. The academicians[153] would have won. But this dulls it, and troubles the dogmatists to the glory of the sceptical crowd, which consists in this doubtful ambiguity, and in a certain doubtful dimness from which our doubts cannot take away all the clearness, nor our own natural lights chase away all the darkness.

393

It is a singular thing to consider that there are people in the world who, having renounced all the laws of God and nature, have made laws for themselves which they strictly obey, as, for instance, the soldiers of Mahomet, robbers, heretics, etc. It is the same with logicians. It seems that their licence must be without any limits or barriers, since they have broken through so many that are so just and sacred.

394

All the principles of sceptics, stoics, atheists, etc., are true. But their conclusions are false, because the opposite principles are also true.

395

Instinct, reason.—We have an incapacity of proof, insurmountable by all dogmatism. We have an idea of truth, invincible to all scepticism. [Pg 107]

396

Two things instruct man about his whole nature; instinct and experience.

397

The greatness of man is great in that he knows himself to be miserable. A tree does not know itself to be miserable. It is then being miserable to know oneself to be miserable; but it is also being great to know that one is miserable.

398

All these same miseries prove man's greatness. They are the miseries of a great lord, of a deposed king.

399

We are not miserable without feeling it. A ruined house is not miserable. Man only is miserable. Ego vir videns.[154]

400

The greatness of man.—We have so great an idea of the soul of man that we cannot endure being despised, or not being esteemed by any soul; and all the happiness of men consists in this esteem.

401

Glory.—The brutes do not admire each other. A horse does not admire his companion. Not that there is no rivalry between them in a race, but that is of no consequence; for, when in the stable, the heaviest and most ill-formed does not give up his oats to another, as men would have others do to them. Their virtue is satisfied with itself.

402

The greatness of man even in his lust, to have known how to extract from it a wonderful code, and to have drawn from it a picture of benevolence.

403

Greatness.—The reasons of effects indicate the greatness of man, in having extracted so fair an order from lust.[Pg 108]

404

The greatest baseness of man is the pursuit of glory. But it is also the greatest mark of his excellence; for whatever possessions he may have on earth, whatever health and essential comfort, he is not satisfied if he has not the esteem of men. He values human reason so highly that, whatever advantages he may have on earth, he is not content if he is not also ranked highly in the judgment of man. This is the finest position in the world. Nothing can turn him from that desire, which is the most indelible quality of man's heart.

And those who most despise men, and put them on a level with the brutes, yet wish to be admired and believed by men, and contradict themselves by their own feelings; their nature, which is stronger than all, convincing them of the greatness of man more forcibly than reason convinces them of their baseness.

405

Contradiction.—Pride counterbalancing all miseries. Man either hides his miseries, or, if he disclose them, glories in knowing them.

406

Pride counterbalances and takes away all miseries. Here is a strange monster, and a very plain aberration. He is fallen from his place, and is anxiously seeking it. This is what all men do. Let us see who will have found it.

407

When malice has reason on its side, it becomes proud, and parades reason in all its splendour. When austerity or stern choice has not arrived at the true good, and must needs return to follow nature, it becomes proud by reason of this return.

408

Evil is easy, and has infinite forms; good is almost unique.[155] But a certain kind of evil is as difficult to find as what we call good; and often on this account such particular evil gets passed off as good. An extraordinary greatness of soul is needed in order to attain to it as well as to good.[Pg 109]

409

The greatness of man.—The greatness of man is so evident, that it is even proved by his wretchedness. For what in animals is nature we call in man wretchedness; by which we recognise that, his nature being now like that of animals, he has fallen from a better nature which once was his.

For who is unhappy at not being a king, except a deposed king? Was Paulus Æmilius[156] unhappy at being no longer consul? On the contrary, everybody thought him happy in having been consul, because the office could only be held for a time. But men thought Perseus so unhappy in being no longer king, because the condition of kingship implied his being always king, that they thought it strange that he endured life. Who is unhappy at having only one mouth? And who is not unhappy at having only one eye? Probably no man ever ventured to mourn at not having three eyes. But any one is inconsolable at having none.

410

Perseus, King of Macedon.—Paulus Æmilius reproached Perseus for not killing himself.

411

Notwithstanding the sight of all our miseries, which press upon us and take us by the throat, we have an instinct which we cannot repress, and which lifts us up.

412

There is internal war in man between reason and the passions.

If he had only reason without passions ...

If he had only passions without reason ...

But having both, he cannot be without strife, being unable to be at peace with the one without being at war with the other. Thus he is always divided against, and opposed to himself.

413

This internal war of reason against the passions has made a division of those who would have peace into two sects. The first would renounce their passions, and become gods; the others would renounce reason, and become brute beasts. (Des Barreaux.)[157] But neither can do so, and reason still remains, to condemn the vileness and injustice of the passions, and to trouble[Pg 110] the repose of those who abandon themselves to them; and the passions keep always alive in those who would renounce them.

414

Men are so necessarily mad, that not to be mad would amount to another form of madness.

415

The nature of man may be viewed in two ways: the one according to its end, and then he is great and incomparable; the other according to the multitude, just as we judge of the nature of the horse and the dog, popularly, by seeing its fleetness, et animum arcendi; and then man is abject and vile. These are the two ways which make us judge of him differently, and which occasion such disputes among philosophers.

For one denies the assumption of the other. One says, "He is not born for this end, for all his actions are repugnant to it." The other says, "He forsakes his end, when he does these base actions."

416

For Port-Royal.[158] Greatness and wretchedness.—Wretchedness being deduced from greatness, and greatness from wretchedness, some have inferred man's wretchedness all the more because they have taken his greatness as a proof of it, and others have inferred his greatness with all the more force, because they have inferred it from his very wretchedness. All that the one party has been able to say in proof of his greatness has only served as an argument of his wretchedness to the others, because the greater our fall, the more wretched we are, and vice versa. The one party is brought back to the other in an endless circle, it being certain that in proportion as men possess light they discover both the greatness and the wretchedness of man. In a word, man knows that he is wretched. He is therefore wretched, because he is so; but he is really great because he knows it.

417

This twofold nature of man is so evident that some have thought that we had two souls. A single subject seemed to them incapable of such sudden variations from unmeasured presumption to a dreadful dejection of heart.[Pg 111]

418

It is dangerous to make man see too clearly his equality with the brutes without showing him his greatness. It is also dangerous to make him see his greatness too clearly, apart from his vileness. It is still more dangerous to leave him in ignorance of both. But it is very advantageous to show him both. Man must not think that he is on a level either with the brutes or with the angels, nor must he be ignorant of both sides of his nature; but he must know both.

419

I will not allow man to depend upon himself, or upon another, to the end that being without a resting-place and without repose ...

420

If he exalt himself, I humble him; if he humble himself, I exalt him; and I always contradict him, till he understands that he is an incomprehensible monster.

421

I blame equally those who choose to praise man, those who choose to blame him, and those who choose to amuse themselves; and I can only approve of those who seek with lamentation.

422

It is good to be tired and wearied by the vain search after the true good, that we may stretch out our arms to the Redeemer.

423

Contraries. After having shown the vileness and the greatness of man.—Let man now know his value. Let him love himself, for there is in him a nature capable of good; but let him not for this reason love the vileness which is in him. Let him despise himself, for this capacity is barren; but let him not therefore despise this natural capacity. Let him hate himself, let him love himself; he has within him the capacity of knowing the truth and of being happy, but he possesses no truth, either constant or satisfactory.

I would then lead man to the desire of finding truth; to be free from passions, and ready to follow it where he may find it,[Pg 112] knowing how much his knowledge is obscured by the passions. I would indeed that he should hate in himself the lust which determined his will by itself, so that it may not blind him in making his choice, and may not hinder him when he has chosen.

424

All these contradictions, which seem most to keep me from the knowledge of religion, have led me most quickly to the true one.

[Pg 113]

SECTION VII

MORALITY AND DOCTRINE

425

Second part.—That man without faith cannot know the true good, nor justice.

All men seek happiness. This is without exception. Whatever different means they employ, they all tend to this end.[159] The cause of some going to war, and of others avoiding it, is the same desire in both, attended with different views. The will never takes the least step but to this object. This is the motive of every action of every man, even of those who hang themselves.

And yet after such a great number of years, no one without faith has reached the point to which all continually look. All complain, princes and subjects, noblemen and commoners, old and young, strong and weak, learned and ignorant, healthy and sick, of all countries, all times, all ages, and all conditions.

A trial so long, so continuous, and so uniform, should certainly convince us of our inability to reach the good by our own efforts. But example teaches us little. No resemblance is ever so perfect that there is not some slight difference; and hence we expect that our hope will not be deceived on this occasion as before. And thus, while the present never satisfies us, experience dupes us, and from misfortune to misfortune leads us to death, their eternal crown.

What is it then that this desire and this inability proclaim to us, but that there was once in man a true happiness of which there now remain to him only the mark and empty trace, which he in vain tries to fill from all his surroundings, seeking from things absent the help he does not obtain in things present? But these are all inadequate, because the infinite abyss can only be filled by an infinite and immutable object, that is to say, only by God Himself.

He only is our true good, and since we have forsaken Him, it[Pg 114] is a strange thing that there is nothing in nature which has not been serviceable in taking His place; the stars, the heavens, earth, the elements, plants, cabbages, leeks, animals, insects, calves, serpents, fever, pestilence, war, famine, vices, adultery, incest. And since man has lost the true good, everything can appear equally good to him, even his own destruction, though so opposed to God, to reason, and to the whole course of nature.

Some seek good in authority, others in scientific research, others in pleasure. Others, who are in fact nearer the truth, have considered it necessary that the universal good, which all men desire, should not consist in any of the particular things which can only be possessed by one man, and which, when shared, afflict their possessor more by the want of the part he has not, than they please him by the possession of what he has. They have learned that the true good should be such as all can possess at once, without diminution and without envy, and which no one can lose against his will. And their reason is that this desire being natural to man, since it is necessarily in all, and that it is impossible not to have it, they infer from it ...

426

True nature being lost, everything becomes its own nature; as the true good being lost, everything becomes its own true good.

427

Man does not know in what rank to place himself. He has plainly gone astray, and fallen from his true place without being able to find it again. He seeks it anxiously and unsuccessfully everywhere in impenetrable darkness.

428

If it is a sign of weakness to prove God by nature, do not despise Scripture; if it is a sign of strength to have known these contradictions, esteem Scripture.

429

The vileness of man in submitting himself to the brutes, and in even worshipping them.

430

For Port Royal. The beginning, after having explained the incomprehensibility.—The greatness and the wretchedness of[Pg 115] man are so evident that the true religion must necessarily teach us both that there is in man some great source of greatness, and a great source of wretchedness. It must then give us a reason for these astonishing contradictions.

In order to make man happy, it must prove to him that there is a God; that we ought to love Him; that our true happiness is to be in Him, and our sole evil to be separated from Him; it must recognise that we are full of darkness which hinders us from knowing and loving Him; and that thus, as our duties compel us to love God, and our lusts turn us away from Him, we are full of unrighteousness. It must give us an explanation of our opposition to God and to our own good. It must teach us the remedies for these infirmities, and the means of obtaining these remedies. Let us therefore examine all the religions of the world, and see if there be any other than the Christian which is sufficient for this purpose.

Shall it be that of the philosophers, who put forward as the chief good, the good which is in ourselves? Is this the true good? Have they found the remedy for our ills? Is man's pride cured by placing him on an equality with God? Have those who have made us equal to the brutes, or the Mahommedans who have offered us earthly pleasures as the chief good even in eternity, produced the remedy for our lusts? What religion, then, will teach us to cure pride and lust? What religion will in fact teach us our good, our duties, the weakness which turns us from them, the cause of this weakness, the remedies which can cure it, and the means of obtaining these remedies?

All other religions have not been able to do so. Let us see what the wisdom of God will do.

"Expect neither truth," she says, "nor consolation from men. I am she who formed you, and who alone can teach you what you are. But you are now no longer in the state in which I formed you. I created man holy, innocent, perfect. I filled him with light and intelligence. I communicated to him my glory and my wonders. The eye of man saw then the majesty of God. He was not then in the darkness which blinds him, nor subject to mortality and the woes which afflict him. But he has not been able to sustain so great glory without falling into pride. He wanted to make himself his own centre, and independent of my help. He withdrew himself from my rule; and, on his making himself equal to me by the desire of finding his happiness in himself, I abandoned him to himself. And setting[Pg 116] in revolt the creatures that were subject to him, I made them his enemies; so that man is now become like the brutes, and so estranged from me that there scarce remains to him a dim vision of his Author. So far has all his knowledge been extinguished or disturbed! The senses, independent of reason, and often the masters of reason, have led him into pursuit of pleasure. All creatures either torment or tempt him, and domineer over him, either subduing him by their strength, or fascinating him by their charms, a tyranny more awful and more imperious.

"Such is the state in which men now are. There remains to them some feeble instinct of the happiness of their former state; and they are plunged in the evils of their blindness and their lust, which have become their second nature.

"From this principle which I disclose to you, you can recognise the cause of those contradictions which have astonished all men, and have divided them into parties holding so different views. Observe, now, all the feelings of greatness and glory which the experience of so many woes cannot stifle, and see if the cause of them must not be in another nature."

For Port-Royal to-morrow (Prosopopœa).—"It is in vain, O men, that you seek within yourselves the remedy for your ills. All your light can only reach the knowledge that not in yourselves will you find truth or good. The philosophers have promised you that, and have been unable to do it. They neither know what is your true good, nor what is your true state. How could they have given remedies for your ills, when they did not even know them? Your chief maladies are pride, which takes you away from God, and lust, which binds you to earth; and they have done nothing else but cherish one or other of these diseases. If they gave you God as an end, it was only to administer to your pride; they made you think that you are by nature like Him, and conformed to Him. And those who saw the absurdity of this claim put you on another precipice, by making you understand that your nature was like that of the brutes, and led you to seek your good in the lusts which are shared by the animals. This is not the way to cure you of your unrighteousness, which these wise men never knew. I alone can make you understand who you are...."

Adam, Jesus Christ.

If you are united to God, it is by grace, not by nature. If you are humbled, it is by penitence, not by nature.

Thus this double capacity ...[Pg 117]

You are not in the state of your creation.

As these two states are open, it is impossible for you not to recognise them. Follow your own feelings, observe yourselves, and see if you do not find the lively characteristics of these two natures. Could so many contradictions be found in a simple subject?

—Incomprehensible.—Not all that is incomprehensible ceases to exist. Infinite number. An infinite space equal to a finite.

—Incredible that God should unite Himself to us.—This consideration is drawn only from the sight of our vileness. But if you are quite sincere over it, follow it as far as I have done, and recognise that we are indeed so vile that we are incapable in ourselves of knowing if His mercy cannot make us capable of Him. For I would know how this animal, who knows himself to be so weak, has the right to measure the mercy of God, and set limits to it, suggested by his own fancy. He has so little knowledge of what God is, that he does not know what he himself is, and, completely disturbed at the sight of his own state, dares to say that God cannot make him capable of communion with Him.

But I would ask him if God demands anything else from him than the knowledge and love of Him, and why, since his nature is capable of love and knowledge, he believes that God cannot make Himself known and loved by him. Doubtless he knows at least that he exists, and that he loves something. Therefore, if he sees anything in the darkness wherein he is, and if he finds some object of his love among the things on earth, why, if God impart to him some ray of His essence, will he not be capable of knowing and of loving Him in the manner in which it shall please Him to communicate Himself to us? There must then be certainly an intolerable presumption in arguments of this sort, although they seem founded on an apparent humility, which is neither sincere nor reasonable, if it does not make us admit that, not knowing of ourselves what we are, we can only learn it from God.

"I do not mean that you should submit your belief to me without reason, and I do not aspire to overcome you by tyranny. In fact, I do not claim to give you a reason for everything. And to reconcile these contradictions, I intend to make you see clearly, by convincing proofs, those divine signs in me, which may convince you of what I am, and may gain authority for me by wonders and proofs which you cannot reject; so that you may[Pg 118] then believe without ... the things which I teach you, since you will find no other ground for rejecting them, except that you cannot know of yourselves if they are true or not.

"God has willed to redeem men, and to open salvation to those who seek it. But men render themselves so unworthy of it, that it is right that God should refuse to some, because of their obduracy, what He grants to others from a compassion which is not due to them. If He had willed to overcome the obstinacy of the most hardened, He could have done so by revealing Himself so manifestly to them that they could not have doubted of the truth of His essence; as it will appear at the last day, with such thunders and such a convulsion of nature, that the dead will rise again, and the blindest will see Him.

"It is not in this manner that He has willed to appear in His advent of mercy, because, as so many make themselves unworthy of His mercy, He has willed to leave them in the loss of the good which they do not want. It was not then right that He should appear in a manner manifestly divine, and completely capable of convincing all men; but it was also not right that He should come in so hidden a manner that He could not be known by those who should sincerely seek Him. He has willed to make Himself quite recognisable by those; and thus, willing to appear openly to those who seek Him with all their heart, and to be hidden from those who flee from Him with all their heart, He so regulates the knowledge of Himself that He has given signs of Himself, visible to those who seek Him, and not to those who seek

Him not. There is enough light for those who only desire to see, and enough obscurity for those who have a contrary disposition."

431

No other religion has recognised that man is the most excellent creature. Some, which have quite recognised the reality of his excellence, have considered as mean and ungrateful the low opinions which men naturally have of themselves; and others, which have thoroughly recognised how real is this vileness, have treated with proud ridicule those feelings of greatness, which are equally natural to man.

"Lift your eyes to God," say the first; "see Him whom you resemble, and who has created you to worship Him. You can make yourselves like unto Him; wisdom will make you equal to Him, if you will follow it." "Raise your heads, free men,"[Pg 119] says Epictetus. And others say, "Bend your eyes to the earth, wretched worm that you are, and consider the brutes whose companion you are."

What, then, will man become? Will he be equal to God or the brutes? What a frightful difference! What, then, shall we be? Who does not see from all this that man has gone astray, that he has fallen from his place, that he anxiously seeks it, that he cannot find it again? And who shall then direct him to it? The greatest men have failed.

432

Scepticism is true; for, after all, men before Jesus Christ did not know where they were, nor whether they were great or small. And those who have said the one or the other, knew nothing about it, and guessed without reason and by chance. They also erred always in excluding the one or the other.

Quod ergo ignorantes, quæritis, religio annuntiat vobis.[160]

433

After having understood the whole nature of man.—That a religion may be true, it must have knowledge of our nature. It ought to know its greatness and littleness, and the reason of both. What religion but the Christian has known this?

434

The chief arguments of the sceptics—I pass over the lesser ones—are that we have no certainty of the truth of these principles apart from faith and revelation, except in so far as we naturally perceive them in ourselves. Now this natural intuition is not a convincing proof of their truth; since, having no certainty, apart from faith, whether man was created by a good God, or by a wicked demon,[161] or by chance, it is doubtful whether these principles given to us are true, or false, or uncertain, according to our origin. Again, no person is certain, apart from faith, whether he is awake or sleeps, seeing that during sleep we believe that we are awake as firmly as we do when we are awake; we believe that we see space, figure, and motion; we are aware of the passage of time, we measure it; and in fact we act as if we were awake. So that half of our life being passed in sleep, we have on our own admission no idea of truth, whatever we may imagine. As all our intuitions are then illusions, who knows[Pg 120] whether the other half of our life, in which we think we are awake, is not another sleep a little different from the former, from which we awake when we suppose ourselves asleep?

[And who doubts that, if we dreamt in company, and the dreams chanced to agree, which is common enough, and if we were always alone when awake, we should believe that matters were reversed? In short, as we often dream that we dream, heaping dream upon dream, may it not be that this half of our life, wherein we think ourselves awake, is itself only a dream on which the others are grafted, from which we wake at death, during which we have as few principles of truth and good as during natural sleep, these different thoughts which disturb us being perhaps only illusions like the flight of time and the vain fancies of our dreams?]

These are the chief arguments on one side and the other.

I omit minor ones, such as the sceptical talk against the impressions of custom, education, manners, country, and the like. Though these influence the majority of common folk, who dogmatise only on shallow foundations, they are upset by the least breath of the sceptics. We have only to see their books if we are not sufficiently convinced of this, and we shall very quickly become so, perhaps too much.

I notice the only strong point of the dogmatists, namely, that, speaking in good faith and sincerely, we cannot doubt natural principles. Against this the sceptics set up in one word the uncertainty of our origin, which includes that of our nature. The dogmatists have been trying to answer this objection ever since the world began.

So there is open war among men, in which each must take a part, and side either with dogmatism or scepticism. For he who thinks to remain neutral is above all a sceptic. This neutrality is the essence of the sect; he who is not against them is essentially for them. [In this appears their advantage.] They are not for themselves; they are neutral, indifferent, in suspense as to all things, even themselves being no exception.

What then shall man do in this state? Shall he doubt everything? Shall he doubt whether he is awake, whether he is being pinched, or whether he is being burned? Shall he doubt whether he doubts? Shall he doubt whether he exists? We cannot go so far as that; and I lay it down as a fact that there never has been a real complete sceptic. Nature sustains our feeble reason, and prevents it raving to this extent.[Pg 121]

Shall he then say, on the contrary, that he certainly possesses truth—he who, when pressed ever so little, can show no title to it, and is forced to let go his hold?

What a chimera then is man! What a novelty! What a monster, what a chaos, what a contradiction, what a prodigy! Judge of all things, imbecile worm of the earth; depositary of truth, a sink of uncertainty and error; the pride and refuse of the universe!

Who will unravel this tangle? Nature confutes the sceptics, and reason confutes the dogmatists. What then will you become, O men! who try to find out by your natural reason what is your true condition? You cannot avoid one of these sects, nor adhere to one of them.

Know then, proud man, what a paradox you are to yourself. Humble yourself, weak reason; be silent, foolish nature; learn that man infinitely transcends man, and learn from your Master your true condition, of which you are ignorant. Hear God.

For in fact, if man had never been corrupt, he would enjoy in his innocence both truth and happiness with assurance; and if man had always been corrupt, he would have no idea of truth or bliss. But, wretched as we are, and more so than if there were no greatness in our condition, we have an idea of happiness, and cannot reach it. We perceive an image of truth, and possess only a lie. Incapable of absolute ignorance and of certain knowledge, we have thus been manifestly in a degree of perfection from which we have unhappily fallen.

It is, however, an astonishing thing that the mystery furthest removed from our knowledge, namely, that of the transmission of sin, should be a fact without which we can have no knowledge of ourselves. For it is beyond doubt that there is nothing which more shocks our reason than to say that the sin of the first man has rendered guilty those, who, being so removed from this source, seem incapable of participation in it. This transmission does not only seem to us impossible, it seems also very unjust. For what is more contrary to the rules of our miserable justice than to damn eternally an infant incapable of will, for a sin wherein he seems to have so little a share, that it was committed six thousand years before he was in existence? Certainly nothing offends us more rudely than this doctrine; and yet, without this mystery, the most incomprehensible of all, we are incomprehensible to ourselves. The knot of our condition takes its twists and turns in this abyss, so that man is more[Pg 122] inconceivable without this mystery than this mystery is inconceivable to man.

[Whence it seems that God, willing to render the difficulty of our existence unintelligible to ourselves, has concealed the knot so high, or, better speaking, so low, that we are quite incapable of reaching it; so that it is not by the proud exertions of our reason, but by the simple submissions of reason, that we can truly know ourselves.

These foundations, solidly established on the inviolable authority of religion, make us know that there are two truths of faith equally certain: the one, that man, in the state of creation, or in that of grace, is raised above all nature, made like unto God and sharing in His divinity; the other, that in the state of corruption and sin, he is fallen from this state and made like unto the beasts.

These two propositions are equally sound and certain. Scripture manifestly declares this to us, when it says in some places: Deliciæ meæ esse cum filiis hominum.[162] Effundam spiritum meum super omnem carnem.[163] Dii estis[164], etc.; and in other places, Omnis caro fænum.[165] Homo assimilatus est jumentis insipientibus, et similis factus est illis.[166] Dixi in corde meo de filiis hominum. Eccles. iii.

Whence it clearly seems that man by grace is made like unto God, and a partaker in His divinity, and that without grace he is like unto the brute beasts.]

435

Without this divine knowledge what could men do but either become elated by the inner feeling of their past greatness which still remains to them, or become despondent at the sight of their present weakness? For, not seeing the whole truth, they could not attain to perfect virtue. Some considering nature as incorrupt, others as incurable, they could not escape either pride or sloth, the two sources of all vice; since they cannot but either abandon themselves to it through cowardice, or escape it by pride. For if they knew the excellence of man, they were ignorant of his corruption; so that they easily avoided sloth, but fell into pride. And if they recognised the infirmity of nature, they were ignorant of its dignity; so that they could easily avoid vanity, but it was to fall into despair. Thence arise the different schools of the Stoics and Epicureans, the Dogmatists, Academicians, etc.[Pg 123]

The Christian religion alone has been able to cure these two vices, not by expelling the one through means of the other according to the wisdom of the world, but by expelling both according to the simplicity of the Gospel. For it teaches the righteous that it raises them even to a participation in divinity itself; that in this lofty state they still carry the source of all corruption, which renders them during all their life subject to error, misery, death, and sin; and it proclaims to the most ungodly that they are capable of the grace of their Redeemer. So making those tremble whom it justifies, and consoling those whom it condemns, religion so justly tempers fear with hope through that double capacity of grace and of sin, common to all, that it humbles infinitely more than reason alone can do, but without despair; and it exalts infinitely more than natural pride, but without inflating; thus making it evident that alone being exempt from error and vice, it alone fulfils the duty of instructing and correcting men.

Who then can refuse to believe and adore this heavenly light? For is it not clearer than day that we perceive within ourselves ineffaceable marks of excellence? And is it not equally true that we experience every hour the results of our deplorable condition? What does this chaos and monstrous confusion proclaim to us but the truth of these two states, with a voice so powerful that it is impossible to resist it?

436

Weakness.—Every pursuit of men is to get wealth; and they cannot have a title to show that they possess it justly, for they have only that of human caprice; nor have they strength to hold it securely. It is the same with knowledge, for disease takes it away. We are incapable both of truth and goodness.

437

We desire truth, and find within ourselves only uncertainty.

We seek happiness, and find only misery and death.

We cannot but desire truth and happiness, and are incapable of certainty or happiness. This desire is left to us, partly to punish us, partly to make us perceive wherefrom we are fallen.

438

If man is not made for God, why is he only happy in God? If man is made for God, why is he so opposed to God?[Pg 124]

439

Nature corrupted.—Man does not act by reason, which constitutes his being.

440

The corruption of reason is shown by the existence of so many different and extravagant customs. It was necessary that truth should come, in order that man should no longer dwell within himself.

441

For myself, I confess that so soon as the Christian religion reveals the principle that human nature is corrupt and fallen from God, that opens my eyes to see everywhere the mark of this truth: for nature is such that she testifies everywhere, both within man and without him, to a lost God and a corrupt nature.

442

Man's true nature, his true good, true virtue, and true religion, are things of which the knowledge is inseparable.

443

Greatness, wretchedness.—The more light we have, the more greatness and the more baseness we discover in man. Ordinary men—those who are more educated: philosophers, they astonish ordinary men—Christians, they astonish philosophers.

Who will then be surprised to see that religion only makes us know profoundly what we already know in proportion to our light?

444

This religion taught to her children what men have only been able to discover by their greatest knowledge.

445

Original sin is foolishness to men, but it is admitted to be such. You must not then reproach me for the want of reason in this doctrine, since I admit it to be without reason. But this foolishness is wiser than all the wisdom of men, sapientius est hominibus.[167] For without this, what can we say that man is? His whole state depends on this imperceptible point. And how should it be perceived by his reason, since it is a thing against reason, and since reason, far from finding it out by her own ways, is averse to it when it is presented to her?[Pg 125]

446

Of original sin.[168] Ample tradition of original sin according to the Jews.

On the saying in Genesis viii, 21: "The imagination of man's heart is evil from his youth."

R. Moses Haddarschan: This evil leaven is placed in man from the time that he is formed.

Massechet Succa: This evil leaven has seven names in Scripture. It is called evil, the foreskin, uncleanness, an enemy, a scandal, a heart of stone, the north wind; all this signifies the malignity which is concealed and impressed in the heart of man.

Midrasch Tillim says the same thing, and that God will deliver the good nature of man from the evil.

This malignity is renewed every day against man, as it is written, Psalm xxxvii, 32: "The wicked watcheth the righteous, and seeketh to slay him"; but God will not abandon him. This malignity tries the heart of man in this life, and will accuse him in the other. All this is found in the Talmud.

Midrasch Tillim on Psalm iv, 4: "Stand in awe and sin not." Stand in awe and be afraid of your lust, and it will not lead you into sin. And on Psalm xxxvi, 1: "The wicked has said within his own heart, Let not the fear of God be before me." That is to say that the malignity natural to man has said that to the wicked.

Midrasch el Kohelet: "Better is a poor and wise child than an old and foolish king who cannot foresee the future."[169] The child is virtue, and the king is the malignity of man. It is called king because all the members obey it, and old because it is in the human heart from infancy to old age, and foolish because it leads man in the way of [perdition], which he does not foresee. The same thing is in Midrasch Tillim.

Bereschist Rabba on Psalm xxxv, 10: "Lord, all my bones shall bless Thee, which deliverest the poor from the tyrant." And is there a greater tyrant than the evil leaven? And on Proverbs xxv, 21: "If thine enemy be hungry, give him bread to eat." That is to say, if the evil leaven hunger, give him the bread of wisdom of which it is spoken in Proverbs ix., and if he be thirsty, give him the water of which it is spoken in Isaiah lv.

Midrasch Tillim says the same thing, and that Scripture in that passage, speaking of the enemy, means the evil leaven; and that, in [giving] him that bread and that water, we heap coals of fire on his head.[Pg 126]

Midrasch el Kohelet on Ecclesiastes ix, 14: "A great king besieged a little city." This great king is the evil leaven; the great bulwarks built against it are temptations; and there has been found a poor wise man who has delivered it—that is to say, virtue.

And on Psalm xli, 1: "Blessed is he that considereth the poor."

And on Psalm lxxviii, 39: "The spirit passeth away, and cometh not again"; whence some have erroneously argued against the immortality of the soul. But the sense is that this spirit is the evil leaven, which accompanies man till death, and will not return at the resurrection.

And on Psalm ciii the same thing.

And on Psalm xvi.

Principles of Rabbinism: two Messiahs.

447

Will it be said that, as men have declared that righteousness has departed the earth, they therefore knew of original sin?—Nemo ante obitum beatus est[170]—that is to say, they knew death to be the beginning of eternal and essential happiness?

448

[Miton] sees well that nature is corrupt, and that men are averse to virtue; but he does not know why they cannot fly higher.

449

Order.—After Corruption to say: "It is right that all those who are in that state should know it, both those who are content with it, and those who are not content with it; but it is not right that all should see Redemption."

450

If we do not know ourselves to be full of pride, ambition, lust, weakness, misery, and injustice, we are indeed blind. And if, knowing this, we do not desire deliverance, what can we say of a man...?

What, then, can we have but esteem for a religion which knows so well the defects of man, and desire for the truth of a religion which promises remedies so desirable?[Pg 127]

451

All men naturally hate one another. They employ lust as far as possible in the service of the public weal. But this is only a [pretence] and a false image of love; for at bottom it is only hate.

452

To pity the unfortunate is not contrary to lust. On the contrary, we can quite well give such evidence of friendship, and acquire the reputation of kindly feeling, without giving anything.

453

From lust men have found and extracted excellent rules of policy, morality, and justice; but in reality this vile root of man, this figmentum malum,[171] is only covered, it is not taken away.

454

Injustice.—They have not found any other means of satisfying lust without doing injury to others.

455

Self is hateful. You, Miton, conceal it; you do not for that reason destroy it; you are, then, always hateful.

—No; for in acting as we do to oblige everybody, we give no more occasion for hatred of us.—That is true, if we only hated in Self the vexation which comes to us from it. But if I hate it because it is unjust, and because it makes itself the centre of everything, I shall always hate it.

In a word, the Self has two qualities: it is unjust in itself since it makes itself the centre of everything; it is inconvenient to others since it would enslave them; for each Self is the enemy, and would like to be the tyrant of all others. You take away its inconvenience, but not its injustice, and so you do not render it lovable to those who hate injustice; you render it lovable only to the unjust, who do not any longer find in it an enemy. And thus you remain unjust, and can please only the unjust.

456

It is a perverted judgment that makes every one place himself above the rest of the world, and prefer his own good, and the continuance of his own good fortune and life, to that of the rest of the world![Pg 128]

457

Each one is all in all to himself; for he being dead, all is dead to him. Hence it comes that each believes himself to be all in all to everybody. We must not judge of nature by ourselves, but by it.

458

"All that is in the world is the lust of the flesh, or the lust of the eyes, or the pride of life; libido sentiendi, libido sciendi, libido dominandi."[172] Wretched is the cursed land which these three rivers of fire enflame rather than water![173] Happy they who, on these rivers, are not overwhelmed nor carried away, but are immovably fixed, not standing but seated on a low and secure base, whence they do not rise before the light, but, having rested in peace, stretch out their hands to Him, who must lift them up, and make them stand upright and firm in the porches of the holy Jerusalem! There pride can no longer assail them nor cast them down; and yet they weep, not to see all those perishable things swept away by the torrents, but at the remembrance of their loved country, the heavenly Jerusalem, which they remember without ceasing during their prolonged exile.

459

The rivers of Babylon rush and fall and sweep away.

O holy Sion, where all is firm and nothing falls!

We must sit upon the waters, not under them or in them, but on them; and not standing but seated; being seated to be humble, and being above them to be secure. But we shall stand in the porches of Jerusalem.

Let us see if this pleasure is stable or transitory; if it pass away, it is a river of Babylon.

460

The lust of the flesh, the lust of the eyes, pride, etc.—There are three orders of things: the flesh, the spirit, and the will. The carnal are the rich and kings; they have the body as their object. Inquirers and scientists; they have the mind as their object. The wise; they have righteousness as their object.

God must reign over all, and all men must be brought back to Him. In things of the flesh lust reigns specially; in intellectual matters, inquiry specially; in wisdom, pride specially. Not that a man cannot boast of wealth or knowledge, but it is not the[Pg 129] place for pride; for in granting to a man that he is learned, it is easy to convince him that he is wrong to be proud. The proper place for pride is in wisdom, for it cannot be granted to a man that he has made himself wise, and that he is wrong to be proud; for that is right. Now God alone gives wisdom, and that is why Qui gloriatur, in Domino glorietur.[174]

461

The three lusts have made three sects; and the philosophers have done no other thing than follow one of the three lusts.

462

Search for the true good.—Ordinary men place the good in fortune and external goods, or at least in amusement. Philosophers have shown the vanity of all this, and have placed it where they could.

463

[Against the philosophers who believe in God without Jesus Christ]

Philosophers.—They believe that God alone is worthy to be loved and admired; and they have desired to be loved and admired of men, and do not know their own corruption. If they feel full of feelings of love and admiration, and find therein their chief delight, very well, let them think themselves good. But if they find themselves averse to Him, if they have no inclination but the desire to establish themselves in the esteem of men, and if their whole perfection consists only in making men—but without constraint—find their happiness in loving them, I declare that this perfection is horrible. What! they have known God, and have not desired solely that men should love Him, but that men should stop short at them! They have wanted to be the object of the voluntary delight of men.

464

Philosophers.—We are full of things which take us out of ourselves.

Our instinct makes us feel that we must seek our happiness outside ourselves. Our passions impel us outside, even when no objects present themselves to excite them. External objects tempt us of themselves, and call to us, even when we are not thinking of them. And thus philosophers have said in vain,[Pg 130] "Retire within yourselves, you will find your good there." We do not believe them, and those who believe them are the most empty and the most foolish.

465

The Stoics say, "Retire within yourselves; it is there you will find your rest." And that is not true.

Others say, "Go out of yourselves; seek happiness in amusement." And this is not true. Illness comes.

Happiness is neither without us nor within us. It is in God, both without us and within us.

466

Had Epictetus seen the way perfectly, he would have said to men, "You follow a wrong road"; he shows that there is another, but he does not lead to it. It is the way of willing what God wills. Jesus Christ alone leads to it: Via, veritas.[175]

The vices of Zeno[176] himself.

467

The reason of effects.—Epictetus.[177] Those who say, "You have a headache;" this is not the same thing. We are assured of health, and not of justice; and in fact his own was nonsense.

And yet he believed it demonstrable, when he said, "It is either in our power or it is not." But he did not perceive that it is not in our power to regulate the heart, and he was wrong to infer this from the fact that there were some Christians.

468

No other religion has proposed to men to hate themselves. No other religion then can please those who hate themselves, and who seek a Being truly lovable. And these, if they had never heard of the religion of a God humiliated, would embrace it at once.

469

I feel that I might not have been; for the Ego consists in my thoughts. Therefore I, who think, would not have been, if my mother had been killed before I had life. I am not then a necessary being. In the same way I am not eternal or infinite; but I see plainly that there exists in nature a necessary Being, eternal and infinite.[Pg 131]

470

"Had I seen a miracle," say men, "I should become converted." How can they be sure they would do a thing of the nature of which they are ignorant? They imagine that this conversion consists in a worship of God which is like commerce, and in a communion such as they picture to themselves. True religion consists in annihilating self before that Universal Being, whom we have so often provoked, and who can justly destroy us at any time; in recognising that we can do nothing without Him, and have deserved nothing from Him but His displeasure. It consists in knowing that there is an unconquerable opposition between us and God, and that without a mediator there can be no communion with Him.

471

It is unjust that men should attach themselves to me, even though they do it with pleasure and voluntarily. I should deceive those in whom I had created this desire; for I am not the end of any, and I have not the wherewithal to satisfy them. Am I not about to die? And thus the object of their attachment will die. Therefore, as I would be blamable in causing a falsehood to be believed, though I should employ gentle persuasion, though it should be believed with pleasure, and though it should give me pleasure; even so I am blamable in making myself loved, and if I attract persons to attach themselves to me. I ought to warn those who are ready to consent to a lie, that they ought not to believe it, whatever advantage comes to me from it; and likewise that they ought not to attach themselves to me; for they ought to spend their life and their care in pleasing God, or in seeking Him.

472

Self-will will never be satisfied, though it should have command of all it would; but we are satisfied from the moment we renounce it. Without it we cannot be discontented; with it we cannot be content.

473

Let us imagine a body full of thinking members.[178]

474

Members, To commence with that.—To regulate the love which we owe to ourselves, we must imagine a body full of[Pg 132] thinking members, for we are members of the whole, and must see how each member should love itself, etc....

475

If the feet and the hands had a will of their own, they could only be in their order in submitting this particular will to the primary will which governs the whole body. Apart from that, they are in disorder and mischief; but in willing only the good of the body, they accomplish their own good.

476

We must love God only and hate self only.

If the foot had always been ignorant that it belonged to the body, and that there was a body on which it depended, if it had only had the knowledge and the love of self, and if it came to know that it belonged to a body on which it depended, what regret, what shame for its past life, for having been useless to the body which inspired its life, which would have annihilated it if it had rejected it and separated it from itself, as it kept itself apart from the body! What prayers for its preservation in it! And with what submission would it allow itself to be governed by the will which rules the body, even to consenting, if necessary, to be cut off, or it would lose its character as member! For every member must be quite willing to perish for the body, for which alone the whole is.

477

It is false that we are worthy of the love of others; it is unfair that we should desire it. If we were born reasonable and impartial, knowing ourselves and others, we should not give this bias to our will. However, we are born with it; therefore born unjust, for all tends to self. This is contrary to all order. We must consider the general good; and the propensity to self is the beginning of all disorder, in war, in politics, in economy, and in the particular body of man. The will is therefore depraved.

If the members of natural and civil communities tend towards the weal of the body, the communities themselves ought to look to another more general body of which they are members. We ought therefore to look to the whole. We are therefore born unjust and depraved.[Pg 133]

478

When we want to think of God, is there nothing which turns us away, and tempts us to think of something else? All this is bad, and is born in us.

479

If there is a God, we must love Him only, and not the creatures of a day. The reasoning of the ungodly in the book of Wisdom[179] is only based upon the non-existence of God. "On that supposition," say they, "let us take delight in the creatures." That is the worst that can happen. But if there were a God to love, they would not have come to this conclusion, but to quite the contrary. And this is the conclusion of the wise: "There is a God, let us therefore not take delight in the creatures."

Therefore all that incites us to attach ourselves to the creatures is bad; since it prevents us from serving God if we know Him, or from seeking Him if we know Him not. Now we are full of lust. Therefore we are full of evil; therefore we ought to hate ourselves and all that excited us to attach ourselves to any other object than God only.

480

To make the members happy, they must have one will, and submit it to the body.

481

The examples of the noble deaths of the Lacedæmonians and others scarce touch us. For what good is it to us? But the example of the death of the martyrs touches us; for they are "our members." We have a common tie with them. Their resolution can form ours, not only by example, but because it has perhaps deserved ours. There is nothing of this in the examples of the heathen. We have no tie with them; as we do not become rich by seeing a stranger who is so, but in fact by seeing a father or a husband who is so.

482

Morality.—God having made the heavens and the earth, which do not feel the happiness of their being, He has willed to make beings who should know it, and who should compose a body of thinking members. For our members do not feel the[Pg 134] happiness of their union, of their wonderful intelligence, of the care which has been taken to infuse into them minds, and to make them grow and endure. How happy they would be if they saw and felt it! But for this they would need to have intelligence to know it, and good-will to consent to that of the universal soul. But if, having received intelligence, they employed it to retain nourishment for themselves without allowing it to pass to the other members, they would hate rather than love themselves; their blessedness, as well as their duty, consisting in their consent to the guidance of the whole soul to which they belong, which loves them better than they love themselves.

483

To be a member is to have neither life, being, nor movement, except through the spirit of the body, and for the body.

The separate member, seeing no longer the body to which it belongs, has only a perishing and dying existence. Yet it believes it is a whole, and seeing not the body on which it depends, it believes it depends only on self, and desires to make itself both centre and body. But not having in itself a principle of life, it only goes astray, and is astonished in the uncertainty of its being; perceiving in fact that it is not a body, and still not seeing that it is a member of a body. In short, when it comes to know itself, it has returned as it were to its own home, and loves itself only for the body. It deplores its past wanderings.

It cannot by its nature love any other thing, except for itself and to subject it to self, because each thing loves itself more than all. But in loving the body, it loves itself, because it only exists in it, by it, and for it. Qui adhæret Deo unus spiritus est.[180]

The body loves the hand; and the hand, if it had a will, should love itself in the same way as it is loved by the soul. All love which goes beyond this is unfair.

Adhærens Deo unus spiritus est. We love ourselves, because we are members of Jesus Christ. We love Jesus Christ, because He is the body of which we are members. All is one, one is in the other, like the Three Persons.

484

Two laws[181] suffice to rule the whole Christian Republic better than all the laws of statecraft.[Pg 135]

485

The true and only virtue, then, is to hate self (for we are hateful on account of lust), and to seek a truly lovable being to love. But as we cannot love what is outside ourselves, we must love a being who is in us, and is not ourselves; and that is true of each and all men. Now, only the Universal Being is such. The kingdom of God is within us;[182] the universal good is within us, is ourselves—and not ourselves.

486

The dignity of man in his innocence consisted in using and having dominion over the creatures, but now in separating himself from them, and subjecting himself to them.

487

Every religion is false, which as to its faith does not worship one God as the origin of everything, and which as to its morality does not love one only God as the object of everything.

488

... But it is impossible that God should ever be the end, if He is not the beginning. We lift our eyes on high, but lean upon the sand; and the earth will dissolve, and we shall fall whilst looking at the heavens.

489

If there is one sole source of everything, there is one sole end of everything; everything through Him, everything for Him. The true religion, then, must teach us to worship Him only, and to love Him only. But as we find ourselves unable to worship what we know not, and to love any other object but ourselves, the religion which instructs us in these duties must instruct us also of this inability, and teach us also the remedies for it. It teaches us that by one man all was lost, and the bond broken between God and us, and that by one man the bond is renewed.

We are born so averse to this love of God, and it is so necessary that we must be born guilty, or God would be unjust.

490

Men, not being accustomed to form merit, but only to recompense it where they find it formed, judge of God by themselves.[Pg 136]

491

The true religion must have as a characteristic the obligation to love God. This is very just, and yet no other religion has commanded this; ours has done so. It must also be aware of human lust and weakness; ours is so. It must have adduced remedies for this; one is prayer. No other religion has asked of God to love and follow Him.

492

He who hates not in himself his self-love, and that instinct which leads him to make himself God, is indeed blinded. Who does not see that there is nothing so opposed to justice and truth? For it is false that we deserve this, and it is unfair and impossible to attain it, since all demand the same thing. It is, then, a manifest injustice which is innate in us, of which we cannot get rid, and of which we must get rid.

Yet no religion has indicated that this was a sin; or that we were born in it; or that we were obliged to resist it; or has thought of giving us remedies for it.

493

The true religion teaches our duties; our weaknesses, pride, and lust; and the remedies, humility and mortification.

494

The true religion must teach greatness and misery; must lead to the esteem and contempt of self, to love and to hate.

495

If it is an extraordinary blindness to live without investigating what we are, it is a terrible one to live an evil life, while believing in God.

496

Experience makes us see an enormous difference between piety and goodness.

497

Against those who, trusting to the mercy of God, live heedlessly, without doing good works.—As the two sources of our sins are pride and sloth, God has revealed to us two of His attributes to cure them, mercy and justice. The property of justice is to[Pg 137] humble pride, however holy may be our works, et non intres in judicium,[183] etc.; and the property of mercy is to combat sloth by exhorting to good works, according to that passage: "The goodness of God leadeth to repentance,"[184] and that other of the Ninevites: "Let us do penance to see if peradventure He will pity us."[185] And thus mercy is so far from authorising slackness, that it is on the contrary the quality which formally attacks it; so that instead of saying, "If there were no mercy in God we should have to make every kind of effort after virtue," we must say, on the contrary, that it is because there is mercy in God, that we must make every kind of effort.

498

It is true there is difficulty in entering into godliness. But this difficulty does not arise from the religion which begins in us, but from the irreligion which is still there. If our senses were not opposed to penitence, and if our corruption were not opposed to the purity of

God, there would be nothing in this painful to us. We suffer only in proportion as the vice which is natural to us resists supernatural grace. Our heart feels torn asunder between these opposed efforts. But it would be very unfair to impute this violence to God, who is drawing us on, instead of to the world, which is holding us back. It is as a child, which a mother tears from the arms of robbers, in the pain it suffers, should love the loving and legitimate violence of her who procures its liberty, and detest only the impetuous and tyrannical violence of those who detain it unjustly. The most cruel war which God can make with men in this life is to leave them without that war which He came to bring. "I came to send war,"[186] He says, "and to teach them of this war. I came to bring fire and the sword."[187] Before Him the world lived in this false peace.

499

External works.—There is nothing so perilous as what pleases God and man. For those states, which please God and man, have one property which pleases God, and another which pleases men; as the greatness of Saint Teresa. What pleased God was her deep humility in the midst of her revelations; what pleased men was her light. And so we torment ourselves to imitate her discourses, thinking to imitate her conditions, and not so much to love what God loves, and to put ourselves in the state which God loves.[Pg 138]

It is better not to fast, and thereby humbled, than to fast and be self-satisfied therewith. The Pharisee and the Publican.[188]

What use will memory be to me, if it can alike hurt and help me, and all depends upon the blessing of God, who gives only to things done for Him, according to His rules and in His ways, the manner being as important as the thing, and perhaps more; since God can bring forth good out of evil, and without God we bring forth evil out of good?

500

The meaning of the words, good and evil.

501

First step: to be blamed for doing evil, and praised for doing good.

Second step: to be neither praised, nor blamed.

502

Abraham[189] took nothing for himself, but only for his servants. So the righteous man takes for himself nothing of the world, nor the applause of the world, but only for his passions, which he uses as their master, saying to the one, "Go," and to another, "Come." Sub te erit appetitus tuus.[190] The passions thus subdued are virtues. Even God attributes to Himself avarice, jealousy, anger; and these are virtues as well as kindness, pity, constancy, which are also passions. We must employ them as slaves, and, leaving to them their food, prevent the soul from taking any of it. For, when the passions become masters, they are vices; and they give their nutriment to the soul, and the soul nourishes itself upon it, and is poisoned.

503

Philosophers have consecrated the vices by placing them in God Himself. Christians have consecrated the virtues.

504

The just man acts by faith in the least things; when he reproves his servants, he desires their conversion by the Spirit of God, and prays God to correct them; and he expects as much from God as from his own reproofs, and prays God to bless his corrections. And so in all his other actions he proceeds with the Spirit of God; and his actions deceive us by reason of the ...[Pg 139] or suspension of the Spirit of God in him; and he repents in his affliction.

505

All things can be deadly to us, even the things made to serve us; as in nature walls can kill us, and stairs can kill us, if we do not walk circumspectly.

The least movement affects all nature; the entire sea changes because of a rock. Thus in grace, the least action affects everything by its consequences; therefore everything is important.

In each action we must look beyond the action at our past, present, and future state, and at others whom it affects, and see the relations of all those things. And then we shall be very cautious.

506

Let God not impute to us our sins, that is to say, all the consequences and results of our sins, which are dreadful, even those of the smallest faults, if we wish to follow them out mercilessly!

507

The spirit of grace; the hardness of the heart; external circumstances.

508

Grace is indeed needed to turn a man into a saint; and he who doubts it does not know what a saint or a man is.

509

Philosophers.—A fine thing to cry to a man who does not know himself, that he should come of himself to God! And a fine thing to say so to a man who does know himself!

510

Man is not worthy of God, but he is not incapable of being made worthy.

It is unworthy of God to unite Himself to wretched man; but it is not unworthy of God to pull him out of his misery.

511

If we would say that man is too insignificant to deserve communion with God, we must indeed be very great to judge of it.[Pg 140]

512

It is, in peculiar phraseology, wholly the body of Jesus Christ, but it cannot be said to be the whole body of Jesus Christ.[191] The union of two things without change does not enable us to say that one becomes the other; the soul thus being united to the body, the fire to the timber, without change. But change is necessary to make the form of the one become the form of the other; thus the union of the Word to man. Because my body without my soul would not make the body of a man; therefore my soul united to any matter whatsoever will make my body. It does not distinguish the necessary condition from the sufficient condition; the union is necessary, but not sufficient. The left arm is not the right.

Impenetrability is a property of matter.

Identity de numers in regard to the same time requires the identity of matter.

Thus if God united my soul to a body in China, the same body, idem numero, would be in China.

The same river which runs there is idem numero as that which runs at the same time in China.

513

Why God has established prayer.

1. To communicate to His creatures the dignity of causality.
2. To teach us from whom our virtue comes.
3. To make us deserve other virtues by work.
(But to keep His own pre-eminence, He grants prayer to whom He pleases.)

Objection: But we believe that we hold prayer of ourselves.

This is absurd; for since, though having faith, we cannot have virtues, how should we have faith? Is there a greater distance between infidelity and faith than between faith and virtue?

Merit. This word is ambiguous.

Meruit habere Redemptorem.

Meruit tam sacra membra tangere.

Digno tam sacra membra tangere.

Non sum dignus.[192]

Qui manducat indignus[193]

Dignus est accipere.[194]

Dignare me.

God is only bound according to His promises. He has[Pg 141] promised to grant justice to prayers; He has never promised prayer only to the children of promise.

Saint Augustine has distinctly said that strength would be taken away from the righteous. But it is by chance that he said it; for it might have happened that the occasion of saying it did not present itself. But his principles make us see that when the occasion for it presented itself, it was impossible that he should not say it, or that he should say anything to the contrary. It is then rather that he was forced to say it, when the occasion presented itself, than that he said it, when the occasion presented itself, the one being of necessity, the other of chance. But the two are all that we can ask.

514

The elect will be ignorant of their virtues, and the outcast of the greatness of their sins: "Lord, when saw we Thee an hungered, thirsty?" etc.[195][196]

515

Romans iii, 27. Boasting is excluded. By what law? Of works? nay, but by faith. Then faith is not within our power like the deeds of the law, and it is given to us in another way.

516

Comfort yourselves. It is not from yourselves that you should expect grace; but, on the contrary, it is in expecting nothing from yourselves, that you must hope for it.

517

Every condition, and even the martyrs, have to fear, according to Scripture.

The greatest pain of purgatory is the uncertainty of the judgment. Deus absconditus.

518

John viii. Multi crediderunt in eum. Dicebat ergo Jesus: "Si manseritis ... VERE mei discipuli eritis, et VERITAS LIBERABIT VOS." Responderunt: "Semen Abrahæ sumus, et nemini servimus unquam."

There is a great difference between disciples and true disciples. We recognise them by telling them that the truth will make[Pg 142] them free; for if they answer that they are free, and that it is in their power to come out of slavery to the devil, they are indeed disciples, but not true disciples.

519

The law has not destroyed nature, but has instructed it; grace has not destroyed the law, but has made it act. Faith received at baptism is the source of the whole life of Christians and of the converted.

520

Grace will always be in the world, and nature also; so that the former is in some sort natural. And thus there will always be Pelagians, and always Catholics, and always strife; because the first birth makes the one, and the grace of the second birth the other.

521

The law imposed what it did not give. Grace gives what is imposes.

522

All faith consists in Jesus Christ and in Adam, and all morality in lust and in grace.

523

There is no doctrine more appropriate to man than this, which teaches him his double capacity of receiving and of losing grace, because of the double peril to which he is exposed, of despair or of pride.

524

The philosophers did not prescribe feelings suitable to the two states.

They inspired feelings of pure greatness, and that is not man's state.

They inspired feelings of pure littleness, and that is not man's state.

There must be feelings of humility, not from nature, but from penitence, not to rest in them, but to go on to greatness. There must be feelings of greatness, not from merit, but from grace, and after having passed through humiliation.[Pg 143]

525

Misery induces despair, pride induces presumption. The Incarnation shows man the greatness of his misery by the greatness of the remedy which he required.

526

The knowledge of God without that of man's misery causes pride. The knowledge of man's misery without that of God causes despair. The knowledge of Jesus Christ constitutes the middle course, because in Him we find both God and our misery.

527

Jesus Christ is a God whom we approach without pride, and before whom we humble ourselves without despair.

528

... Not a degradation which renders us incapable of good, nor a holiness exempt from evil.

529

A person told me one day that on coming from confession he felt great joy and confidence. Another told me that he remained in fear. Whereupon I thought that these two together would make one good man, and that each was wanting in that he had not the feeling of the other. The same often happens in other things.

530

He who knows the will of his master will be beaten with more blows, because of the power he has by his knowledge. Qui justus est, justificetur adhuc,[197] because of the power he has by justice. From him who has received most, will the greatest reckoning be demanded, because of the power he has by this help.

531

Scripture has provided passages of consolation and of warning for all conditions.

Nature seems to have done the same thing by her two infinities, natural and moral; for we shall always have the higher and the lower, the more clever and the less clever, the most exalted and the meanest, in order to humble our pride, and exalt our humility.[Pg 144]

532

Comminutum cor (Saint Paul). This is the Christian character. Alba has named you, I know you no more (Corneille).[198] That is the inhuman character. The human character is the opposite.

533

There are only two kinds of men: the righteous who believe themselves sinners; the rest, sinners, who believe themselves righteous.

534

We owe a great debt to those who point out faults. For they mortify us. They teach us that we have been despised. They do not prevent our being so in the future; for we have many other faults for which we may be despised. They prepare for us the exercise of correction and freedom from fault.

535

Man is so made that by continually telling him he is a fool he believes it, and by continually telling it to himself he makes himself believe it. For man holds an inward talk with his self alone, which it behoves him to regulate well: Corrumpunt bonos mores colloquia prava.[199] We must keep silent as much as possible and talk with ourselves only of God, whom we know to be true; and thus we convince ourselves of the truth.

536

Christianity is strange. It bids man recognise that he is vile, even abominable, and bids him desire to be like God. Without such a counterpoise, this dignity would make him horribly vain, or this humiliation would make him terribly abject.

537

With how little pride does a Christian believe himself united to God! With how little humiliation does he place himself on a level with the worms of earth!

A glorious manner to welcome life and death, good and evil!

538

What difference in point of obedience is there between a soldier and a Carthusian monk? For both are equally under[Pg 145] obedience and dependent, both engaged in equally painful exercises. But the soldier always hopes to command, and never attains this, for even captains and princes are ever slaves and dependants; still he ever hopes and ever works to attain this. Whereas the Carthusian monk makes a vow to be always dependent. So they do not differ in their perpetual thraldom, in which both of them always exist, but in the hope, which one always has, and the other never.

539

The hope which Christians have of possessing an infinite good is mingled with real enjoyment as well as with fear; for it is not as with those who should hope for a kingdom, of which they, being subjects, would have nothing; but they hope for holiness, for freedom from injustice, and they have something of this.

540

None is so happy as a true Christian, nor so reasonable, virtuous, or amiable.

541

The Christian religion alone makes man altogether lovable and happy. In honesty, we cannot perhaps be altogether lovable and happy.

542

Preface.—The metaphysical proofs of God are so remote from the reasoning of men, and so complicated, that they make little impression; and if they should be of service to some, it would be only during the moment that they see such demonstration; but an hour afterwards they fear they have been mistaken.

Quod curiositate cognoverunt superbia amiserunt.[200]

This is the result of the knowledge of God obtained without Jesus Christ; it is communion without a mediator with the God whom they have known without a mediator. Whereas those who have known God by a mediator know their own wretchedness.

543

The God of the Christians is a God who makes the soul feel that He is her only good, that her only rest is in Him, that her[Pg 146] only delight is in loving Him; and who makes her at the same time abhor the obstacles which keep her back, and prevent her from loving God with all her strength. Self-love and lust, which hinder us, are unbearable to her. Thus God makes her feel that she has this root of self-love which destroys her, and which He alone can cure.

544

Jesus Christ did nothing but teach men that they loved themselves, that they were slaves, blind, sick, wretched, and sinners; that He must deliver them, enlighten, bless, and heal them; that this would be effected by hating self, and by following Him through suffering and the death on the cross.

545

Without Jesus Christ man must be in vice and misery; with Jesus Christ man is free from vice and misery; in Him is all our virtue and all our happiness. Apart from Him there is but vice, misery, darkness, death, despair.

546

We know God only by Jesus Christ. Without this mediator all communion with God is taken away; through Jesus Christ we know God. All those who have claimed to know God, and to prove Him without Jesus Christ, have had only weak proofs. But in proof of Jesus Christ we have the prophecies, which are solid and palpable proofs. And these prophecies, being accomplished and proved true by the event, mark the certainty of these truths, and therefore the divinity of Christ. In Him then, and through Him, we know God. Apart from Him, and without the Scripture, without original sin, without a necessary Mediator promised and come, we cannot absolutely prove God, nor teach right doctrine and right morality. But through Jesus Christ, and in Jesus Christ, we prove God, and teach morality and doctrine. Jesus Christ is then the true God of men.

But we know at the same time our wretchedness; for this God is none other than the Saviour of our wretchedness. So we can only know God well by knowing our iniquities. Therefore those who have known God, without knowing their wretchedness, have not glorified Him, but have glorified themselves. Quia ... non cognovit per sapientiam ... placuit Deo per stultitiam prædicationis salvos facere. [Pg 147][201]

547

Not only do we know God by Jesus Christ alone, but we know ourselves only by Jesus Christ. We know life and death only through Jesus Christ. Apart from Jesus Christ, we do not know what is our life, nor our death, nor God, nor ourselves.

Thus without the Scripture, which has Jesus Christ alone for its object, we know nothing, and see only darkness and confusion in the nature of God, and in our own nature.

548

It is not only impossible but useless to know God without Jesus Christ. They have not departed from Him, but approached; they have not humbled themselves, but ...

Quo quisque optimus est, pessimus, si hoc ipsum, quod optimus est, adscribat sibi.

549

I love poverty because He loved it. I love riches because they afford me the means of helping the very poor. I keep faith with everybody; I do not render evil to those who wrong me, but I wish them a lot like mine, in which I receive neither evil nor good from men. I try to be just, true, sincere, and faithful to all men; I have a tender heart for those to whom God has more closely united me; and whether I am alone, or seen of men, I do all my actions in the sight of God, who must judge of them, and to whom I have consecrated them all.

These are my sentiments; and every day of my life I bless my Redeemer, who has implanted them in me, and who, of a man full of weakness, of miseries, of lust, of pride, and of ambition, has made a man free from all these evils by the power of His grace, to which all the glory of it is due, as of myself I have only misery and error.

550

Dignior plagis quam osculis non timeo quia amo.

551

The Sepulchre of Jesus Christ.—Jesus Christ was dead, but seen on the Cross. He was dead, and hidden in the Sepulchre.

Jesus Christ was buried by the saints alone.

Jesus Christ wrought no miracle at the Sepulchre.

Only the saints entered it.[Pg 148]

It is there, not on the Cross, that Jesus Christ takes a new life.

It is the last mystery of the Passion and the Redemption.

Jesus Christ had nowhere to rest on earth but in the Sepulchre.

His enemies only ceased to persecute Him at the Sepulchre.

552

The Mystery of Jesus.—Jesus suffers in His passions the torments which men inflict upon Him; but in His agony He suffers the torments which He inflicts on Himself; turbare semetipsum.[202] This is a suffering from no human, but an almighty hand, for He must be almighty to bear it.

Jesus seeks some comfort at least in His three dearest friends, and they are asleep. He prays them to bear with Him for a little, and they leave Him with entire indifference, having so little compassion that it could not prevent their sleeping even for a moment. And thus Jesus was left alone to the wrath of God.

Jesus is alone on the earth, without any one not only to feel and share His suffering, but even to know of it; He and Heaven were alone in that knowledge.

Jesus is in a garden, not of delight as the first Adam, where he lost himself and the whole human race, but in one of agony, where He saved Himself and the whole human race.

He suffers this affliction and this desertion in the horror of night.

I believe that Jesus never complained but on this single occasion; but then He complained as if he could no longer bear His extreme suffering. "My soul is sorrowful, even unto death."[203]

Jesus seeks companionship and comfort from men. This is the sole occasion in all His life, as it seems to me. But He receives it not, for His disciples are asleep.

Jesus will be in agony even to the end of the world. We must not sleep during that time.

Jesus, in the midst of this universal desertion, including that of His own friends chosen to watch with Him, finding them asleep, is vexed because of the danger to which they expose, not Him, but themselves; He cautions them for their own safety and their own good, with a sincere tenderness for them during their ingratitude, and warns them that the spirit is willing and the flesh weak.

Jesus, finding them still asleep, without being restrained by any consideration for themselves or for Him, has the kindness not to waken them, and leaves them in repose.[Pg 149]

Jesus prays, uncertain of the will of His Father, and fears death; but, when He knows it, He goes forward to offer Himself to death. Eamus. Processit[204] (John).

Jesus asked of men and was not heard.

Jesus, while His disciples slept, wrought their salvation. He has wrought that of each of the righteous while they slept, both in their nothingness before their birth, and in their sins after their birth.

He prays only once that the cup pass away, and then with submission; and twice that it come if necessary.

Jesus is weary.

Jesus, seeing all His friends asleep and all His enemies wakeful, commits Himself entirely to His Father.

Jesus does not regard in Judas his enmity, but the order of God, which He loves and admits, since He calls him friend.

Jesus tears Himself away from His disciples to enter into His agony; we must tear ourselves away from our nearest and dearest to imitate Him.

Jesus being in agony and in the greatest affliction, let us pray longer.

We implore the mercy of God, not that He may leave us at peace in our vices, but that He may deliver us from them.

If God gave us masters by His own hand, oh! how necessary for us to obey them with a good heart! Necessity and events follow infallibly.

—"Console thyself, thou wouldst not seek Me, if thou hadst not found Me.

"I thought of thee in Mine agony, I have sweated such drops of blood for thee.

"It is tempting Me rather than proving thyself, to think if thou wouldst do such and such a thing on an occasion which has not happened; I shall act in thee if it occur.

"Let thyself be guided by My rules; see how well I have led the Virgin and the saints who have let Me act in them.

"The Father loves all that I do.

"Dost thou wish that it always cost Me the blood of My humanity, without thy shedding tears?

"Thy conversion is My affair; fear not, and pray with confidence as for Me.

"I am present with thee by My Word in Scripture, by My Spirit in the Church and by inspiration, by My power in the priests, by My prayer in the faithful.[Pg 150]

"Physicians will not heal thee, for thou wilt die at last. But it is I who heal thee, and make the body immortal.

"Suffer bodily chains and servitude, I deliver thee at present only from spiritual servitude.

"I am more a friend to thee than such and such an one, for I have done for thee more than they, they would not have suffered what I have suffered from thee, and they would not have died for thee as I have done in the time of thine infidelities and cruelties, and as I am ready to do, and do, among my elect and at the Holy Sacrament."

"If thou knewest thy sins, thou wouldst lose heart."

—I shall lose it then, Lord, for on Thy assurance I believe their malice.

—"No, for I, by whom thou learnest, can heal thee of them, and what I say to thee is a sign that I will heal thee. In proportion to thy expiation of them, thou wilt know them, and it will be said to thee: 'Behold, thy sins are forgiven thee.' Repent, then, for thy hidden sins, and for the secret malice of those which thou knowest."

—Lord, I give Thee all.

—"I love thee more ardently than thou hast loved thine abominations, ut immundus pro luto.

"To Me be the glory, not to thee, worm of the earth.

"Ask thy confessor, when My own words are to thee occasion of evil, vanity, or curiosity."

—I see in me depths of pride, curiosity, and lust. There is no relation between me and God, nor Jesus Christ the Righteous. But He has been made sin for me; all Thy scourges are fallen upon Him. He is more abominable than I, and, far from abhorring me, He holds Himself honoured that I go to Him and succour Him.

But He has healed Himself, and still more so will He heal me.

I must add my wounds to His, and join myself to Him; and He will save me in saving Himself. But this must not be postponed to the future.

Eritis sicut dii scientes bonum et malum.[205] Each one creates his god, when judging, "This is good or bad"; and men mourn or rejoice too much at events.

Do little things as though they were great, because of the majesty of Jesus Christ who does them in us, and who lives our life; and do the greatest things as though they were little and easy, because of His omnipotence.[Pg 151]

553

It seems to me that Jesus Christ only allowed His wounds to be touched after His resurrection: Noli me tangere.[206] We must unite ourselves only to His sufferings.

At the Last Supper He gave Himself in communion as about to die; to the disciples at Emmaus as risen from the dead; to the whole Church as ascended into heaven.

554

"Compare not thyself with others, but with Me. If thou dost not find Me in those with whom thou comparest thyself, thou comparest thyself to one who is abominable. If thou findest Me in them, compare thyself to Me. But whom wilt thou compare? Thyself, or Me in thee? If it is thyself, it is one who is abominable. If it is I, thou comparest Me to Myself. Now I am God in all.

"I speak to thee, and often counsel thee, because thy director cannot speak to thee, for I do not want thee to lack a guide.

"And perhaps I do so at his prayers, and thus he leads thee without thy seeing it. Thou wouldst not seek Me, if thou didst not possess Me.

"Be not therefore troubled."

[Pg 152]

SECTION VIII

THE FUNDAMENTALS OF THE CHRISTIAN RELIGION

555

... Men blaspheme what they do not know. The Christian religion consists in two points. It is of equal concern to men to know them, and it is equally dangerous to be ignorant to them. And it is equally of God's mercy that He has given indications of both.

And yet they take occasion to conclude that one of these points does not exist, from that which should have caused them to infer the other. The sages who have said there is only one God have been persecuted, the Jews were hated, and still more the Christians. They have seen by the light of nature that if there be a true religion on earth, the course of all things must tend to it as to a centre.

The whole course of things must have for its object the establishment and the greatness of religion. Men must have within them feelings suited to what religion teaches us. And, finally, religion must so be the object and centre to which all things tend, that whoever knows the principles of religion can give an explanation both of the whole nature of man in particular, and of the whole course of the world in general.

And on this ground they take occasion to revile the Christian religion, because they misunderstand it. They imagine that it consists simply in the worship of a God considered as great, powerful, and eternal; which is strictly deism, almost as far removed from the Christian religion as atheism, which is its exact opposite. And thence they conclude that this religion is not true, because they do not see that all things concur to the establishment of this point, that God does not manifest Himself to men with all the evidence which He could show.

But let them conclude what they will against deism, they will conclude nothing against the Christian religion, which properly consists in the mystery of the Redeemer, who, uniting in Himself the two natures, human and divine, has redeemed men from the[Pg 153] corruption of sin in order to reconcile them in His divine person to God.

The Christian religion, then, teaches men these two truths; that there is a God whom men can know, and that there is a corruption in their nature which renders them unworthy of Him. It is equally important to men to know both these points; and it is equally dangerous for man to know God without knowing his own wretchedness, and to know his own wretchedness without knowing the Redeemer who can free him from it. The knowledge of only one of these points gives rise either to the pride of philosophers, who have known God, and not their own wretchedness, or to the despair of atheists, who know their own wretchedness, but not the Redeemer.

And, as it is alike necessary to man to know these two points, so is it alike merciful of God to have made us know them. The Christian religion does this; it is in this that it consists.

Let us herein examine the order of the world, and see if all things do not tend to establish these two chief points of this religion: Jesus Christ is the end of all, and the centre to which all tends. Whoever knows Him knows the reason of everything.

Those who fall into error err only through failure to see one of these two things. We can then have an excellent knowledge of God without that of our own wretchedness, and of our own wretchedness without that of God. But we cannot know Jesus Christ without knowing at the same time both God and our own wretchedness.

Therefore I shall not undertake here to prove by natural reasons either the existence of God, or the Trinity, or the immortality of the soul, or anything of that nature; not only because I should not feel myself sufficiently able to find in nature arguments to convince hardened atheists, but also because such knowledge without Jesus Christ is useless and barren. Though a man should be convinced that numerical proportions are immaterial truths, eternal and dependent on a first truth, in which they subsist, and which is called God, I should not think him far advanced towards his own salvation.

The God of Christians is not a God who is simply the author of mathematical truths, or of the order of the elements; that is the view of heathens and Epicureans. He is not merely a God who exercises His providence over the life and fortunes of men, to bestow on those who worship Him a long and happy life. That was the portion of the Jews. But the God of Abraham,[Pg 154] the God of Isaac, the God of

Jacob, the God of Christians, is a God of love and of comfort, a God who fills the soul and heart of those whom He possesses, a God who makes them conscious of their inward wretchedness, and His infinite mercy, who unites Himself to their inmost soul, who fills it with humility and joy, with confidence and love, who renders them incapable of any other end than Himself.

All who seek God without Jesus Christ, and who rest in nature, either find no light to satisfy them, or come to form for themselves a means of knowing God and serving Him without a mediator. Thereby they fall either into atheism, or into deism, two things which the Christian religion abhors almost equally.

Without Jesus Christ the world would not exist; for it should needs be either that it would be destroyed or be a hell.

If the world existed to instruct man of God, His divinity would shine through every part in it in an indisputable manner; but as it exists only by Jesus Christ, and for Jesus Christ, and to teach men both their corruption and their redemption, all displays the proofs of these two truths.

All appearance indicates neither a total exclusion nor a manifest presence of divinity, but the presence of a God who hides Himself. Everything bears this character.

... Shall he alone who knows his nature know it only to be miserable? Shall he alone who knows it be alone unhappy?

... He must not see nothing at all, nor must he see sufficient for him to believe he possesses it; but he must see enough to know that he has lost it. For to know of his loss, he must see and not see; and that is exactly the state in which he naturally is.

... Whatever part he takes, I shall not leave him at rest ...

556

... It is then true that everything teaches man his condition, but he must understand this well. For it is not true that all reveals God, and it is not true that all conceals God. But it is at the same time true that He hides Himself from those who tempt Him, and that He reveals

Himself to those who seek Him, because men are both unworthy and capable of God; unworthy by their corruption capable by their original nature.

557

What shall we conclude from all our darkness, but our unworthiness? [Pg 155]

558

If there never had been any appearance of God, this eternal deprivation would have been equivocal, and might have as well corresponded with the absence of all divinity, as with the unworthiness of men to know Him; but His occasional, though not continual, appearances remove the ambiguity, If He appeared once, He exists always; and thus we cannot but conclude both that there is a God, and that men are unworthy of Him.

559

We do not understand the glorious state of Adam, nor the nature of his sin, nor the transmission of it to us. These are matters which took place under conditions of a nature altogether different from our own, and which transcend our present understanding.

The knowledge of all this is useless to us as a means of escape from it; and all that we are concerned to know, is that we are miserable, corrupt, separated from God, but ransomed by Jesus Christ, whereof we have wonderful proofs on earth.

So the two proofs of corruption and redemption are drawn from the ungodly, who live in indifference to religion, and from the Jews who are irreconcilable enemies.

560

There are two ways of proving the truths of our religion; one by the power of reason, the other by the authority of him who speaks.

We do not make use of the latter, but of the former. We do not say, "This must be believed, for Scripture, which says it, is divine." But we say that it must be believed for such and such a reason, which are feeble arguments, as reason may be bent to everything.

561

There is nothing on earth that does not show either the wretchedness of man, or the mercy of God; either the weakness of man without God, or the strength of man with God.

562

It will be one of the confusions of the damned to see that they are condemned by their own reason, by which they claimed to condemn the Christian religion.[Pg 156]

563

The prophecies, the very miracles and proofs of our religion, are not of such a nature that they can be said to be absolutely convincing. But they are also of such a kind that it cannot be said that it is unreasonable to believe them. Thus there is both evidence and obscurity to enlighten some and confuse others. But the evidence is such that it surpasses, or at least equals, the evidence to the contrary; so that it is not reason which can determine men not to follow it, and thus it can only be lust or malice of heart. And by this means there is sufficient evidence to condemn, and insufficient to convince; so that it appears in those who follow it, that it is grace, and not reason, which makes them follow it; and in those who shun it, that it is lust, not reason, which makes them shun it.

Vere discipuli, vere Israëlita, vere liberi, vere cibus.[207]

564

Recognise, then, the truth of religion in the very obscurity of religion, in the little light we have of it, and in the indifference which we have to knowing it.

565

We understand nothing of the works of God, if we do not take as a principle that He has willed to blind some, and enlighten others.

566

The two contrary reasons. We must begin with that; without that we understand nothing, and all is heretical; and we must even add at the end of each truth that the opposite truth is to be remembered.

567

Objection. The Scripture is plainly full of matters not dictated by the Holy Spirit.—Answer. Then they do not harm faith.—Objection. But the Church has decided that all is of the Holy Spirit.—Answer. I answer two things: first, the Church has not so decided; secondly, if she should so decide, it could be maintained.

Do you think that the prophecies cited in the Gospel are related to make you believe? No, it is to keep you from believing.[Pg 157]

568

Canonical.—The heretical books in the beginning of the Church serve to prove the canonical.

569

To the chapter on the Fundamentals must be added that on Typology touching the reason of types: why Jesus Christ was prophesied as to His first coming; why prophesied obscurely as to the manner.

570

The reason why. Types.—[They had to deal with a carnal people and to render them the depositary of the spiritual covenant.] To give faith to the Messiah, it was necessary there should have been precedent prophecies, and that these should be conveyed by persons above suspicion, diligent, faithful, unusually zealous, and known to all the world.

To accomplish all this, God chose this carnal people, to whom He entrusted the prophecies which foretell the Messiah as a deliverer, and as a dispenser of those carnal goods which this people loved. And thus they have had an extraordinary passion for their prophets, and, in sight of the whole world, have had charge of these books which foretell their Messiah, assuring all nations that He should come, and in the way foretold in the books, which they held open to the whole world. Yet this people, deceived by the poor and ignominious advent of the Messiah, have been His most cruel enemies. So that they, the people least open to suspicion in the world of favouring us, the most strict and most zealous that can be named for their law and their prophets, have kept the books incorrupt. Hence those who have rejected and crucified Jesus Christ, who has been to them an offence, are those who have charge of the books which testify of Him, and state that He will be an offence and rejected. Therefore they have shown it was He by rejecting Him, and He has been alike proved both by the righteous Jews who received Him, and by the unrighteous who rejected Him, both facts having been foretold.

Wherefore the prophecies have a hidden and spiritual meaning, to which this people were hostile, under the carnal meaning which they loved. If the spiritual meaning had been revealed, they would not have loved it, and, unable to bear it, they would not have been zealous of the preservation of their books and their[Pg 158] ceremonies; and if they had loved these spiritual promises, and had preserved them incorrupt till the time of the Messiah, their testimony would have had no force, because they had been his friends.

Therefore it was well that the spiritual meaning should be concealed; but, on the other hand, if this meaning had been so hidden as not to appear at all, it could not have served as a proof of the Messiah. What then was done? In a crowd of passages it has been hidden under the temporal meaning, and in a few has been clearly revealed; besides that the time and the state of the world have been so clearly foretold that it is clearer than the sun. And in some places this spiritual meaning is so clearly expressed, that it would require a blindness like that which the flesh imposes on the spirit when it is subdued by it, not to recognise it.

See, then, what has been the prudence of God. This meaning is concealed under another in an infinite number of passages, and in some, though rarely, it is revealed; but yet so that the passages in which it is concealed are equivocal, and can suit both meanings; whereas the passages where it is disclosed are unequivocal, and can only suit the spiritual meaning.

So that this cannot lead us into error, and could only be misunderstood by so carnal a people.

For when blessings are promised in abundance, what was to prevent them from understanding the true blessings, but their covetousness, which limited the meaning to worldly goods? But those whose only good was in God referred them to God alone. For there are two principles, which divide the wills of men, covetousness and charity. Not that covetousness cannot exist along with faith in God, nor charity with worldly riches; but covetousness uses God, and enjoys the world, and charity is the opposite.

Now the ultimate end gives names to things. All which prevents us from attaining it, is called an enemy to us. Thus the creatures, however good, are the enemies of the righteous, when they turn them away from God, and God Himself is the enemy of those whose covetousness He confounds.

Thus as the significance of the word "enemy" is dependent on the ultimate end, the righteous understood by it their passions, and the carnal the Babylonians; and so these terms were obscure only for the unrighteous. And this is what Isaiah says: Signa legem in electis meis, [208] and that Jesus Christ shall be a stone of[Pg 159] stumbling. But, "Blessed are they who shall not be offended in him." Hosea, [209] ult., says excellently, "Where is the wise? and he shall understand what I say. The righteous shall know them, for the ways of God are right; but the transgressors shall fall therein."

571

Hypothesis that the apostles were impostors.—The time clearly, the manner obscurely.—Five typical proofs.

{1600 prophets.
2000 {
{ 400 scattered.

572

Blindness of Scripture.—"The Scripture," said the Jews, "says that we shall not know whence Christ will come (John vii, 27, and xii, 34). The Scripture says that Christ abideth for ever, and He said that He should die." Therefore, says Saint John,[210] they believed not, though He had done so many miracles, that the word of Isaiah might be fulfilled: "He hath blinded them," etc.

573

Greatness.—Religion is so great a thing that it is right that those who will not take the trouble to seek it, if it be obscure, should be deprived of it. Why, then, do any complain, if it be such as can be found by seeking?

574

All things work together for good to the elect, even the obscurities of Scripture; for they honour them because of what is divinely clear. And all things work together for evil to the rest of the world, even what is clear; for they revile such, because of the obscurities which they do not understand.

575

The general conduct of the world towards the Church: God willing to blind and to enlighten.—The event having proved the divinity of these prophecies, the rest ought to be believed. And thereby we see the order of the world to be of this kind. The miracles of the Creation and the Deluge being forgotten, God sends the law and the miracles of Moses, the prophets who prophesied particular things; and to prepare a lasting miracle,[Pg 160] He prepares prophecies and their fulfilment; but, as the prophecies could be suspected, He desires to make them above suspicion, etc.

576

God has made the blindness of this people subservient to the good of the elect.

577

There is sufficient clearness to enlighten the elect, and sufficient obscurity to humble them. There is sufficient obscurity to blind the reprobate, and sufficient clearness to condemn them, and make them inexcusable.—Saint Augustine, Montaigne, Sébond.

The genealogy of Jesus Christ in the Old Testament is intermingled with so many others that are useless, that it cannot be distinguished. If Moses had kept only the record of the ancestors of Christ, that might have been too plain. If he had not noted that of Jesus Christ, it might not have been sufficiently plain. But, after all, whoever looks closely sees that of Jesus Christ expressly traced through Tamar,[211] Ruth,[212] etc.

Those who ordained these sacrifices, knew their uselessness; those who have declared their uselessness, have not ceased to practise them.

If God had permitted only one religion, it had been too easily known; but when we look at it closely, we clearly discern the truth amidst this confusion.

The premiss.—Moses was a clever man. If, then, he ruled himself by his reason, he would say nothing clearly which was directly against reason.

Thus all the very apparent weaknesses are strength. Example; the two genealogies in Saint Matthew and Saint Luke. What can be clearer than that this was not concerted?

578

God (and the Apostles), foreseeing that the seeds of pride would make heresies spring up, and being unwilling to give them occasion to arise from correct expressions, has put in Scripture and the prayers of the Church contrary words and sentences to produce their fruit in time.

So in morals He gives charity, which produces fruits contrary to lust. [Pg 161]

579

Nature has some perfections to show that she is the image of God, and some defects to show that she is only His image.

580

God prefers rather to incline the will than the intellect. Perfect clearness would be of use to the intellect, and would harm the will. To humble pride.

581

We make an idol of truth itself; for truth apart from charity is not God, but His image and idol, which we must neither love nor worship; and still less must we love or worship its opposite, namely, falsehood.

I can easily love total darkness; but if God keeps me in a state of semi-darkness, such partial darkness displeases me, and, because I do not see therein the advantage of total darkness, it is unpleasant to me. This is a fault, and a sign that I make for myself an idol of darkness, apart from the order of God. Now only His order must be worshipped.

582

The feeble-minded are people who know the truth, but only affirm it so far as consistent with their own interest. But, apart from that, they renounce it.

583

The world exists for the exercise of mercy and judgment, not as if men were placed in it out of the hands of God, but as hostile to God; and to them He grants by grace sufficient light, that they may return to Him, if they desire to seek and follow Him; and also that they may be punished, if they refuse to seek or follow Him.

584

That God has willed to hide Himself.—If there were only one religion, God would indeed be manifest. The same would be the case, if there were no martyrs but in our religion.

God being thus hidden, every religion which does not affirm that God is hidden, is not true; and every religion which does not give the reason of it, is not instructive. Our religion does, all this: Vere tu es Deus absconditus.[Pg 162]

585

If there were no obscurity, man would not be sensible of his corruption; if there were no light, man would not hope for a remedy. Thus, it is not only fair, but advantageous to us, that God be partly hidden and partly revealed; since it is equally dangerous to man to know God without knowing his own wretchedness, and to know his own wretchedness without knowing God.

586

This religion, so great in miracles, saints, blameless Fathers, learned and great witnesses, martyrs, established kings as David, and Isaiah, a prince of the blood, and so great in science, after having displayed all her miracles and all her wisdom, rejects all this, and declares that she has neither wisdom nor signs, but only the cross and foolishness.

For those, who, by these signs and that wisdom, have deserved your belief, and who have proved to you their character, declare to you that nothing of all this can change you, and render you capable of knowing and loving God, but the power of the foolishness of the cross without wisdom and signs, and not the signs without this power. Thus our religion is foolish in respect to the effective cause, and wise in respect to the wisdom which prepares it.

587

Our religion is wise and foolish. Wise, because it is the most learned, and the most founded on miracles, prophecies, etc. Foolish, because it is not all this which makes us belong to it. This makes us indeed condemn those who do not belong to it; but it does not cause belief in those who do belong to it. It is the cross that makes them believe, ne evacuata sit crux. And so Saint Paul, who came with wisdom and signs, says that he has come neither with wisdom nor with signs; for he came to convert. But those who come only to convince, can say that they come with wisdom and with signs.

[Pg 163]

SECTION IX

PERPETUITY

588

On the fact that the Christian religion is not the only religion.—So far is this from being a reason for believing that it is not the true one, that, on the contrary, it makes us see that it is so.

589

Men must be sincere in all religions; true heathens, true Jews, true Christians.

590

```
      J. C.
Heathens __|__ Mahomet
      \   /
     Ignorance
      of God.
```

591

The falseness of other religions.—They have no witnesses. Jews have. God defies other religions to produce such signs: Isaiah xliii, 9; xliv, 8.

592

History of China.[213]-I believe only the histories, whose witnesses got themselves killed.

[Which is the more credible of the two, Moses or China?]

It is not a question of seeing this summarily. I tell you there is in it something to blind, and something to enlighten.

By this one word I destroy all your reasoning. "But China obscures," say you; and I answer, "China obscures, but there is clearness to be found; seek it."

Thus all that you say makes for one of the views, and not at all against the other. So this serves, and does no harm.

We must then see this in detail; we must put the papers on the table. [Pg 164]

593

Against the history of China. The historians of Mexico, the five suns, [214] of which the last is only eight hundred years old.

The difference between a book accepted by a nation, and one which makes a nation.

594

Mahomet was without authority. His reasons then should have been very strong, having only their own force. What does he say then, that we must believe him?

595

The Psalms are chanted throughout the whole world.

Who renders testimony to Mahomet? Himself. Jesus Christ[215] desires His own testimony to be as nothing.

The quality of witnesses necessitates their existence always and everywhere; and he, miserable creature, is alone.

596

Against Mahomet.—The Koran is not more of Mahomet than the Gospel is of Saint Matthew, for it is cited by many authors from age to age. Even its very enemies, Celsus and Porphyry, never denied it.

The Koran says Saint Matthew was an honest man.[216] Therefore Mahomet was a false prophet for calling honest men wicked, or for not agreeing with what they have said of Jesus Christ.

597

It is not by that which is obscure in Mahomet, and which may be interpreted in a mysterious sense, that I would have him judged, but by what is clear, as his paradise and the rest. In that he is ridiculous.

And since what is clear is ridiculous, it is not right to take his obscurities for mysteries.

It is not the same with the Scripture. I agree that there are in it obscurities as strange as those of Mahomet; but there are admirably clear passages, and the prophecies are manifestly fulfilled. The cases are therefore not on a par. We must not confound, and put on one level things which only resemble each other in their obscurity, and not in the clearness, which requires us to reverence the obscurities.[Pg 165]

598

The difference between Jesus Christ and Mahomet.—Mahomet was not foretold; Jesus Christ was foretold.

Mahomet slew; Jesus Christ caused His own to be slain.

Mahomet forbade reading; the Apostles ordered reading.

In fact the two are so opposed, that if Mahomet took the way to succeed from a worldly point of view, Jesus Christ, from the same point of view, took the way to perish. And instead of concluding that, since Mahomet succeeded, Jesus Christ might well have succeeded, we ought to say that since Mahomet succeeded, Jesus Christ should have failed.

599

Any man can do what Mahomet has done; for he performed no miracles, he was not foretold. No man can do what Christ has done.

600

The heathen religion has no foundation [at the present day. It is said once to have had a foundation by the oracles which spoke. But what are the books which assure us of this? Are they so worthy of belief on account of the virtue of their authors? Have they been preserved with such care that we can be sure that they have not been meddled with?]

The Mahometan religion has for a foundation the Koran and Mahomet. But has this prophet, who was to be the last hope of the world, been foretold? What sign has he that every other man has not, who chooses to call himself a prophet? What miracles does he himself say that he has done? What mysteries has he taught, even according to his own tradition? What was the morality, what the happiness held out by him?

The Jewish religion must be differently regarded in the tradition of the Holy Bible, and in the tradition of the people. Its morality and happiness are absurd in the tradition of the people, but are admirable in that of the Holy Bible. (And all religion is the same; for the Christian religion is very different in the Holy Bible and in the casuists.) The foundation is admirable; it is the most ancient book in the world, and the most authentic; and whereas Mahomet, in order to make his own book continue in existence, forbade men to read it, Moses,[217] for the same reason, ordered every one to read his.[Pg 166]

Our religion is so divine that another divine religion has only been the foundation of it.

601

Order.—To see what is clear and indisputable in the whole state of the Jews.

602

The Jewish religion is wholly divine in its authority, its duration, its perpetuity, its morality, its doctrine, and its effects.

603

The only science contrary to common sense and human nature is that alone which has always existed among men.

604

The only religion contrary to nature, to common sense, and to our pleasure, is that alone which has always existed.

605

No religion but our own has taught that man is born in sin. No sect of philosophers has said this. Therefore none have declared the truth.

No sect or religion has always existed on earth, but the Christian religion.

606

Whoever judges of the Jewish religion by its coarser forms will misunderstand it. It is to be seen in the Holy Bible, and in the tradition of the prophets, who have made it plain enough that they did not interpret the law according to the letter. So our religion is divine in the Gospel, in the Apostles, and in tradition; but it is absurd in those who tamper with it.

The Messiah, according to the carnal Jews, was to be a great temporal prince. Jesus Christ, according to carnal Christians,[218] has come to dispense us from the love of God, and to give us sacraments which shall do everything without our help. Such is not the Christian religion, nor the Jewish. True Jews and true Christians have always expected a Messiah who should make them love God, and by that love triumph over their enemies.[Pg 167]

607

The carnal Jews hold a midway place between Christians and heathens. The heathens know not God, and love the world only. The Jews know the true God, and love the world only. The Christians know the true God, and love not the world. Jews and heathens love the same good. Jews and Christians know the same God.

The Jews were of two kinds; the first had only heathen affections, the other had Christian affections.

608

There are two kinds of men in each religion: among the heathen, worshippers of beasts, and the worshippers of the one only God of natural religion; among the Jews, the carnal, and the spiritual, who were the Christians of the old law; among Christians, the coarser-minded, who are the Jews of the new law. The carnal Jews looked for a carnal Messiah; the coarser Christians believe that the Messiah has dispensed them from the love of God; true Jews and true Christians worship a Messiah who makes them love God.

609

To show that the true Jews and the true Christians have but the same religion.—The religion of the Jews seemed to consist essentially in the fatherhood of Abraham, in circumcision, in sacrifices, in ceremonies, in the Ark, in the temple, in Jerusalem, and, finally, in the law, and in the covenant with Moses.

I say that it consisted in none of those things, but only in the love of God, and that God disregarded all the other things.

That God did not accept the posterity of Abraham.

That the Jews were to be punished like strangers, if they transgressed. Deut. viii, 19; "If thou do at all forget the Lord thy God, and walk after other gods, I testify against you this day that ye shall surely perish, as the nations which the Lord destroyeth before your face."

That strangers, if they loved God, were to be received by Him as the Jews. Isaiah lvi, 3: "Let not the stranger say, 'The Lord will not receive me.' The strangers who join themselves unto the Lord to serve Him and love Him, will I bring unto my holy mountain, and accept therein sacrifices, for mine house is a house of prayer."[Pg 168]

That the true Jews considered their merit to be from God only, and not from Abraham. Isaiah lxiii, 16; "Doubtless thou art our Father, though Abraham be ignorant of us, and Israel acknowledge us not. Thou art our Father and our Redeemer."

Moses himself told them that God would not accept persons. Deut. x, 17: "God," said he, "regardeth neither persons nor sacrifices."

The Sabbath was only a sign, Exod. xxxi, 13; and in memory of the escape from Egypt, Deut. v, 19. Therefore it is no longer necessary, since Egypt must be forgotten.

Circumcision was only a sign, Gen. xvii, 11. And thence it came to pass that, being in the desert, they were not circumcised because they could not be confounded with other peoples; and after Jesus Christ came, it was no longer necessary.

That the circumcision of the heart is commanded. Deut. x, 16; Jeremiah iv, 4: "Be ye circumcised in heart; take away the superfluities of your heart, and harden yourselves not. For your God is a mighty God, strong and terrible, who accepteth not persons."

That God said He would one day do it. Deut. xxx, 6; "God will circumcise thine heart, and the heart of thy seed, that thou mayest love Him with all thine heart."

That the uncircumcised in heart shall be judged. Jeremiah ix, 26: For God will judge the uncircumcised peoples, and all the people of Israel, because he is "uncircumcised in heart."

That the external is of no avail apart from the internal. Joel ii, 13: Scindite corda vestra, etc.; Isaiah lviii, 3, 4, etc.

The love of God is enjoined in the whole of Deuteronomy. Deut. xxx, 19: "I call heaven and earth to record that I have set before you life and death, that you should choose life, and love God, and obey Him, for God is your life."

That the Jews, for lack of that love, should be rejected for their offences, and the heathen chosen in their stead. Hosea i, 10; Deut. xxxii, 20. "I will hide myself from them in view of their latter sins, for they are a froward generation without faith. They have moved me to jealousy with that which is not God, and I will move them to jealousy with those which are not a people, and with an ignorant and foolish nation." Isaiah lxv, 1.

That temporal goods are false, and that the true good is to be united to God. Psalm cxliii, 15.

That their feasts are displeasing to God. Amos v, 21.[Pg 169]

That the sacrifices of the Jews displeased God. Isaiah lxvi. 1-3; i, II; Jer. vi, 20; David, Miserere.—Even on the part of the good, Expectavi. Psalm xlix, 8, 9, 10, 11, 12, 13 and 14.

That He has established them only for their hardness. Micah, admirably, vi; 1 Kings xv, 22; Hosea vi, 6.

That the sacrifices of the Gentiles will be accepted of God, and that God will take no pleasure in the sacrifices of the Jews. Malachi i, II.

That God will make a new covenant with the Messiah, and the old will be annulled. Jer. xxxi, 31. Mandata non bona. Ezek.

That the old things will be forgotten. Isaiah xliii, 18, 19; lxv 17, 10.

That the Ark will no longer be remembered. Jer. iii, 15, 16.

That the temple should be rejected. Jer. vii, 12, 13, 14.

That the sacrifices should be rejected, and other pure sacrifices established. Malachi i, II.

That the order of Aaron's priesthood should be rejected, and that of Melchizedek introduced by the Messiah. Ps. Dixit Dominus.

That this priesthood should be eternal. Ibid.

That Jerusalem should be rejected, and Rome admitted. Ps. Dixit Dominus.

That the name of the Jews should be rejected, and a new name given. Isaiah lxv, 15.

That this last name should be more excellent than that of the Jews, and eternal. Isaiah lvi, 5.

That the Jews should be without prophets (Amos), without a king, without princes, without sacrifice, without an idol.

That the Jews should nevertheless always remain a people. Jer. xxxi, 36.

610

Republic.—The Christian republic—and even the Jewish—has only had God for ruler, as Philo the Jew notices, On Monarchy.

When they fought, it was for God only; their chief hope was in God only; they considered their towns as belonging to God only, and kept them for God. 1 Chron. xix, 13.

611

Gen. xvii, 7. Statuam pactum meum inter me et te fœdere sempiterno ... ut sim Deus tuus ...

Et tu ergo custodies pactum meum.[Pg 170]

612

Perpetuity.—That religion has always existed on earth, which consists in believing that man has fallen from a state of glory and of communion with God into a state of sorrow, penitence, and estrangement from God, but that after this life we shall be restored by a Messiah who should have come. All things have passed away, and this has endured, for which all things are.

Men have in the first age of the world been carried away into every kind of debauchery, and yet there were saints, as Enoch, Lamech, and others, who waited patiently for the Christ promised from the beginning of the world. Noah saw the wickedness of men at its height; and he was held worthy to save the world in his person, by the hope of the Messiah of whom he was the type. Abraham was surrounded by idolaters, when God made known to him the mystery of the Messiah, whom he welcomed from afar.[219] In the time of Isaac and Jacob abomination was spread over all the earth; but these saints lived in faith; and Jacob, dying and blessing his children, cried in a transport which made him break off his discourse, "I await, O my God, the Saviour whom Thou hast promised. Salutare taum expectabo, Domine."[220] The Egyptians were infected both with idolatry and magic; the very people of God were led astray by their example. Yet Moses and others believed Him whom they saw not, and worshipped Him, looking to the eternal gifts which He was preparing for them.

The Greeks and Latins then set up false deities; the poets made a hundred different theologies, while the philosophers separated into a thousand different sects; and yet in the heart of Judæa there were always chosen men who foretold the coming of this Messiah, which was known to them alone.

He came at length in the fullness of time, and time has since witnessed the birth of so many schisms and heresies, so many political revolutions, so many changes in all things; yet this Church, which worships Him who has always been worshipped, has endured uninterruptedly. It is a wonderful, incomparable, and altogether divine fact that this religion, which has always endured, has always been attacked. It has been a thousand times on the eve of universal destruction, and every time it has been in that state, God has restored it by extraordinary acts of His power. This is astonishing, as also that it has preserved itself without yielding to the will of tyrants. For it is not strange that a State endures, when its laws are sometimes made[Pg 171] to give way to necessity, but that ... (See the passage indicated in Montaigne.)

613

States would perish if they did not often make their laws give way to necessity. But religion has never suffered this, or practised it. Indeed, there must be these compromises, or miracles. It is not strange to be saved by yieldings, and this is not strictly self-preservation; besides, in the end they perish entirely. None has endured a thousand years. But the fact that this religion has always maintained itself, inflexible as it is, proves its divinity.

614

Whatever may be said, it must be admitted that the Christian religion has something astonishing in it. Some will say, "This is because you were born in it." Far from it; I stiffen myself against it for this very reason, for fear this prejudice bias me. But although I am born in it, I cannot help finding it so.

615

Perpetuity.—The Messiah has always been believed in. The tradition from Adam was fresh in Noah and in Moses. Since then the prophets have foretold him, while at the same time foretelling other things, which, being from time to time fulfilled in the sight of men, showed the truth of their mission, and consequently that of their promises touching the Messiah. Jesus Christ performed miracles, and the Apostles also, who converted all the heathen; and all the prophecies being thereby fulfilled, the Messiah is for ever proved.

616

Perpetuity.—Let us consider that since the beginning of the world the expectation of worship of the Messiah has existed uninterruptedly; that there have been found men, who said that God had revealed to them that a Redeemer was to be born, who should save His people; that Abraham came afterwards, saying that he had had a revelation that the Messiah was to spring from him by a son, whom he should have; that Jacob declared that, of his twelve sons, the Messiah would spring from Judah; that Moses and the prophets then came to declare the time and the manner of His coming; that they said their law was only temporary till that of the Messiah, that it should endure till[Pg 172] then, but that the other should last for ever; that thus either their law, or that of the Messiah, of which it was the promise, would be always upon the earth; that, in fact, it has always endured; that at last Jesus Christ came with all the circumstances foretold. This is wonderful.

617

This is positive fact. While all philosophers separate into different sects, there is found in one corner of the world the most ancient people in it, declaring that all the world is in error, that God has revealed to them the truth, that they will always exist on the earth. In fact, all other sects come to an end, this one still endures, and has done so for four thousand years.

They declare that they hold from their ancestors that man has fallen from communion with God, and is entirely estranged from God, but that He has promised to redeem them; that this doctrine shall always exist on the earth; that their law has a double signification; that during sixteen hundred years they have had people, whom they believed prophets, foretelling both the time and the manner; that four hundred years after they were scattered everywhere, because Jesus Christ was to be everywhere announced; that Jesus Christ came in the manner, and at the time foretold; that the Jews have since been scattered abroad under a curse, and nevertheless still exist.

618

I see the Christian religion founded upon a preceding religion, and this is what I find as a fact.

I do not here speak of the miracles of Moses, of Jesus Christ, and of the Apostles, because they do not at first seem convincing, and because I only wish here to put in evidence all those foundations of the Christian religion which are beyond doubt, and which cannot be called in question by any person whatsoever. It is certain that we see in many places of the world a peculiar people, separated from all other peoples of the world, and called the Jewish people.

I see then a crowd of religions in many parts of the world and in all times; but their morality cannot please me, nor can their proofs convince me. Thus I should equally have rejected the religion of Mahomet and of China, of the ancient Romans and of the Egyptians, for the sole reason, that none having more[Pg 173] marks of truth than another, nor anything which should necessarily persuade me, reason cannot incline to one rather than the other.

But, in thus considering this changeable and singular variety of morals and beliefs at different times, I find in one corner of the world a peculiar people, separated from all other peoples on earth, the most ancient of all, and whose histories are earlier by many generations than the most ancient which we possess.

I find, then, this great and numerous people, sprung from a single man, who worship one God, and guide themselves by a law which they say that they obtained from His own hand. They maintain that they are the only people in the world to whom God has revealed His mysteries; that all men are corrupt and in disgrace with God; that they are all abandoned to their senses and their own imagination, whence come the strange errors and continual changes which happen among them, both of religions and of morals, whereas they themselves remain firm in their conduct; but that God will not leave other nations in this darkness for ever; that there will come a Saviour for all; that they are in the world to announce Him to men; that they are expressly formed to be forerunners and heralds of this great event, and to summon all nations to join with them in the expectation of this Saviour.

To meet with this people is astonishing to me, and seems to me worthy of attention. I look at the law which they boast of having obtained from God, and I find it admirable. It is the first law of all, and is of such a kind that, even before the term law was in currency among the Greeks, it had, for nearly a thousand years earlier, been uninterruptedly accepted and observed by the Jews. I likewise think it strange that the first law of the world happens to be the most perfect; so that the greatest legislators have borrowed their laws from it, as is apparent from the law of the Twelve Tables at Athens,[221] afterwards taken by the Romans, and as it would be easy to prove, if Josephus[222] and others had not sufficiently dealt with this subject.

619

Advantages of the Jewish people.—In this search the Jewish people at once attracts my attention by the number of wonderful and singular facts which appear about them.

I first see that they are a people wholly composed of brethren,[Pg 174] and whereas all others are formed by the assemblage of an infinity of families, this, though so wonderfully fruitful, has all sprung from one man alone, and, being thus all one flesh, and members one of another, they constitute a powerful state of one family. This is unique.

This family, or people, is the most ancient within human knowledge, a fact which seems to me to inspire a peculiar veneration for it, especially in view of our present inquiry; since if God had from all time revealed Himself to men, it is to these we must turn for knowledge of the tradition.

This people is not eminent solely by their antiquity, but is also singular by their duration, which has always continued from their origin till now. For whereas the nations of Greece and of Italy, of Lacedæmon, of Athens and of Rome, and others who came long after, have long since perished, these ever remain, and in spite of the endeavours of many powerful kings who have a hundred times tried to destroy them, as their historians testify, and as it is easy to conjecture from the natural order of things during so long a space of years, they have nevertheless been preserved (and this preservation has been foretold); and extending from the earliest times to the latest, their history comprehends in its duration all our histories [which it preceded by a long time].

The law by which this people is governed is at once the most ancient law in the world, the most perfect, and the only one which has been always observed without a break in a state. This is what Josephus admirably proves, against Apion,[223] and also Philo[224] the Jew, in different places, where they point out that it is so ancient that the very name of law was only known by the oldest nation more than a thousand years afterwards; so that Homer, who has written the history of so many states, has never used the term. And it is easy to judge of its perfection by simply reading it; for we see that it has provided for all things with so great wisdom, equity, and judgment, that the most ancient legislators, Greek and Roman, having had some knowledge of it, have borrowed from it their principal laws; this is evident from what are called the Twelve Tables, and from the other proofs which Josephus gives.

But this law is at the same time the severest and strictest of all in respect to their religious worship, imposing on this people, in order to keep them to their duty, a thousand peculiar and painful observances, on pain of death. Whence it is very[Pg 175] astonishing that it has been constantly preserved during many centuries by a people, rebellious and impatient as this one was; while all other states have changed their laws from time to time, although these were far more lenient.

The book which contains this law, the first of all, is itself the most ancient book in the world, those of Homer, Hesiod, and others, being six or seven hundred years later.

620

The creation and the deluge being past, and God no longer requiring to destroy the world, nor to create it anew, nor to give such great signs of Himself, He began to establish a people on the earth, purposely formed, who were to last until the coming of the people whom the Messiah should fashion by His spirit.

621

The creation of the world beginning to be distant, God provided a single contemporary historian, and appointed a whole people as guardians of this book, in order that this history might be the most authentic in the world, and that all men might thereby learn a fact so necessary to know, and which could only be known through that means.

622

[Japhet begins the genealogy.]

Joseph folds his arms, and prefers the younger.[225]

623

Why should Moses make the lives of men so long, and their generations so few?

Because it is not the length of years, but the multitude of generations, which renders things obscure. For truth is perverted only by the change of men. And yet he puts two things, the most memorable that were ever imagined, namely, the creation and the deluge, so near that we reach from one to the other.

624

Shem, who saw Lamech, who saw Adam, saw also Jacob, who saw those who saw Moses; therefore the deluge and the creation are true. This is conclusive among certain people who understand it rightly.[Pg 176]

625

The longevity of the patriarchs, instead of causing the loss of past history, conduced, on the contrary, to its preservation. For the reason why we arc sometimes insufficiently instructed in the history of our ancestors, is that we have never lived long with them, and that they are often dead before we have attained the age of reason. Now, when men lived so long, children lived long with their parents. They conversed long with them. But what else could be the subject of their talk save the history of their ancestors, since to that all history was reduced, and men did not study science or art, which now form a large part of daily conversation? We see also that in these days tribes took particular care to preserve their genealogies.

626

I believe that Joshua was the first of God's people to have this name, as Jesus Christ was the last of God's people.

627

Antiquity of the Jews.—What a difference there is between one book and another! I am not astonished that the Greeks made the Iliad, nor the Egyptians and the Chinese their histories.

We have only to see how this originates. These fabulous historians are not contemporaneous with the facts about which they write. Homer composes a romance, which he gives out as such, and which is received as such; for nobody doubted that Troy and Agamemnon no more existed than did the golden apple. Accordingly he did not think of making a history, but solely a book to amuse; he is the only writer of his time; the beauty of the work has made it last, every one learns it and talks of it, it is necessary to know it, and each one knows it by heart. Four hundred years afterwards the witnesses of these facts are no longer alive, no one knows of his own knowledge if it be a fable or a history; one has only learnt it from his ancestors, and this can pass for truth.

Every history which is not contemporaneous, as the books of the Sibyls and Trismegistus,[226] and so many others which have been believed by the world, are false, and found to be false in the course of time. It is not so with contemporaneous writers.

There is a great difference between a book which an individual writes, and publishes to a nation, and a book which itself creates a nation. We cannot doubt that the book is as old as the people.[Pg 177]

628

Josephus hides the shame of his nation.

Moses does not hide his own shame.

Quis mihi det ut omnes prophetent?[227]

He was weary of the multitude.

629

The sincerity of the Jews.—Maccabees,[228] after they had no more prophets; the Masorah, since Jesus Christ.

This book will be a testimony for you.[229]

Defective and final letters.

Sincere against their honour, and dying for it; this has no example in the world, and no root in nature.

630

Sincerity of the Jews.—They preserve lovingly and carefully the book in which Moses declares that they have been all their life ungrateful to God, and that he knows they will be still more so after his death; but that he calls heaven and earth to witness against them, and that he has [taught] them enough.

He declares that God, being angry with them, shall at last scatter them among all the nations of the earth; that as they have offended Him by worshipping gods who were not their God, so He will provoke them by calling a people who are not His people; that He desires that all His words be preserved for ever, and that His book be placed in the Ark of the Covenant to serve for ever as a witness against them.

Isaiah says the same thing, xxx.

631

On Esdras.—The story that the books were burnt with the temple proved false by Maccabees: "Jeremiah gave them the law."

The story that he recited the whole by heart. Josephus and Esdras point out that he read the book. Baronius, Ann., p. 180: Nullus penitus Hebræorum antiquorum reperitur qui tradiderit libros periisse et per Esdram esse restitutos, nisi in IV Esdræ.

The story that he changed the letters.

Philo, in Vita Moysis: Illa lingua ac character quo antiquitus scripta est lex sic permansit usque ad LXX.[Pg 178]

Josephus says that the Law was in Hebrew when it was translated by the Seventy.

Under Antiochus and Vespasian, when they wanted to abolish the books, and when there was no prophet, they could not do so. And under the Babylonians, when no persecution had been made, and when there were so many prophets, would they have let them be burnt?

Josephus laughs at the Greeks who would not bear ...

Tertullian.[230]—Perinde potuit abolefactam eam violentia cataclysmi in spiritu rursus reformare, quemadmodum et Hierosolymis Babylonia expugnatione deletis, omne instrumentum Judaicæ literaturæ per Esdram constat restauratum.

He says that Noah could as easily have restored in spirit the book of Enoch, destroyed by the Deluge, as Esdras could have restored the Scriptures lost during the Captivity.

(Θεὸς) ἐν τῇ ἐπὶ Ναβουχοδόνοσορ αἰcγμαλωίᾳ τοῦ λαοῦ, διαφθαρεισῶν τῶν γραφῶν ... ἐνέπνευσε Εσδρᾷ τῶ ἱερεἱ ἐκ τῆς φυλῆς Λευὶ τοῦς τῶν προγελονότων προφητῶν πα'ντας ἀνατάξασθαι λόγους, καὶ ἀποκαταστῆσαι τῷ λαῳ τὴν διὰ Μωυσέως νομοθεσίαν. [231] He alleges this to prove that it is not incredible that the Seventy may have explained the holy Scriptures with that uniformity which we admire in them. And he took that from Saint Irenæus.[232]

Saint Hilary, in his preface to the Psalms, says that Esdras arranged the Psalms in order.

The origin of this tradition comes from the 14th chapter of the fourth book of Esdras. Deus glorificatus est, et Scripturæ vere divinæ creditæ sunt, omnibus eandem et eisdem verbis et eisdem nominibus recitantibus ab initio usque ad finem, uti et præsentes gentes cognoscerent quoniam per inspirationem Dei interpretatæ sunt Scripturæ, et non esset mirabile Deum hoc in eis operatum: quando in ea captivitate populi quæ facta est a Nabuchodonosor, corruptis scripturis et post 70 annos Judæis descendentibus in regionem suam, et post deinde temporibus Artaxerxis Persarum regis, inspiravit Esdræ sacerdoti tribus Levi præteritorum prophetarum omnes rememorare sermones, et restituere populo eam legem quæ data est per Moysen.

632

Against the story in Esdras, 2 Maccab. ii;—Josephus, Antiquities, II, i —Cyrus took occasion from the prophecy of Isaiah to release the people. The Jews held their property in[Pg 179] peace under Cyrus in Babylon; hence they could well have the Law.

Josephus, in the whole history of Esdras, does not say one word about this restoration.—2 Kings xvii, 27.

633

If the story in Esdras[233] is credible, then it must be believed that the Scripture is Holy Scripture; for this story is based only on the authority of those who assert that of the Seventy, which shows that the Scripture is holy.

Therefore if this account be true, we have what we want therein; if not, we have it elsewhere. And thus those who would ruin the truth of our religion, founded on Moses, establish it by the same authority by which they attack it. So by this providence it still exists.

634

Chronology of Rabbinism. (The citations of pages are from the book Pugio.)

Page 27. R. Hakadosch (anno 200), author of the Mischna, or vocal law, or second law.

Commentaries on the Mischna (anno 340): { The one Siphra.
{ Barajetot.
{ Talmud Hierosol.
{ Tosiphtot.
Bereschit Rabah, by R. Osaiah Rabah, commentary on the Mischna.

Bereschit Rabah, Bar Naconi, are subtle and pleasant discourses, historical and theological. This same author wrote the books called Rabot.

A hundred years after the Talmud Hierosol was composed the Babylonian Talmud, by R. Ase, A.D. 440, by the universal consent of all the Jews, who are necessarily obliged to observe all that is contained therein.

The addition of R. Ase is called the Gemara, that is to say, the "commentary" on the Mischna.

And the Talmud includes together the Mischna and the Gemara.

635

If does not indicate indifference: Malachi, Isaiah.

Is., Si volumus, etc.

In quacumque die.[Pg 180]

636

Prophecies.—The sceptre was not interrupted by the captivity in Babylon, because the return was promised and foretold.

637

Proofs of Jesus Christ.—Captivity, with the assurance of deliverance within seventy years, was not real captivity. But now they are captives without any hope.

God has promised them that even though He should scatter them to the ends of the earth, nevertheless if they were faithful to His law, He would assemble them together again. They are very faithful to it, and remain oppressed.

638

When Nebuchadnezzar carried away the people, for fear they should believe that the sceptre had departed from Judah, they were told beforehand that they would be there for a short time, and that they would be restored. They were always consoled by the prophets; and their kings continued. But the second destruction is without promise of restoration, without prophets, without kings, without consolation, without hope, because the sceptre is taken away for ever.

639

It is a wonderful thing, and worthy of particular attention, to see this Jewish people existing so many years in perpetual misery, it being necessary as a proof of Jesus Christ, both that they should exist to prove Him, and that they should be miserable because they crucified Him; and though to be miserable and to exist are contradictory, they nevertheless still exist in spite of their misery.

640

They are visibly a people expressly created to serve as a witness to the Messiah (Isaiah, xliii, 9; xliv, 8). They keep the books, and love them, and do not understand them. And all this was foretold; that God's judgments are entrusted to them, but as a sealed book.

[Pg 181]

SECTION X

TYPOLOGY

641

Proof of the two Testaments at once.—To prove the two at one stroke, we need only see if the prophecies in one are fulfilled in the other. To examine the prophecies, we must understand them. For if we believe they have only one meaning, it is certain that the Messiah has not come; but if they have two meanings, it is certain that He has come in Jesus Christ.

The whole problem then is to know if they have two meanings.

That the Scripture has two meanings, which Jesus Christ and the Apostles have given, is shown by the following proofs:

1. Proof by Scripture itself.

2. Proof by the Rabbis. Moses Maimonides says that it has two aspects, and that the prophets have prophesied Jesus Christ only.

3. Proof by the Kabbala.[234]

4. Proof by the mystical interpretation which the Rabbis themselves give to Scripture.

5. Proof by the principles of the Rabbis, that there are two meanings; that there are two advents of the Messiah, a glorious and an humiliating one, according to their desert; that the prophets have prophesied of the Messiah only—the Law is not eternal, but must change at the coming of the Messiah—that then they shall no more remember the Red Sea; that the Jews and the Gentiles shall be mingled.

[6. Proof by the key which Jesus Christ and the Apostles give us.]

642

Isaiah, li. The Red Sea an image of the Redemption. Ut sciatis quod filius hominis habet potestatem remittendi peccata, tibi dico: Surge.[235] God, wishing to show that He could form a people holy with an invisible holiness, and fill them with an eternal glory, made visible things. As nature is an image of[Pg 182] grace, He has done in the bounties of nature what He would do in those of grace, in order that we might judge that He could make the invisible, since He made the visible excellently.

Therefore He saved this people from the deluge; He has raised them up from Abraham, redeemed them from their enemies, and set them at rest.

The object of God was not to save them from the deluge, and raise up a whole people from Abraham, only in order to bring them into a rich land.

And even grace is only the type of glory, for it is not the ultimate end. It has been symbolised by the law, and itself symbolises [glory]. But it is the type of it, and the origin or cause.

The ordinary life of men is like that of the saints. They all seek their satisfaction, and differ only in the object in which they place it; they call those their enemies who hinder them, etc. God has then shown the power which He has of giving invisible blessings, by that which He has shown Himself to have over things visible.

643

Types.—God, wishing to form for Himself an holy people, whom He should separate from all other nations, whom He should deliver from their enemies, and should put into a place of rest, has promised to do so, and has foretold by His prophets the time and the manner of His coming. And yet, to confirm the hope of His elect, He has made them see in it an image through all time, without leaving them devoid of assurances of His power and of His will to save them. For, at the creation of man, Adam was the witness, and guardian of the promise of a Saviour, who should be born of woman, when men were still so near the creation that they could not have forgotten their creation and their fall. When those who had seen Adam were no longer in the world, God sent Noah whom He saved, and drowned the whole earth by a miracle which sufficiently indicated the power which He had to save the world, and the will which He had to do so, and to raise up from the seed of woman Him whom He had promised. This miracle was enough to confirm the hope of men.

The memory of the deluge being so fresh among men, while Noah was still alive, God made promises to Abraham, and, while Shem was still living, sent Moses, etc....[Pg 183]

644

Types.—God, willing to deprive His own of perishable blessings, created the Jewish people in order to show that this was not owing to lack of power.

645

The Synagogue did not perish, because it was a type. But because it was only a type, it fell into servitude. The type existed till the truth came, in order that the Church should be always visible, either in the sign which promised it, or in substance.

646

That the law was figurative.

647

Two errors: 1. To take everything literally. 2. To take everything spiritually.

648

To speak against too greatly figurative language.

649

There are some types clear and demonstrative, but others which seem somewhat far-fetched, and which convince only those who are already persuaded. These are like the Apocalyptics. But the difference is that they have none which are certain, so that nothing is so unjust as to claim that theirs are as well founded as some of ours; for they have none so demonstrative as some of ours. The comparison is unfair. We must not put on the same level, and confound things, because they seem to agree in one point, while they are so different in another. The clearness in divine things requires us to revere the obscurities in them.

[It is like men, who employ a certain obscure language among themselves. Those who should not understand it, would understand only a foolish meaning.]

650

Extravagances of the Apocalyptics, Preadamites, Millenarians, etc.—He who would base extravagant opinions on Scripture, will, for example, base them on this. It is said that "this generation[Pg 184] shall not pass till all these things be fulfilled."[236] Upon that I will say that after that generation will come another generation, and so on ever in succession.

Solomon and the King are spoken of in the second book of Chronicles, as if they were two different persons. I will say that they were two.

651

Particular Types.—A double law, double tables of the law, a double temple, a double captivity.

652

Types.—The prophets prophesied by symbols of a girdle, a beard and burnt hair, etc.

653

Difference between dinner and supper.[237]

In God the word does not differ from the intention, for He is true; nor the word from the effect, for He is powerful; nor the means from the effect, for He is wise. Bern., Ult. Sermo in Missam.

Augustine, De Civit. Dei, v, 10. This rule is general. God can do everything, except those things, which if He could do, He would not be almighty, as dying, being deceived, lying, etc.

Several Evangelists for the confirmation of the truth; their difference useful.

The Eucharist after the Lord's Supper. Truth after the type.

The ruin of Jerusalem, a type of the ruin of the world, forty years after the death of Jesus. "I know not," as a man, or as an ambassador (Mark xiii, 32). (Matthew xxiv, 36.)

Jesus condemned by the Jews and the Gentiles.

The Jews and the Gentiles typified by the two sons. Aug., De Civ., xx, 29.

654

The six ages, the six Fathers of the six ages, the six wonders at the beginning of the six ages, the six mornings at the beginning of the six ages.[238]

655

Adam forma futuri.[239] The six days to form the one, the six ages to form the other. The six days, which Moses represents[Pg 185] for the formation of Adam, are only the picture of the six ages to form Jesus Christ and the Church. If Adam had not sinned, and Jesus Christ had not come, there had been only one covenant, only one age of men, and the creation would have been represented as accomplished at one single time.

656

Types.—The Jewish and Egyptian peoples were plainly foretold by the two individuals whom Moses met; the Egyptian beating the Jew, Moses avenging him and killing the Egyptian, and the Jew being ungrateful.

657

The symbols of the Gospel for the state of the sick soul are sick bodies; but because one body cannot be sick enough to express it well, several have been needed. Thus there are the deaf, the dumb, the blind, the paralytic, the dead Lazarus, the possessed. All this crowd is in the sick soul.

658

Types.—To show that the Old Testament is only figurative, and that the prophets understood by temporal blessings other blessings, this is the proof:

First, that this would be unworthy of God.

Secondly, that their discourses express very clearly the promise of temporal blessings, and that they say nevertheless that their discourses are obscure, and that their meaning will not be understood. Whence it appears that this secret meaning was not that which they openly expressed, and that consequently they meant to speak of other sacrifices, of another deliverer, etc. They say that they will be understood only in the fullness of time (Jer. xxx, ult.).

The third proof is that their discourses are contradictory, and neutralise each other; so that if we think that they did not mean by the words "law" and "sacrifice" anything else than that of Moses, there is a plain and gross contradiction. Therefore they meant something else, sometimes contradicting themselves in the same chapter. Now, to understand the meaning of an author ...

659

Lust has become natural to us, and has made our second nature. Thus there are two natures in us—the one good, the[Pg 186] other bad. Where is God? Where you are not, and the kingdom of God is within you. The Rabbis.

660

Penitence, alone of all these mysteries, has been manifestly declared to the Jews, and by Saint John, the Forerunner; and then the other mysteries; to indicate that in each man, as in the entire world, this order must be observed.

661

The carnal Jews understood neither the greatness nor the humiliation of the Messiah foretold in their prophecies. They misunderstood Him in His foretold greatness, as when He said that the Messiah should be lord of David, though his son, and that He was before Abraham, who had seen Him. They did not believe Him so great as to be eternal, and they likewise misunderstood Him in His humiliation and in His death. "The Messiah," said they, "abideth for ever, and this man says that he shall die."[240] Therefore they believed Him neither mortal nor eternal; they only sought in Him for a carnal greatness.

662

Typical.—Nothing is so like charity as covetousness, and nothing is so opposed to it. Thus the Jews, full of possessions which flattered their covetousness, were very like Christians, and very contrary. And by this means they had the two qualities which it was necessary they should have, to be very like the Messiah to typify Him, and very contrary not to be suspected witnesses.

663

Typical.—God made use of the lust of the Jews to make them minister to Jesus Christ, [who brought the remedy for their lust].

664

Charity is not a figurative precept. It is dreadful to say that Jesus Christ, who came to take away types in order to establish the truth, came only to establish the type of charity, in order to take away the existing reality which was there before.

"If the light be darkness, how great is that darkness!"[Pg 187][241]

665

Fascination. Somnum suum.[242] Figura hujus mundi.[243]

The Eucharist. Comedes panem tuum.[244] Panem nostrum.

Inimici Dei terram lingent.[245] Sinners lick the dust, that is to say, love earthly pleasures.

The Old Testament contained the types of future joy, and the New contains the means of arriving at it. The types were of joy; the means of penitence; and nevertheless the Paschal Lamb was eaten with bitter herbs, cum amaritudinibus.[246]

Singularis sum ego donec transeam.[247]—Jesus Christ before His death was almost the only martyr.

666

Typical.—The expressions, sword, shield. Potentissime.

667

We are estranged, only by departing from charity. Our prayers and our virtues are abominable before God, if they are not the prayers and the virtues of Jesus Christ. And our sins will never be the object of [mercy], but of the justice of God, if they are not [those of] Jesus Christ. He has adopted our sins, and has [admitted] us into union [with Him], for virtues are [His own, and] sins are foreign to Him; while virtues [are] foreign to us, and our sins are our own.

Let us change the rule which we have hitherto chosen for judging what is good. We had our own will as our rule. Let us now take the will of [God]; all that He wills is good and right to us, all that He does not will is [bad].

All that God does not permit is forbidden. Sins are forbidden by the general declaration that God has made, that He did not allow them. Other things which He has left without general prohibition, and which for that reason are said to be permitted, are nevertheless not always permitted. For when God removed some one of them from us, and when, by the event, which is a manifestation of the will of God, it appears that God does not will that we should have a thing, that is then forbidden to us as sin; since the will of God is that we should not have one more than another. There is this sole difference between these two things, that it is certain that God will never allow sin, while it is not certain that He will never allow the other. But so long as God does not permit it, we ought to regard it as sin; so long[Pg 188] as the absence of God's will, which alone is all goodness and all justice, renders it unjust and wrong.

668

To change the type, because of our weakness.

669

Types.—The Jews had grown old in these earthly thoughts, that God loved their father Abraham, his flesh and what sprung from it; that on account of this He had multiplied them, and distinguished them from all other nations, without allowing them to intermingle; that when they were languishing in Egypt, He brought them out with all these great signs in their favour; that He fed them with manna in the desert, and led them into a very rich land; that He gave them kings and a well-built temple, in order to offer up beasts before Him, by the shedding of whose blood they should be purified; and that at last He was to send them the Messiah to make them masters of all the world, and foretold the time of His coming.

The world having grown old in these carnal errors, Jesus Christ came at the time foretold, but not with the expected glory; and thus men did not think it was He. After His death, Saint Paul[248] came to teach men that all these things had happened in allegory; that the kingdom of God did not consist in the flesh, but in the spirit; that the enemies of men were not the Babylonians, but the passions; that God delighted not in temples made with hands, but in a pure and contrite heart; that the circumcision of the body was unprofitable, but that of the heart was needed; that Moses had not given them the bread from heaven, etc.[249]

But God, not having desired to reveal these things to this people who were unworthy of them, and having nevertheless desired to foretell them, in order that they might be believed, foretold the time clearly, and expressed the things sometimes clearly, but very often in figures, in order that those who loved symbols might consider them, and those who loved what was symbolised might see it therein.

All that tends not to charity is figurative.

The sole aim of the Scripture is charity.

All which tends not to the sole end is the type of it. For since there is only one end, all which does not lead to it in express terms is figurative.[Pg 189]

God thus varies that sole precept of charity to satisfy our curiosity, which seeks for variety, by that variety which still leads us to the one thing needful. For one thing alone is needful,[250] and we love variety; and God satisfies both by these varieties, which lead to the one thing needful.

The Jews have so much loved the shadows, and have so strictly expected them, that they have misunderstood the reality, when it came in the time and manner foretold.

The Rabbis take the breasts of the Spouse[251] for types, and all that does not express the only end they have, namely, temporal good.

And Christians take even the Eucharist as a type of the glory at which they aim.

670

The Jews, who have been called to subdue nations and kings, have been the slaves of sin; and the Christians, whose calling has been to be servants and subjects, are free children.[252]

671

A formal point.—When Saint Peter and the Apostles deliberated about abolishing circumcision, where it was a question of acting against the law of God, they did not heed the prophets, but simply the reception of the Holy Spirit in the persons uncircumcised.[253]

They thought it more certain that God approved of those whom He filled with His Spirit, than it was that the law must be obeyed. They knew that the end of the law was only the Holy Spirit; and that thus, as men certainly had this without circumcision, it was not necessary.

672

Fac secundum exemplar quod tibi ostensum est in monte.[254]—The Jewish religion then has been formed on its likeness to the truth of the Messiah; and the truth of the Messiah has been recognised by the Jewish religion, which was the type of it.

Among the Jews the truth was only typified; in heaven it is revealed.

In the Church it is hidden, and recognised by its resemblance to the type.

The type has been made according to the truth, and the truth has been recognised according to the type.[Pg 190]

Saint Paul[255] says himself that people will forbid to marry, and he himself speaks of it to the Corinthians in a way which is a snare. For if a prophet had said the one, and Saint Paul had then said the other, he would have been accused.

673

Typical.—"Do all things according to the pattern which has been shown thee on the mount." On which Saint Paul says that the Jews have shadowed forth heavenly things.[256]

674

... And yet this Covenant, made to blind some and enlighten others, indicated in those very persons, whom it blinded, the truth which should be recognised by others. For the visible blessings which they received from God were so great and so divine, that He indeed appeared able to give them those that are invisible, and a Messiah.

For nature is an image of Grace, and visible miracles are images of the invisible. Ut sciatis ... tibi dico: Surge.

Isaiah says that Redemption will be as the passage of the Red Sea.

God has then shown by the deliverance from Egypt, and from the sea, by the defeat of kings, by the manna, by the whole genealogy of Abraham, that He was able to save, to send down bread from heaven, etc.; so that the people hostile to Him are the type and the representation of the very Messiah whom they know not, etc.

He has then taught us at last that all these things were only types, and what is "true freedom," a "true Israelite," "true circumcision," "true bread from heaven," etc.

In these promises each one finds what he has most at heart, temporal benefits or spiritual, God or the creatures; but with this difference, that those who therein seek the creatures find them, but with many contradictions, with a prohibition against loving them, with the command to worship God only, and to love Him only, which is the same thing, and, finally, that the Messiah came not for them; whereas those who therein seek God find Him, without any contradiction, with the command to love Him only, and that the Messiah came in the time foretold, to give them the blessings which they ask.

Thus the Jews had miracles and prophecies, which they say fulfilled and the teaching of their law was to worship and[Pg 191] love God only; it was also perpetual. Thus it had all the marks of the true religion; and so it was. But the Jewish teaching must be distinguished from the teaching of the Jewish law. Now the Jewish teaching was not true, although it had miracles and prophecy and perpetuity, because it had not this other point of worshipping and loving God only.

675

The veil, which is upon these books for the Jews, is there also for evil Christians, and for all who do not hate themselves.

But how well disposed men are to understand them and to know Jesus Christ, when they truly hate themselves!

676

A type conveys absence and presence, pleasure and pain.

A cipher has a double meaning, one clear, and one in which it is said that the meaning is hidden.

677

Types.—A portrait conveys absence and presence, pleasure and pain. The reality excludes absence and pain.

To know if the law and the sacrifices are a reality or a type, we must see if the prophets, in speaking of these things, confined their view and their thought to them, so that they saw only the old covenant; or if they saw therein something else of which they were the representation, for in a portrait we see the thing figured. For this we need only examine what they say of them.

When they say that it will be eternal, do they mean to speak of that covenant which they say will be changed; and so of the sacrifices, etc.?

A cipher has two meanings. When we find out an important letter in which we discover a clear meaning, and in which it is nevertheless said that the meaning is veiled and obscure, that it is hidden, so that we might read the letter without seeing it, and interpret it without understanding it, what must we think but that here is a cipher with a double meaning, and the more so if we find obvious contradictions in the literal meaning? The prophets have clearly said that Israel would be always loved by God, and that the law would be eternal; and they have said that their meaning would not be understood, and that it was veiled.

How greatly then ought we to value those who interpret the[Pg 192] cipher, and teach us to understand the hidden meaning, especially if the principles which they educe are perfectly clear and natural! This is what Jesus Christ did, and the Apostles. They broke the seal; He rent the veil, and revealed the spirit. They have taught us through this that the enemies of man are his passions; that the Redeemer would be spiritual, and His reign spiritual; that there would be two advents, one in lowliness to humble the proud, the other in glory to exalt the humble; that Jesus Christ would be both God and man.

678

Types.—Jesus Christ opened their mind to understand the Scriptures.

Two great revelations are these. (1) All things happened to them in types: vere Israëlitæ, vere liberi, true bread from Heaven. (2) A God humbled to the Cross. It was necessary that Christ should suffer in order to enter into glory, "that He should destroy death through death."[257] Two advents.

679

Types.—When once this secret is disclosed, it is impossible not to see it. Let us read the Old Testament in this light, and let us see if the sacrifices were real; if the fatherhood of Abraham was the true cause of the friendship of God; and if the promised land was the true place of rest. No. They are therefore types. Let us in the same way examine all those ordained ceremonies, all those commandments which are not of charity, and we shall see that they are types.

All these sacrifices and ceremonies were then either types or nonsense. Now these are things too clear, and too lofty, to be thought nonsense.

To know if the prophets confined their view in the Old Testament, or saw therein other things.

680

Typical.—The key of the cipher. Veri adoratores.[258]—Ecce agnus Dei qui tollit peccata mundi.[259]

681

Is. i, 21. Change of good into evil, and the vengeance of God. Is. x, I; xxvi, 20; xxviii, I. Miracles: Is. xxxiii, 9; xl, 17; xli, 26; xliii, 13.

Jer. xi, 21; xv, 12; xvii, 9. Pravum est cor omnium et[Pg 193] incrustabile; quis cognoscet illud? that is to say, Who can know all its evil? For it is already known to be wicked. Ego dominus, etc.—vii, 14, Faciam domui huic, etc. Trust in external sacrifices—vii, 22, Quia non sum locutus, etc. Outward sacrifice is not the essential point—xi, 13, Secundum numerum, etc. A multitude of doctrines.

Is. xliv, 20-24; liv, 8; lxiii, 12-17; lxvi, 17. Jer. ii, 35; iv, 22-24; v, 4, 29-31; vi, 16; xxiii, 15-17.

682

Types,—The letter kills. All happened in types. Here is the cipher which Saint Paul gives us. Christ must suffer. An humiliated God. Circumcision of the heart, true fasting, true sacrifice, a true temple. The prophets have shown that all these must be spiritual.

Not the meat which perishes, but that which does not perish.

"Ye shall be free indeed."[260] Then the other freedom was only a type of freedom.

"I am the true bread from Heaven."[261]

683

Contradiction.—We can only describe a good character by reconciling all contrary qualities, and it is not enough to keep up a series of harmonious qualities, without reconciling contradictory ones. To understand the meaning of an author, we must make all the contrary passages agree.

Thus, to understand Scripture, we must have a meaning in which all the contrary passages are reconciled. It is not enough to have one which suits many concurring passages; but it is necessary to have one which reconciles even contradictory passages.

Every author has a meaning in which all the contradictory passages agree, or he has no meaning at all. We cannot affirm the latter of Scripture and the prophets; they undoubtedly are full of good sense. We must then seek for a meaning which reconciles all discrepancies.

The true meaning then is not that of the Jews; but in Jesus Christ all the contradictions are reconciled.

The Jews could not reconcile the cessation of the royalty and principality, foretold by Hosea, with the prophecy of Jacob.

If we take the law, the sacrifices, and the kingdom as realities, we cannot reconcile all the passages. They must then necessarily[Pg 194] be only types. We cannot even reconcile the passages of the same author, nor of the same book, nor sometimes of the same chapter, which indicates copiously what was the meaning of the author. As when Ezekiel, chap, xx, says that man will not live by the commandments of God and will live by them.

684

Types.—If the law and the sacrifices are the truth, it must please God, and must not displease Him. If they are types, they must be both pleasing and displeasing.

Now in all the Scripture they are both pleasing and displeasing. It is said that the law shall be changed; that the sacrifice shall be changed; that they shall be without law, without a prince, and without a sacrifice; that a new covenant shall be made; that the law shall be renewed; that the precepts which they have received are not good;

that their sacrifices are abominable; that God has demanded none of them.

It is said, on the contrary, that the law shall abide for ever; that this covenant shall be for ever; that sacrifice shall be eternal; that the sceptre shall never depart from among them, because it shall not depart from them till the eternal King comes.

Do all these passages indicate what is real? No. Do they then indicate what is typical? No, but what is either real or typical. But the first passages, excluding as they do reality, indicate that all this is only typical.

All these passages together cannot be applied to reality; all can be said to be typical; therefore they are not spoken of reality, but of the type.

Agnus occisus est ab origine mundi.[262] A sacrificing judge.

685

Contradictions.—The sceptre till the Messiah—without king or prince.

The eternal law—changed.

The eternal covenant—a new covenant.

Good laws—bad precepts. Ezekiel.

686

Types.—When the word of God, which is really true, is false literally, it is true spiritually. Sede a dextris meis:[263] this is false literally, therefore it is true spiritually.

In these expressions, God is spoken of after the manner of[Pg 195] men; and this means nothing else but that the intention which men have in giving a seat at their right hand, God will have also. It is then an indication of the intention of God, not of His manner of carrying it out.

Thus when it is said, "God has received the odour of your incense, and will in recompense give you a rich land," that is equivalent to saying that the same intention which a man would have, who, pleased with your perfumes, should in recompense give you a rich land, God will have towards you, because you have had the same intention as a man has towards him to whom he presents perfumes. So iratus est, a "jealous God,"[264] etc. For, the things of God being inexpressible, they cannot be spoken of otherwise, and the Church makes use of them even to-day: Quia confortavil seras,[265] etc.

It is not allowable to attribute to Scripture the meaning which is not revealed to us that it has. Thus, to say that the closed mem[266] of Isaiah signifies six hundred, has not been revealed. It might be said that the final tsade and he deficientes may signify mysteries. But it is not allowable to say so, and still less to say this is the way of the philosopher's stone. But we say that the literal meaning is not the true meaning, because the prophets have themselves said so.

687

I do not say that the mem is mystical.

688

Moses (Deut. xxx) promises that God will circumcise their heart to render them capable of loving Him.

689

One saying of David, or of Moses, as for instance that "God will circumcise the heart," enables us to judge of their spirit. If all their other expressions were ambiguous, and left us in doubt whether they were philosophers or Christians, one saying of this kind would in fact determine all the rest, as one sentence of Epictetus decides the meaning of all the rest to be the opposite. So far ambiguity exists, but not afterwards.

690

If one of two persons, who are telling silly stories, uses language with a double meaning, understood in his own circle, while the[Pg 196] other uses it with only one meaning, any one not in the secret, who hears them both talk in this manner, will pass upon them the same judgment. But if afterwards, in the rest of their conversation one says angelic things, and the other always dull commonplaces, he will judge that the one spoke in mysteries, and not the other; the one having sufficiently shown that he is incapable of such foolishness, and capable of being mysterious; and the other that he is incapable of mystery, and capable of foolishness.

The Old Testament is a cipher.

691

There are some that see clearly that man has no other enemy than lust, which turns him from God, and not God; and that he has no other good than God, and not a rich land. Let those who believe that the good of man is in the flesh, and evil in what turns him away from sensual pleasures, [satiate] themselves with them, and [die] in them. But let those who seek God with all their heart, who are only troubled at not seeing Him, who desire only to possess Him, and have as enemies only those who turn them away from Him, who are grieved at seeing themselves surrounded and overwhelmed with such enemies, take comfort. I proclaim to them happy news. There exists a Redeemer for them. I shall show Him to them. I shall show that there is a God for them. I shall not show Him to others. I shall make them see that a Messiah has been promised, who should deliver them from their enemies, and that One has come to free them from their iniquities, but not from their enemies.

When David foretold that the Messiah would deliver His people from their enemies, one can believe that in the flesh these would be the Egyptians; and then I cannot show that the prophecy was fulfilled. But one can well believe also that the enemies would be their sins; for indeed the Egyptians were not their enemies, but their sins were so. This word, enemies, is therefore ambiguous. But if he says elsewhere, as he does, that He will deliver His people from their sins, as indeed do Isaiah and others, the ambiguity is removed, and the double meaning of enemies is reduced to the simple meaning of iniquities. For if he had sins in his mind, he could well denote them as enemies; but if he thought of enemies, he could not designate them as iniquities.[Pg 197]

Now Moses, David, and Isaiah used the same terms. Who will say then that they have not the same meaning, and that David's meaning, which is plainly iniquities when he spoke of enemies, was not the same as [that of] Moses when speaking of enemies?

Daniel (ix) prays for the deliverance of the people from the captivity of their enemies. But he was thinking of sins, and, to show this, he says that Gabriel came to tell him that his prayer was heard, and that there were only seventy weeks to wait, after which the people would be freed from iniquity, sin would have an end, and the Redeemer, the Holy of Holies, would bring eternal justice, not legal, but eternal.

[Pg 198]

SECTION XI

THE PROPHECIES

692

When I see the blindness and the wretchedness of man, when I regard the whole silent universe, and man without light, left to himself, and, as it were, lost in this corner of the universe, without knowing who has put him there, what he has come to do, what will become of him at death, and incapable of all knowledge, I become terrified, like a man who should be carried in his sleep to a dreadful desert island, and should awake without knowing where he is, and without means of escape. And thereupon I wonder how people in a condition so wretched do not fall into despair. I see other persons around me of a like nature. I ask them if they are better informed than I am. They tell me that they are not. And thereupon these wretched and lost beings, having looked around them, and seen some pleasing objects, have given and attached themselves to them. For my own part, I have not been able to attach myself to them, and, considering how strongly it appears that there is something else than what I see, I have examined whether this God has not left some sign of Himself.

I see many contradictory religions, and consequently all false save one. Each wants to be believed on its own authority, and threatens unbelievers. I do not therefore believe them. Every one can say this; every one can call himself a prophet. But I see that Christian religion wherein prophecies are fulfilled; and that is what every one cannot do.

693

And what crowns all this is prediction, so that it should not be said that it is chance which has done it.

Whosoever, having only a week to live, will not find out that it is expedient to believe that all this is not a stroke of chance ...

Now, if the passions had no hold on us, a week and a hundred years would amount to the same thing.[Pg 199]

694

Prophecies.—Great Pan is dead.[267]

695

Susceperunt verbum cum omni aviditate, scrutantes Scripturas, si ita se haberent.[268]

696

Prodita lege.—Impleta cerne.—Implenda collige.

697

We understand the prophecies only when we see the events happen. Thus the proofs of retreat, discretion, silence, etc. are proofs only to those who know and believe them.

Joseph so internal in a law so external.

Outward penances dispose to inward, as humiliations to humility. Thus the ...

698

The synagogue has preceded the church; the Jews, the Christians. The prophets have foretold the Christians; Saint John, Jesus Christ.

699

It is glorious to see with the eyes of faith the history of Herod and of Cæsar.

700

The zeal of the Jews for their law and their temple (Josephus, and Philo the Jew, Ad Caïum). What other people had such a zeal? It was necessary they should have it.

Jesus Christ foretold as to the time and the state of the world. The ruler taken from the thigh,[269] and the fourth monarchy. How lucky we are to see this light amidst this darkness!

How fine it is to see, with the eyes of faith, Darius and Cyrus, Alexander, the Romans, Pompey and Herod working, without knowing it, for the glory of the Gospel!

701

Zeal of the Jewish people for the law, especially after there were no more prophets.[Pg 200]

702

While the prophets were for maintaining the law, the people were indifferent. But since there have been no more prophets, zeal has succeeded them.

703

The devil troubled the zeal of the Jews before Jesus Christ, because he would have been their salvation, but not since.

The Jewish people scorned by the Gentiles; the Christian people persecuted.

704

Proof.—Prophecies with their fulfilment; what has preceded and what has followed Jesus Christ.

705

The prophecies are the strongest proof of Jesus Christ. It is for them also that God has made most provision; for the event which has fulfilled them is a miracle existing since the birth of the Church to the end. So God has raised up prophets during sixteen hundred years, and, during four hundred years afterwards, He has scattered all these prophecies among all the Jews, who carried them into all parts of the world. Such was the preparation for the birth of Jesus Christ, and, as His Gospel was to be believed by all the world, it was not only necessary that there should be prophecies to make it believed, but that these prophecies should exist throughout the whole world, in order to make it embraced by the whole world.

706

But it was not enough that the prophecies should exist. It was necessary that they should be distributed throughout all places, and preserved throughout all times. And in order that this agreement might not be taken for an effect of chance, it was necessary that this should be foretold.

It is far more glorious for the Messiah that the Jews should be the spectators, and even the instruments of His glory, besides that God had reserved them.

707

Prophecies.—The time foretold by the state of the Jewish people, by the state of the heathen, by the state of the temple, by the number of years.[Pg 201]

708

One must be bold to predict the same thing in so many ways. It was necessary that the four idolatrous or pagan monarchies, the end of the kingdom of Judah, and the seventy weeks, should happen at the same time, and all this before the second temple was destroyed.

709

Prophecies.—If one man alone had made a book of predictions about Jesus Christ, as to the time and the manner, and Jesus Christ had come in conformity to these prophecies, this fact would have infinite weight.

But there is much more here. Here is a succession of men during four thousand years, who, consequently and without variation, come, one after another, to foretell this same event. Here is a whole people who announce it, and who have existed for four thousand years, in order to give corporate testimony of the assurances which they have, and from which they cannot be diverted by whatever threats and persecutions people may make against them. This is far more important.

710

Predictions of particular things.—They were strangers in Egypt, without any private property, either in that country or elsewhere. [There was not the least appearance, either of the royalty which had previously existed so long, or of that supreme council of seventy judges which they called the Sanhedrin, and which, having been instituted by Moses, lasted to the time of Jesus Christ. All these things were as far removed from their state at that time as they could be], when Jacob, dying, and blessing his twelve children, declared to them, that they would be proprietors of a great land, and foretold in particular to the family of Judah, that the kings, who would one day rule them, should be of his race; and that all his brethren should be their subjects; [and that even the Messiah, who was to be the expectation of nations, should spring from him; and that the kingship should not be taken away from Judah, nor the ruler and law-giver of his descendants, till the expected Messiah should arrive in his family].

This same Jacob, disposing of this future land as though he had been its ruler, gave a portion to Joseph more than to the others. "I give you," said he, "one part more than to your[Pg 202] brothers." And blessing his two children, Ephraim and Manasseh, whom Joseph had presented to him, the elder, Manasseh, on his right, and the young Ephraim on his left, he put his arms crosswise, and placing his right hand on the head of Ephraim, and his left on Manasseh, he blessed them in this manner. And, upon Joseph's representing to him that he was preferring the younger, he replied to him with admirable resolution: "I know it well, my son; but Ephraim will increase more than Manasseh." This has been indeed so true in the result, that, being alone almost as fruitful as the two entire lines which composed a whole kingdom, they have been usually called by the name of Ephraim alone.

This same Joseph, when dying, bade his children carry his bones with them when they should go into that land, to which they only came two hundred years afterwards.

Moses, who wrote all these things so long before they happened, himself assigned to each family portions of that land before they entered it, as though he had been its ruler. [In fact he declared that God was to raise up from their nation and their race a prophet, of whom he was the type; and he foretold them exactly all that was to happen to them in the land which they were to enter after his death, the victories which God would give them, their ingratitude towards God, the punishments which they would receive for it, and the rest of their adventures.] He gave them judges who should make the division. He prescribed the entire form of political government which they should observe, the cities of refuge which they should build, and ...

711

The prophecies about particular things are mingled with those about the Messiah, so that the prophecies of the Messiah should not be without proofs, nor the special prophecies without fruit.

712

Perpetual captivity of the Jews.—Jer. xi, 11: "I will bring evil upon Judah from which they shall not be able to escape."

Types.—Is. v: "The Lord had a vineyard, from which He looked for grapes; and it brought forth only wild grapes. I will therefore lay it waste, and destroy it; the earth shall only bring forth thorns, and I will forbid the clouds from [raining] upon it. The vineyard of the Lord is the house of Israel, and[Pg 203] the men of Judah His pleasant plant. I looked that they should do justice, and they bring forth only iniquities."

Is. viii: "Sanctify the Lord with fear and trembling; let Him be your only dread, and He shall be to you for a sanctuary, but for a stone of stumbling and a rock of offence to both the houses of Israel, for a gin and for a snare to the inhabitants of Jerusalem; and many among them shall stumble against that stone, and fall, and be broken, and be snared, and perish. Hide my words, and cover my law for my disciples.

"I will then wait in patience upon the Lord that hideth and concealeth Himself from the house of Jacob."

Is. xxix: "Be amazed and wonder, people of Israel; stagger and stumble, and be drunken, but not with wine; stagger, but not with strong drink. For the Lord hath poured out upon you the spirit of deep sleep. He will close your eyes; He will cover your princes and your prophets that have visions." (Daniel xii: "The wicked shall not understand, but the wise shall understand." Hosea, the last chapter, the last verse, after many temporal blessings, says: "Who is wise, and he shall understand these things, etc.?") "And the visions of all the prophets are become unto you as a sealed book, which men deliver to one that is learned, and who can read; and he saith, I cannot read it, for it is sealed. And when the book is delivered to them that are not learned, they say I am not learned.

"Wherefore the Lord said, Forasmuch as this people with their lips do honour me, but have removed their heart far from me,"—there is the reason and the cause of it; for if they adored God in their hearts, they would understand the prophecies,— "and their fear towards me is taught by the precept of man. Therefore, behold, I will proceed to do a marvellous work among this people, even a marvellous work and a wonder; for the wisdom of their wise men shall perish, and their understanding shall be [hid]."

Prophecies. Proofs of Divinity.—Is. xli: "Shew the things that are to come hereafter, that we may know that ye are gods: we will incline our heart unto your words. Teach us the things that have been at the beginning, and declare us things for to come.

"By this we shall know that ye are gods. Yea, do good or do evil, if you can. Let us then behold it and reason together. Behold, ye are of nothing, and only an abomination, etc. Who," (among contemporary writers), "hath declared from the[Pg 204] beginning that we may know of the things done from the beginning and origin? that we may say, You are righteous. There is none that teacheth us, yea, there is none that declareth the future."

Is. xlii: "I am the Lord, and my glory will I not give to another. I have foretold the things which have come to pass, and things that are to come do I declare. Sing unto God a new song in all the earth.

"Bring forth the blind people that have eyes and see not, and the deaf that have ears and hear not. Let all the nations be gathered together. Who among them can declare this, and shew us former things, and things to come? Let them bring forth their witnesses, that they may be justified; or let them hear, and say, It is truth.

"Ye are my witnesses, saith the Lord, and my servant whom I have chosen; that ye may know and believe me, and understand that I am He.

"I have declared, and have saved, and I alone have done wonders before your eyes: ye are my witnesses, said the Lord, that I am God.

"For your sake I have brought down the forces of the Babylonians. I am the Lord, your Holy One and creator.

"I have made a way in the sea, and a path in the mighty waters. I am He that drowned and destroyed for ever the mighty enemies that have resisted you.

"Remember ye not the former things, neither consider the things of old.

"Behold, I will do a new thing; now it shall spring forth; shall ye not know it? I will even make a way in the wilderness, and rivers in the desert.

"This people have I formed for myself; I have established them to shew forth my praise, etc.

"I, even I, am He that blotteth out thy transgressions for mine own sake, and will not remember thy sins. Put in remembrance your ingratitude: see thou, if thou mayest be justified. Thy first father hath sinned, and thy teachers have transgressed against me."

Is. xliv: "I am the first, and I am the last, saith the Lord. Let him who will equal himself to me, declare the order of things since I appointed the ancient people, and the things that are coming. Fear ye not: have I not told you all these things? Ye are my witnesses."[Pg 205]

Prophecy of Cyrus.—Is. xlv, 4: "For Jacob's sake, mine elect, I have called thee by thy name."

Is. xlv, 21: "Come and let us reason together. Who hath declared this from ancient time? Who hath told it from that time? Have not I, the Lord?"

Is. xlvi: "Remember the former things of old, and know there is none like me, declaring the end from the beginning, and from ancient times the things that are not yet done, saying, My counsel shall stand, and I will do all my pleasure."

Is. xlii: "Behold, the former things are come to pass, and new things do I declare; before they spring forth I tell you of them."

Is. xlviii, 3: "I have declared the former things from the beginning; I did them suddenly; and they came to pass. Because I know that thou art obstinate, that thy spirit is rebellious, and thy brow brass; I have even declared it to thee before it came to pass: lest thou shouldst say that it was the work of thy gods, and the effect of their commands.

"Thou hast seen all this; and will not ye declare it? I have shewed thee new things from this time, even hidden things, and thou didst not know them. They are created now, and not from the beginning; I have kept them hidden from thee; lest thou shouldst say, Behold, I knew them.

"Yea, thou knewest not; yea, thou heardest not; yea, from that time that thine ear was not opened: for I knew that thou couldst deal very treacherously, and wast called a transgressor from the womb."

Reprobation of the Jews and conversion of the Gentiles.—Is. lxv: "I am sought of them that asked not for me; I am found of them that sought me not; I said, Behold me, behold me, behold me, unto a nation that did not call upon my name.

"I have spread out my hands all the day unto an unbelieving people, which walketh in a way that was not good, after their own thoughts; a people that provoketh me to anger continually by the sins they commit in my face; that sacrificeth to idols, etc.

"These shall be scattered like smoke in the day of my wrath, etc.

"Your iniquities, and the iniquities of your fathers, will I assemble together, and will recompense you for all according to your works.

"Thus saith the Lord, As the new wine is found in the cluster, and one saith, Destroy it not, for a blessing is in it [and the[Pg 206] promise of fruit]: for my servants' sake I will not destroy all Israel.

"Thus I will bring forth a seed out of Jacob and out of Judah, an inheritor of my mountains, and mine elect and my servants shall inherit it, and my fertile and abundant plains; but I will destroy all others, because you have forgotten your God to serve strange gods. I called, and ye did not answer; I spake, and ye did not hear; and ye did choose the thing which I forbade.

"Therefore thus saith the Lord, Behold, my servants shall eat, but ye shall be hungry; my servants shall rejoice, but ye shall be ashamed; my servants shall sing for joy of heart, but ye shall cry and howl for vexation of spirit.

"And ye shall leave your name for a curse unto my chosen: for the Lord shall slay thee, and call His servants by another name, that he who blesseth himself in the earth shall bless himself in God, etc., because the former troubles are forgotten.

"For, behold, I create new heavens and a new earth; and the former things shall not be remembered, nor come into mind.

"But be ye glad and rejoice for ever in that which I create; for, behold, I create Jerusalem a rejoicing, and her people a joy.

"And I will rejoice in Jerusalem and joy in my people; and the voice of weeping shall no more be heard in her, nor the voice of crying.

"Before they call, I will answer; and while they are yet speaking, I will hear. The wolf and the lamb shall feed together, and the lion shall eat straw like the bullock; and dust shall be the serpent's meat. They shall not hurt nor destroy in all my holy mountain."

Is. lvi, 3: "Thus saith the Lord, Keep ye judgment, and do justice: for my salvation is near to come, and my righteousness to be revealed.

"Blessed is the man that doeth this, that keepeth the Sabbath, and keepeth his hand from doing any evil.

"Neither let the strangers that have joined themselves to me, say, God will separate me from His people. For thus saith the Lord: Whoever will keep my Sabbath, and choose the things that please me, and take hold of my covenant; even unto them will I give in mine house a place and a name better than that of sons and of daughters: I will give them an everlasting name, that shall not be cut off."

Is. lix, 9: "Therefore for our iniquities is justice far from us: we wait for light, but behold obscurity; for brightness, but we[Pg 207] walk in darkness. We grope for the wall like the blind; we stumble at noon day as in the night: we are in desolate places as dead men.

"We roar all like bears, and mourn sore like doves; we look for judgment, but there is none; for salvation, but it is far from us."

Is. lxvi, 18: "But I know their works and their thoughts; it shall come that I will gather all nations and tongues, and they shall see my glory.

"And I will set a sign among them, and I will send those that escape of them unto the nations, to Africa, to Lydia, to Italy, to Greece, and to the people that have not heard my fame, neither have seen my glory. And they shall bring your brethren."

Jer. vii. Reprobation of the Temple: "Go ye unto Shiloth, where I set my name at the first, and see what I did to it for the wickedness of my people. And now, because ye have done all these works, saith the Lord, I will do unto this house, wherein my name is called upon, wherein ye trust, and unto the place which I gave to your priests, as I have done to Shiloth." (For I have rejected it, and made myself a temple elsewhere.)

"And I will cast you out of my sight, as I have cast out all your brethren, even the seed of Ephraim." (Rejected for ever.) "Therefore pray not for this people."

Jer. vii, 22: "What avails it you to add sacrifice to sacrifice? For I spake not unto your fathers, when I brought them out of the land of Egypt, concerning burnt offerings or sacrifices. But this thing commanded I them, saying, Obey and be faithful to my commandments, and I will be your God, and ye shall be my people." (It was only after they had sacrificed to the golden calf that I gave myself sacrifices to turn into good an evil custom.)

Jer. vii, 4: "Trust ye not in lying words, saying, The temple of the Lord, the temple of the Lord, the temple of the Lord, are these."

713

The Jews witnesses for God. Is. xliii, 9; xliv, 8.

Prophecies fulfilled.—I Kings xiii, 2.—I Kings xxiii, 16.— Joshua vi, 26.—I Kings xvi, 34.—Deut. xxiii.

Malachi i, II. The sacrifice of the Jews rejected, and the sacrifice of the heathen, (even out of Jerusalem,) and in all places.[Pg 208]

Moses, before dying, foretold the calling of the Gentiles, Deut. xxxii, 21, and the reprobation of the Jews.

Moses foretold what would happen to each tribe.

Prophecy.—"Your name shall be a curse unto mine elect, and I will give them another name."

"Make their heart fat,"[270] and how? by flattering their lust and making them hope to satisfy it.

714

Prophecy.—Amos and Zechariah. They have sold the just one, and therefore will not be recalled.—Jesus Christ betrayed.

They shall no more remember Egypt. See Is. xliii, 16, 17, 18, 19. Jer. xxiii, 6, 7.

Prophecy.—The Jews shall be scattered abroad. Is. xxvii, 6.—A new law, Jerem. xxxi, 32.

Malachi. Grotius.—The second temple glorious.—Jesus Christ will come. Haggai ii, 7, 8, 9, 10.

The calling of the Gentiles. Joel ii, 28. Hosea ii, 24. Deut. xxxii, 21. Malachi i, 11.

715

Hosea iii.—Is. xlii, xlviii, liv, lx, lxi, last verse. "I foretold it long since that they might know that it is I." Jaddus to Alexander.

716

[Prophecies.—The promise that David will always have descendants. Jer. xiii, 13.]

717

The eternal reign of the race of David, 2 Chron., by all the prophecies, and with an oath. And it was not temporally fulfilled. Jer. xxiii, 20.

718

We might perhaps think that, when the prophets foretold that the sceptre should not depart from Judah until the eternal King came, they spoke to flatter the people, and that their prophecy was proved false by Herod. But to show that this was not their meaning, and that, on the contrary, they knew well that this temporal kingdom should cease, they said that they would be without a king and without a prince, and for a long time. Hosea iii, 4.[Pg 209]

719

Non habemus regem nisi Cæsarem.[271] Therefore Jesus Christ was the Messiah, since they had no longer any king but a stranger, and would have no other.

720

We have no king but Cæsar.

721

Daniel ii: "All thy soothsayers and wise men cannot shew unto thee the secret which thou hast demanded. But there is a God in heaven who can do so, and that hath revealed to thee in thy dream what shall be in the latter days," (This dream must have caused him much misgiving.)

"And it is not by my own wisdom that I have knowledge of this secret, but by the revelation of this same God, that hath revealed it to me, to make it manifest in thy presence.

"Thy dream was then of this kind. Thou sawest a great image, high and terrible, which stood before thee. His head was of gold, his breast and arms of silver, his belly and his thighs of brass, his legs of iron, his feet part of iron and part of clay. Thus thou sawest till that a stone was cut out without hands, which smote the image upon his feet, that were of iron and of clay, and brake them to pieces.

"Then was the iron, the clay, the brass, the silver, and the gold broken to pieces together, and the wind carried them away; but this stone that smote the image became a great mountain, and filled the whole earth. This is the dream, and now I will give thee the interpretation thereof.

"Thou who art the greatest of kings, and to whom God hath given a power so vast that thou art renowned among all peoples, art the head of gold which thou hast seen. But after thee shall arise another kingdom inferior to thee, and another third kingdom of brass, which shall bear rule over all the earth.

"But the fourth kingdom shall be strong as iron, and even as iron breaketh in pieces and subdueth all things, so shall this empire break in pieces and bruise all.

"And whereas thou sawest the feet and toes, part of clay and part of iron, the kingdom shall be divided; but there shall be in it of the strength of iron and of the weakness of clay.

"But as iron cannot be firmly mixed with clay, so they who[Pg 210] are represented by the iron and by the clay, shall not cleave one to another though united by marriage.

"Now in the days of these kings shall God set up a kingdom, which shall never be destroyed, nor ever be delivered up to other people. It shall break in pieces and consume all these kingdoms, and it shall stand for ever, according as thou sawest that the stone was cut out of the mountain without hands, and that it fell from the mountain, and brake in pieces the iron, the clay, the silver, and the gold. God hath made known to thee what shall come to pass hereafter. This dream is certain, and the interpretation thereof sure.

"Then Nebuchadnezzar fell upon his face towards the earth," etc.

Daniel viii, 8. "Daniel having seen the combat of the ram and of the he-goat, who vanquished him and ruled over the earth, whereof the principal horn being broken four others came up toward the four winds of heaven, and out of one of them came forth a little horn, which waxed exceedingly great toward the south, and toward the east, and toward the land of Israel, and it waxed great even to the host of heaven; and it cast down some of the stars, and stamped upon them, and at last overthrew the prince, and by him the daily sacrifice was taken away, and the place of his sanctuary was cast down.

"This is what Daniel saw. He sought the meaning of it, and a voice cried in this manner, 'Gabriel, make this man to understand the vision,' And Gabriel said:

"The ram which thou sawest is the king of the Medes and Persians, and the he-goat is the king of Greece, and the great horn that is between his eyes is the first king of this monarchy.

"Now that being broken, whereas four stood up for it, four kingdoms shall stand up out of the nation, but not in his power.

"And in the latter time of their kingdom, when iniquities are come to the full, there shall arise a king, insolent and strong, but not by his own power, to whom all things shall succeed after his own will; and he shall destroy the holy people, and through his policy also he shall cause craft to prosper in his hand, and he shall destroy many. He shall also stand up against the Prince of princes, but he shall perish miserably, and nevertheless by a violent hand."

Daniel ix, 20. "Whilst I was praying with all my heart, and confessing my sin and the sin of all my people, and prostrating myself before my God, even Gabriel, whom I had seen in the[Pg 211] vision at the beginning, came to me and touched me about the time of the evening oblation, and he informed me and said, O Daniel, I am now come forth to give thee the knowledge of things. At the beginning of thy supplications I came to shew that which thou didst desire, for thou are greatly beloved: therefore understand the matter, and consider the vision. Seventy weeks are determined upon thy people, and upon thy holy city, to finish the transgression, and to make an end of sins, and to abolish iniquity, and to bring in everlasting righteousness; to accomplish the vision and the prophecies, and to anoint the Most Holy. (After which this people shall be no more thy people, nor this city the holy city. The times of wrath shall be passed, and the years of grace shall come for ever.)

"Know therefore, and understand, that, from the going forth of the commandment to restore and to build Jerusalem unto the Messiah the Prince, shall be seven weeks, and three score and two weeks." (The Hebrews were accustomed to divide numbers, and to place the small first. Thus, 7 and 62 make 69. Of this 70 there will then remain the 70th, that is to say, the 7 last years of which he will speak next.)

"The street shall be built again, and the wall, even in troublous times. And after three score and two weeks," (which have followed the first seven. Christ will then be killed after the sixty-nine weeks, that is to say, in the last week), "the Christ shall be cut off, and a people of the prince that shall come shall destroy the city and the sanctuary, and overwhelm all, and the end of that war shall accomplish the desolation."

"Now one week," (which is the seventieth, which remains), "shall confirm the covenant with many, and in the midst of the week," (that is to say, the last three and a half years), "he shall cause the sacrifice and the oblation to cease, and for the overspreading of abominations he shall make it desolate, even until the consummation, and that determined shall be poured upon the desolate."

Daniel xi. "The angel said to Daniel: There shall stand up yet," (after Cyrus, under whom this still is), "three kings in Persia," (Cambyses, Smerdis, Darius); "and the fourth who shall then come," (Xerxes) "shall be far richer than they all, and far stronger, and shall stir up all his people against the Greeks.

"But a mighty king shall stand up," (Alexander), "that shall rule with great dominion, and do according to his will. And[Pg 212] when he shall stand up, his kingdom shall be broken, and shall be divided in four parts toward the four winds of heaven," (as he had said above, vii, 6; viii, 8), "but not his posterity; and his successors shall not equal his power, for his kingdom shall be plucked up, even for others besides these," (his four chief successors).

"And the king of the south," (Ptolemy, son of Lagos, Egypt), "shall be strong; but one of his princes shall be strong above him, and his dominion shall be a great dominion," (Seleucus, King of Syria. Appian says that he was the most powerful of Alexander's successors).

"And in the end of years they shall join themselves together, and the king's daughter of the south," (Berenice, daughter of Ptolemy Philadelphus, son of the other Ptolemy), "shall come to the king of the north," (to Antiochus Deus, King of Syria and of Asia, son of Seleucus Lagidas), "to make peace between these princes.

"But neither she nor her seed shall have a long authority; for she and they that brought her, and her children, and her friends, shall be delivered to death." (Berenice and her son were killed by Seleucus Callinicus.)

"But out of a branch of her roots shall one stand up," (Ptolemy Euergetes was the issue of the same father as Berenice), "which shall come with a mighty army into the land of the king of the north, where he shall put all under subjection, and he shall also carry captive into Egypt their gods, their princes, their gold, their silver, and all their precious spoils," (if he had not been called into Egypt by domestic reasons, says Justin, he would have entirely stripped

Seleucus); "and he shall continue several years when the king of the north can do nought against him.

"And so he shall return into his kingdom. But his sons shall be stirred up, and shall assemble a multitude of great forces," (Seleucus Ceraunus, Antiochus the Great). "And their army shall come and overthrow all; wherefore the king of the south shall be moved with choler, and shall also form a great army, and fight him," (Ptolemy Philopator against Antiochus the Great at Raphia), "and conquer; and his troops shall become insolent, and his heart shall be lifted up," (this Ptolemy desecrated the temple; Josephus): "he shall cast down many ten thousands, but he shall not be strengthened by it. For the king of the north," (Antiochus the Great), "shall return with a[Pg 213] greater multitude than before, and in those times also a great number of enemies shall stand up against the king of the south," (during the reign of the young Ptolemy Epiphanes); "also the apostates and robbers of thy people shall exalt themselves to establish the vision; but they shall fall." (Those who abandon their religion to please Euergetes, when he will send his troops to Scopas; for Antiochus will again take Scopas, and conquer them.) "And the king of the north shall destroy the fenced cities, and the arms of the south shall not withstand, and all shall yield to his will; he shall stand in the land of Israel, and it shall yield to him. And thus he shall think to make himself master of all the empire of Egypt," (despising the youth of Epiphanes, says Justin). "And for that he shall make alliance with him, and give his daughter" (Cleopatra, in order that she may betray her husband. On which Appian says that doubting his ability to make himself master of Egypt by force, because of the protection of the Romans, he wished to attempt it by cunning). "He shall wish to corrupt her, but she shall not stand on his side, neither be for him. Then he shall turn his face to other designs, and shall think to make himself master of some isles," (that is to say, seaports), "and shall take many," (as Appian says).

"But a prince shall oppose his conquests," (Scipio Africanus, who stopped the progress of Antiochus the Great, because he offended the Romans in the person of their allies), "and shall cause the reproach offered by him to cease. He shall then return into his kingdom and there perish, and be no more." (He was slain by his soldiers.)

"And he who shall stand up in his estate," (Seleucus Philopator or Soter, the son of Antiochus the Great), "shall be a tyrant, a raiser of taxes in the glory of the kingdom," (which means the people), "but within a few days he shall be destroyed, neither in anger nor in battle. And in his place shall stand up a vile person, unworthy of the honour of the kingdom, but he shall come in cleverly by flatteries. All armies shall bend before him; he shall conquer them, and even the prince with whom he has made a covenant. For having renewed the league with him, he shall work deceitfully, and enter with a small people into his province, peaceably and without fear. He shall take the fattest places, and shall do that which his fathers have not done, and ravage on all sides. He shall forecast great devices during his time."[Pg 214]

722

Prophecies.—The seventy weeks of Daniel are ambiguous as regards the term of commencement, because of the terms of the prophecy; and as regards the term of conclusion, because of the differences among chronologists. But all this difference extends only to two hundred years.

723

Predictions.—That in the fourth monarchy, before the destruction of the second temple, before the dominion of the Jews was taken away, in the seventieth week of Daniel, during the continuance of the second temple, the heathen should be instructed, and brought to the knowledge of the God worshipped by the Jews; that those who loved Him should be delivered from their enemies, and filled with His fear and love.

And it happened that in the fourth monarchy, before the destruction of the second temple, etc., the heathen in great number worshipped God, and led an angelic life. Maidens dedicated their virginity and their life to God. Men renounced their pleasures. What Plato could only make acceptable to a few men, specially chosen and instructed, a secret influence imparted, by the power of a few words, to a hundred million ignorant men.

The rich left their wealth. Children left the dainty homes of their parents to go into the rough desert. (See Philo the Jew.) All this was foretold a great while ago. For two thousand years no heathen had worshipped the God of the Jews; and at the time foretold, a great number of the heathen worshipped this only God. The temples were destroyed. The very kings made submission to the cross. All this was due to the Spirit of God, which was spread abroad upon the earth.

No heathen, since Moses until Jesus Christ, believed according to the very Rabbis. A great number of the heathen, after Jesus Christ, believed in the books of Moses, kept them in substance and spirit, and only rejected what was useless.

724

Prophecies.—The conversion of the Egyptians (Isaiah xix, 19); an altar in Egypt to the true God.

725

Prophecies.—In Egypt.—Pugio Fidei, p. 659. Talmud.

"It is a tradition among us, that, when the Messiah shall[Pg 215] come, the house of God, destined for the dispensation of His Word, shall be full of filth and impurity; and that the wisdom of the scribes shall be corrupt and rotten. Those who shall be afraid to sin, shall be rejected by the people, and treated as senseless fools."

Is. xlix: "Listen, O isles, unto me, and hearken, ye people, from afar: The Lord hath called me by my name from the womb of my mother; in the shadow of His hand hath He hid me, and hath made my words like a sharp sword, and said unto me, Thou art my servant in whom I will be glorified. Then I said, Lord, have I laboured in vain? have I spent my strength for nought? yet surely my judgment is with Thee, O Lord, and my work with Thee. And now, saith the Lord, that formed me from the womb to be His servant, to bring Jacob and Israel again to Him, Thou shalt be glorious in my sight, and I will be thy strength. It is a light thing that thou shouldst convert the tribes of Jacob; I have raised thee up for a light to the Gentiles, that thou mayest be my salvation unto the ends of the earth. Thus saith the Lord to him whom man despiseth, to him whom the nation abhorreth, to a servant of rulers, Princes and kings shall worship thee, because the Lord is faithful that hath chosen thee.

"Again saith the Lord unto me, I have heard thee in the days of salvation and of mercy, and I will preserve thee for a covenant of the people, to cause to inherit the desolate nations, that thou mayest say to the prisoners: Go forth; to them that are in darkness show yourselves, and possess these abundant and fertile lands. They shall not hunger nor thirst, neither shall the heat nor sun smite them; for he that hath mercy upon them shall lead them, even by the springs of waters shall he guide them, and make the mountains a way before them. Behold, the peoples shall come from all parts, from the east and from the west, from the north and from the south. Let the heavens give glory to God; let the earth be joyful; for it hath pleased the Lord to comfort His people, and He will have mercy upon the poor who hope in Him.

"Yet Sion dared to say: The Lord hath forsaken me, and hath forgotten me. Can a woman forget her child, that she should not have compassion on the son of her womb? but if she forget, yet will not I forget thee, O Sion. I will bear thee always between my hands, and thy walls are continually before me. They that shall build thee are come, and thy destroyers shall[Pg 216] go forth of thee. Lift up thine eyes round about, and behold; all these gather themselves together, and come to thee. As I live, saith the Lord, thou shalt surely clothe thee with them all, as with an ornament. Thy waste and thy desolate places, and the land of thy destruction, shall even now be too narrow by reason of the inhabitants, and the children thou shalt have after thy barrenness shall say again in thy ears: The place is too strait for me: give place to me that I may dwell. Then shalt thou say in thy heart: Who hath begotten me these, seeing I have lost my children, and am desolate, a captive, and removing to and fro? and who brought up these? Behold, I was left alone; these, where had they been? And the Lord shall say to thee: Behold, I will lift up mine hand to the Gentiles, and set up my standard to the people; and they shall bring thy sons in their arms and in their bosoms. And kings shall be their nursing fathers, and queens their nursing mothers; they shall bow down to thee with their face toward the earth, and lick up the dust of thy feet; and thou shalt know that I am the Lord; for they shall not be ashamed that wait for me. Shall the prey be taken from the mighty? But even if the captives be taken away from the strong, nothing shall hinder me from saving thy children, and from destroying thy enemies; and all flesh shall know that I am the Lord, thy Saviour and thy Redeemer, the mighty One of Jacob.

"Thus saith the Lord: What is the bill of this divorcement, wherewith I have put away the synagogue? and why have I delivered it into the hands of your enemies? Is it not for your iniquities and for your transgressions that I have put it away?

"For I came, and no man received me; I called and there was none to hear. Is my arm shortened, that I cannot redeem?

"Therefore I will show the tokens of mine anger; I will clothe the heavens with darkness, and make sackcloth their covering.

"The Lord hath given me the tongue of the learned that I should know how to speak a word in season to him that is weary. He hath opened mine ear, and I have listened to Him as a master.

"The Lord hath revealed His will, and I was not rebellious.

"I gave my body to the smiters, and my cheeks to outrage; I hid not my face from shame and spitting. But the Lord hath helped me; therefore I have not been confounded.

"He is near that justifieth me; who will contend with me? who will be mine adversary, and accuse me of sin, God himself being my protector?[Pg 217]

"All men shall pass away, and be consumed by time; let those that fear God hearken to the voice of His servant; let him that languisheth in darkness put his trust in the Lord. But as for you, ye do but kindle the wrath of God upon you; ye walk in the light of your fire and in the sparks that ye have kindled. This shall ye have of mine hand; ye shall lie down in sorrow.

"Hearken to me, ye that follow after righteousness, ye that seek the Lord: look unto the rock whence ye are hewn, and to the hole of the pit whence ye are digged. Look unto Abraham, your father, and unto Sarah that bare you: for I called him alone, when childless, and increased him. Behold, I have comforted Zion, and heaped upon her blessings and consolations.

"Hearken unto me, my people, and give ear unto me: for a law shall proceed from me, and I will make my judgment to rest for a light of the Gentiles."

Amos viii. The prophet, having enumerated the sins of Israel, said that God had sworn to take vengeance on them.

He says this: "And it shall come to pass in that day, saith the Lord, that I will cause the sun to go down at noon, and I will darken the earth in the clear day; and I will turn your feasts into mourning, and all your songs into lamentation.

"You all shall have sorrow and suffering, and I will make this nation mourn as for an only son, and the end therefore as a bitter day. Behold, the days come, saith the Lord, that I will send a famine in the land, not a famine of bread, nor a thirst for water, but of hearing the words of the Lord. And they shall wander from sea to sea, and from the north even to the east; they shall run to and fro to seek the word of the Lord, and shall not find it.

"In that day shall the fair virgins and young men faint for thirst. They that have followed the idols of Samaria, and sworn by the god of Dan, and followed the manner of Beersheba, shall fall, and never rise up again."

Amos iii, 2: "Ye only have I known of all the families of the earth for my people."

Daniel xii, 7. Having described all the extent of the reign of the Messiah, he says: "All these things shall be finished, when the scattering of the people of Israel shall be accomplished."

Haggai ii, 4: "Ye who, comparing this second house with the glory of the first, despise it, be strong, saith the Lord, be strong, O Zerubbabel, and O Jesus, the high priest, be strong, all ye[Pg 218] people of the land, and work. For I am with you, saith the Lord of hosts; according to the word that I covenanted with you when ye came out of Egypt, so my spirit remaineth among you. Fear ye not. For thus saith the Lord of hosts: Yet one little while, and I will shake the heavens, and the earth, and the sea, and the dry land," (a way of speaking to indicate a great and an extraordinary change); "and I will shake all nations, and the desire of all the Gentiles shall come; and I will fill this house with glory, saith the Lord.

"The silver is mine, and the gold is mine, saith the Lord," (that is to say, it is not by that that I wish to be honoured; as it is said elsewhere:

All the beasts of the field are mine, what advantages me that they are offered me in sacrifice?). "The glory of this latter house shall be greater than of the former, saith the Lord of hosts; and in this place will I establish my house, saith the Lord.

"According to all that thou desiredst in Horeb in the day of the assembly, saying, Let us not hear again the voice of the Lord, neither let us see this fire any more, that we die not.[272] And the Lord said unto me, Their prayer is just. I will raise them up a prophet from among their brethren, like unto thee, and will put my words in his mouth; and he shall speak unto them all that I shall command him. And it shall come to pass, that whosoever will not hearken unto my words which he will speak in my name, I will require it of him."

Genesis xlix: "Judah, thou art he whom thy brethren shall praise, and thou shalt conquer thine enemies; thy father's children shall bow down before thee. Judah is a lion's whelp: from the prey, my son, thou art gone up, and art couched as a lion, and as a lioness that shall be roused up.

"The sceptre shall not depart from Judah, nor a lawgiver from between his feet, until Shiloh come; and unto him shall the gathering of the people be."

726

During the life of the Messiah.—Ænigmatis.—Ezek. xvii.

His forerunner. Malachi iii.

He will be born an infant. Is. ix.

He will be born in the village of Bethlehem. Micah v. He will appear chiefly in Jerusalem, and will be a descendant of the family of Judah and of David.

He is to blind the learned and the wise, Is. vi, viii, xxix, etc.;[Pg 219] and to preach the Gospel to the lowly, Is. xxix; to open the eyes of the blind, give health to the sick, and bring light to those that languish in darkness. Is. lxi.

He is to show the perfect way, and be the teacher of the Gentiles. Is. lv; xlii, 1-7.

The prophecies are to be unintelligible to the wicked, Dan. xii; Hosea xiv, 10; but they are to be intelligible to those who are well informed.

The prophecies, which represent Him as poor, represent Him as master of the nations. Is. lii, 14, etc.; liii; Zech. ix, 9.

The prophecies, which foretell the time, foretell Him only as master of the nations and suffering, and not as in the clouds nor as judge. And those, which represent Him thus as judge and in glory, do not mention the time. When the Messiah is spoken of as great and glorious, it is as the judge of the world, and not its Redeemer.

He is to be the victim for the sins of the world. Is. xxxix, liii, etc.

He is to be the precious corner-stone. Is. xxviii, 16.

He is to be a stone of stumbling and offence. Is. viii. Jerusalem is to dash against this stone.

The builders are to reject this stone. Ps. cxvii, 22.

God is to make this stone the chief corner-stone.

And this stone is to grow into a huge mountain, and fill the whole earth. Dan. ii.

So He is to be rejected, despised, betrayed (Ps. cviii, 8), sold (Zech. xi, 12), spit upon, buffeted, mocked, afflicted in innumerable ways, given gall to drink (Ps. lxviii), pierced (Zech. xii), His feet and His hands pierced, slain, and lots cast for His raiment.

He will raise again (Ps. xv) the third day (Hosea vi, 3).

He will ascend to heaven to sit on the right hand. Ps. cx.

The kings will arm themselves against Him. Ps. ii.

Being on the right hand of the Father, He will be victorious over His enemies.

The kings of the earth and all nations will worship Him. Is. lx.

The Jews will continue as a nation. Jeremiah.

They will wander, without kings, etc. (Hosea iii), without prophets (Amos), looking for salvation and finding it not (Isaiah).

Calling of the Gentiles by Jesus Christ. Is. lii, 15; lv, 5; lx, etc. Ps. lxxxi.

Hosea i, 9: "Ye are not my people, and I will not be your[Pg 220] God, when ye are multiplied after the dispersion. In the places where it was said, Ye are not my people, I will call them my people."

727

It was not lawful to sacrifice outside of Jerusalem, which was the place that the Lord had chosen, nor even to eat the tithes elsewhere. Deut. xii, 5, etc.; Deut. xiv, 23, etc.; xv, 20; xvi, 2, 7, 11, 15.

Hosea foretold that they should be without a king, without a prince, without a sacrifice, and without an idol; and this prophecy is now fulfilled, as they cannot make a lawful sacrifice out of Jerusalem.

728

Predictions.—It was foretold that, in the time of the Messiah, He should come to establish a new covenant, which should make them forget the escape from Egypt (Jer. xxiii, 5; Is. xliii, 10); that He should place His law not in externals, but in the heart; that He should put His fear, which had only been from without, in the midst of the heart. Who does not see the Christian law in all this?

729

... That then idolatry would be overthrown; that this Messiah would cast down all idols, and bring men into the worship of the true God.

That the temples of the idols would be cast down, and that among all nations, and in all places of the earth, He would be offered a pure sacrifice, not of beasts.

That He would be king of the Jews and Gentiles. And we see this king of the Jews and Gentiles oppressed by both, who conspire His death; and ruler of both, destroying the worship of Moses in Jerusalem, which was its centre, where He made His first Church; and also the worship of idols in Rome, the centre of it, where He made His chief Church.

730

Prophecies.—That Jesus Christ will sit on the right hand, till God has subdued His enemies.

Therefore He will not subdue them Himself.

731

"... Then they shall teach no more every man his neighbour, saying, Here is the Lord, for God shall make Himself known to all."[Pg 221][273]

"... Your sons shall prophesy."[274] "I will put my spirit and my fear in your heart."

All that is the same thing. To prophesy is to speak of God, not from outward proofs, but from an inward and immediate feeling.

732

That He would teach men the perfect way.

And there has never come, before Him nor after Him, any man who has taught anything divine approaching to this.

733

... That Jesus Christ would be small in His beginning, and would then increase. The little stone of Daniel.

If I had in no wise heard of the Messiah, nevertheless, after such wonderful predictions of the course of the world which I see fulfilled, I see that He is divine. And if I knew that these same books foretold a

Messiah, I should be sure that He would come; and seeing that they place His time before the destruction of the second temple, I should say that He had come.

734

Prophecies.—That the Jews would reject Jesus Christ, and would be rejected of God, for this reason, that the chosen vine brought forth only wild grapes. That the chosen people would be fruitless, ungrateful, and unbelieving, populum non credentem et contradicentem.[275] That God would strike them with blindness, and in full noon they would grope like the blind; and that a forerunner would go before Him.

735

Transfixerunt. Zech. xii, 10.

That a deliverer should come, who would crush the demon's head, and free His people from their sins, ex omnibus iniquitatibus; that there should be a New Covenant, which would be eternal; that there should be another priesthood after the order of Melchisedek, and it should be eternal; that the Christ should be glorious, mighty, strong, and yet so poor that He would not be recognised, nor taken for what He is, but rejected and slain; that His people who denied Him should no longer be His people; that the idolaters should receive Him, and take refuge in Him; that He should leave Zion to reign in the centre of idolatry; that nevertheless the Jews should continue for ever; that He should be of Judah, and when there should be no longer a king.

[Pg 222]

SECTION XII

PROOFS OF JESUS CHRIST

736

... Therefore I reject all other religions. In that way I find an answer to all objections. It is right that a God so pure should only reveal Himself to those whose hearts are purified. Hence this religion is lovable to me, and I find it now sufficiently justified by so divine a morality. But I find more in it.

I find it convincing that, since the memory of man has lasted, it was constantly announced to men that they were universally corrupt, but that a Redeemer should come; that it was not one man who said it, but innumerable men, and a whole nation expressly made for the purpose, and prophesying for four thousand years. This is a nation which is more ancient than every other nation. Their books, scattered abroad, are four thousand years old.

The more I examine them, the more truths I find in them: an entire nation foretell Him before His advent, and an entire nation worship Him after His advent; what has preceded and what has followed; in short, people without idols and kings, this synagogue which was foretold, and these wretches who frequent it, and who, being our enemies, are admirable witnesses of the truth of these prophecies, wherein their wretchedness and even their blindness are foretold.

I find this succession, this religion, wholly divine in its authority, in its duration, in its perpetuity, in its morality, in its conduct, in its doctrine, in its effects. The frightful darkness of the Jews was foretold: Eris palpans in meridie.[276] Dabitur liber scienti literas, et dicet: Non possum legere.[277] While the sceptre was still in the hands of the first foreign usurper, there is the report of the coming of Jesus Christ.

So I hold out my arms to my Redeemer, who, having been foretold for four thousand years, has come to suffer and to die for me on earth, at the time and under all the circumstances foretold. By His grace, I await death in peace, in the hope of[Pg 223] being eternally united to Him. Yet I live with joy, whether in the prosperity which it pleases Him to bestow upon me, or in the adversity which He sends for my good, and which He has taught me to bear by His example.

737

The prophecies having given different signs which should all happen at the advent of the Messiah, it was necessary that all these signs should occur at the same time. So it was necessary that the fourth monarchy should have come, when the seventy weeks of Daniel were ended; and that the sceptre should have then departed from Judah.

And all this happened without any difficulty. Then it was necessary that the Messiah should come; and Jesus Christ then came, who was called the Messiah. And all this again was without difficulty. This indeed shows the truth of the prophecies.

738

The prophets foretold, and were not foretold. The saints again were foretold, but did not foretell. Jesus Christ both foretold and was foretold.

739

Jesus Christ, whom the two Testaments regard, the Old as its hope, the New as its model, and both as their centre.

740

The two oldest books in the world are those of Moses and Job, the one a Jew and the other a Gentile. Both of them look upon Jesus Christ as their common centre and object: Moses in relating the promises of God to Abraham, Jacob, etc., and his prophecies; and Job, Quis mihi det ut,[278] etc. Scio enim quod redemptor meus vivit, etc.

741

The Gospel only speaks of the virginity of the Virgin up to the time of the birth of Jesus Christ. All with reference to Jesus Christ.

742

Proofs of Jesus Christ.

Why was the book of Ruth preserved?

Why the story of Tamar?

[Pg 224]

743

"Pray that ye enter not into temptation."[279] It is dangerous to be tempted; and people are tempted because they do not pray.

Et tu conversus confirma fratres tuos. But before, conversus Jesus respexit Petrum.

Saint Peter asks permission to strike Malchus, and strikes before hearing the answer. Jesus Christ replies afterwards.

The word, Galilee, which the Jewish mob pronounced as if by chance, in accusing Jesus Christ before Pilate, afforded Pilate a reason for sending Jesus Christ to Herod. And thereby the mystery was accomplished, that He should be judged by Jews and Gentiles. Chance was apparently the cause of the accomplishment of the mystery.

744

Those who have a difficulty in believing seek a reason in the fact that the Jews do not believe. "Were this so clear," say they, "why did the Jews not believe?" And they almost wish that they had believed, so as not to be kept back by the example of their refusal. But it is their very refusal that is the foundation of our faith. We should be much less disposed to the faith, if they were on our side. We should then have a more ample pretext. The wonderful thing is to have made the Jews great lovers of the things foretold, and great enemies of their fulfilment.

745

The Jews were accustomed to great and striking miracles, and so, having had the great miracles of the Red Sea and of the land of Canaan as an epitome of the great deeds of their Messiah, they therefore looked for more striking miracles, of which those of Moses were only the patterns.

746

The carnal Jews and the heathen have their calamities, and Christians also. There is no Redeemer for the heathen, for they do not so much as hope for one. There is no Redeemer for the Jews; they hope for

Him in vain. There is a Redeemer only for Christians. (See Perpetuity.)

747

In the time of the Messiah the people divided themselves. The spiritual embraced the Messiah, and the coarser-minded remained to serve as witnesses of Him.[Pg 225]

748

"If this was clearly foretold to the Jews, how did they not believe it, or why were they not destroyed for resisting a fact so clear?"

I reply: in the first place, it was foretold both that they would not believe a thing so clear, and that they would not be destroyed. And nothing is more to the glory of the Messiah; for it was not enough that there should be prophets; their prophets must be kept above suspicion. Now, etc.

749

If the Jews had all been converted by Jesus Christ, we should have none but questionable witnesses. And if they had been entirely destroyed, we should have no witnesses at all.

750

What do the prophets say of Jesus Christ? That He will be clearly God? No; but that He is a God truly hidden; that He will be slighted; that none will think that it is He; that He will be a stone of stumbling, upon which many will stumble, etc. Let people then reproach us no longer for want of clearness, since we make profession of it.

But, it is said, there are obscurities.—And without that, no one would have stumbled over Jesus Christ, and this is one of the formal pronouncements of the prophets: Excæca[280] ...

751

Moses first teaches the Trinity, original sin, the Messiah.

David: a great witness; a king, good, merciful, a beautiful soul, a sound mind, powerful. He prophesies, and his wonder comes to pass. This is infinite.

He had only to say that he was the Messiah, if he had been vain; for the prophecies are clearer about him than about Jesus Christ. And the same with Saint John.

752

Herod was believed to be the Messiah. He had taken away the sceptre from Judah, but he was not of Judah. This gave rise to a considerable sect.

Curse of the Greeks upon those who count three periods of time.[Pg 226]

In what way should the Messiah come, seeing that through Him the sceptre was to be eternally in Judah, and at His coming the sceptre was to be taken away from Judah?

In order to effect that seeing they should not see, and hearing they should not understand, nothing could be better done.

753

Homo existens te Deum facit.

Scriptum est, Dii estis, et non potest solvi Scriptura.

Hæc infirmitas non est ad vitam et est ad mortem.

Lazarus dormit, et deinde dixit: Lazarus mortuus est.[281]

754

The apparent discrepancy of the Gospels.[282]

755

What can we have but reverence for a man who foretells plainly things which come to pass, and who declares his intention both to blind and to enlighten, and who intersperses obscurities among the clear things which come to pass?

756

The time of the first advent was foretold; the time of the second is not so; because the first was to be obscure, and the second is to be brilliant, and so manifest that even His enemies will recognise it. But, as He was first to come only in obscurity, and to be known only of those who searched the Scriptures ...

757

God, in order to cause the Messiah to be known by the good and not to be known by the wicked, made Him to be foretold in this manner. If the manner of the Messiah had been clearly foretold, there would have been no obscurity, even for the wicked. If the time had been obscurely foretold, there would have been obscurity, even for the good. For their [goodness of heart] would not have made them understand, for instance, that the closed mem signifies six hundred years. But the time has been clearly foretold, and the manner in types.

By this means, the wicked, taking the promised blessings for material blessings, have fallen into error, in spite of the clear prediction of the time; and the good have not fallen in[Pg 227] error. For the understanding of the promised blessings depends on the heart, which calls "good" that which it loves; but the understanding of the promised time does not depend on the heart. And thus the clear prediction of the time, and the obscure prediction of the blessings, deceive the wicked alone.

758

[Either the Jews or the Christians must be wicked.]

759

The Jews reject Him, but not all. The saints receive Him, and not the carnal-minded. And so far is this from being against His glory, that it is the last touch which crowns it. For their argument, the only one found in all their writings, in the Talmud and in the Rabbinical writings, amounts only to this, that Jesus Christ has not subdued the nations with sword in hand, gladiumt uum, potentissime.[283] (Is this all they have to say? Jesus Christ has been slain, say they. He has failed. He has not subdued the heathen with His might. He has not bestowed upon us their spoil. He does not give riches. Is this all they have to say? It is in this respect that He is lovable to me. I would not desire Him whom they fancy.) It is evident that it is only His life which has prevented them from accepting Him; and through this rejection they are irreproachable witnesses, and, what is more, they thereby accomplish the prophecies.

[By means of the fact that this people have not accepted Him, this miracle here has happened. The prophecies were the only lasting miracles which could be wrought, but they were liable to be denied.]

760

The Jews, in slaying Him in order not to receive Him as the Messiah, have given Him the final proof of being the Messiah.

And in continuing not to recognise Him, they made themselves irreproachable witnesses. Both in slaying Him, and in continuing to deny Him, they have fulfilled the prophecies (Isa. lx; Ps. lxxi).

761

What could the Jews, His enemies, do? If they receive Him, they give proof of Him by their reception; for then the guardians[Pg 228] of the expectation of the Messiah receive Him. If they reject Him, they give proof of Him by their rejection.

762

The Jews, in testing if He were God, have shown that He was man.

763

The Church has had as much difficulty in showing that Jesus Christ was man, against those who denied it, as in showing that he was God; and the probabilities were equally great.

764

Source of contradictions.—A God humiliated, even to the death on the cross; a Messiah triumphing over death by his own death. Two natures in Jesus Christ, two advents, two states of man's nature.

765

Types.—Saviour, father, sacrificer, offering, food, king, wise, law-giver, afflicted, poor, having to create a people whom He must lead and nourish, and bring into His land....

Jesus Christ. Offices.—He alone had to create a great people, elect, holy, and chosen; to lead, nourish, and bring it into the place of rest and holiness; to make it holy to God; to make it the temple of God; to reconcile it to, and save it from, the wrath of God; to free it from the slavery of sin, which visibly reigns in man; to give laws to this people, and engrave these laws on their heart; to offer Himself to God for them, and sacrifice Himself for them; to be a victim without blemish, and Himself the sacrificer, having to offer Himself, His body, and His blood, and yet to offer bread and wine to God ...

Ingrediens mundum.[284]

"Stone upon stone."[285]

What preceded and what followed. All the Jews exist still, and are wanderers.

766

Of all that is on earth, He partakes only of the sorrows, not of the joys. He loves His neighbours, but His love does not confine itself within these bounds, and overflows to His own enemies, and then to those of God.[Pg 229]

767

Jesus Christ typified by Joseph, the beloved of his father, sent by his father to see his brethren, etc., innocent, sold by his brethren for twenty pieces of silver, and thereby becoming their lord, their saviour, the saviour of strangers, and the saviour of the world; which had not been but for their plot to destroy him, their sale and their rejection of him.

In prison Joseph innocent between two criminals; Jesus Christ on the cross between two thieves. Joseph foretells freedom to the one, and death to the other, from the same omens. Jesus Christ saves the elect, and condemns the outcast for the same sins. Joseph foretells only; Jesus Christ acts. Joseph asks him who will be saved to remember him, when he comes into his glory; and he whom Jesus Christ saves asks that He will remember him, when He comes into His kingdom.

768

The conversion of the heathen was only reserved for the grace of the Messiah. The Jews have been so long in opposition to them without success; all that Solomon and the prophets said has been useless. Sages, like Plato and Socrates, have not been able to persuade them.

769

After many persons had gone before, Jesus Christ at last came to say: [286] "Here am I, and this is the time. That which the prophets have said was to come in the fullness of time, I tell you My apostles will do. The Jews shall be cast out. Jerusalem shall be soon destroyed. And the heathen shall enter into the knowledge of God. My apostles shall do this after you have slain the heir of the vineyard."

Then the apostles said to the Jews: "You shall be accursed," (Celsus laughed at it); and to the heathen, "You shall enter into the knowledge of God." And this then came to pass.

770

Jesus Christ came to blind those who saw clearly, and to give sight to the blind; to heal the sick, and leave the healthy to die; to call to repentance, and to justify sinners, and to leave the righteous in their sins; to fill the needy, and leave the rich empty.[Pg 230]

771

Holiness.—Effundam spiritum meum.[287] All nations were in unbelief and lust. The whole world now became fervent with love.

Princes abandoned their pomp; maidens suffered martyrdom. Whence came this influence? The Messiah was come. These were the effect and sign of His coming.

772

Destruction of the Jews and heathen by Jesus Christ: Omnes gentes venient et adorabunt eum.[288] Parum est ut,[289] etc. Postula a me.[290] Adorabunt eum omnes reges.[291] Testes iniqui.[292] Dabit maxillam percutienti.[293] Dederunt fel in escam.[294]

773

Jesus Christ for all, Moses for a nation.

The Jews blessed in Abraham: "I will bless those that bless thee."[295] But: "All nations blessed in his seed."[296] Parum est ut, etc.

Lumen ad revelationem gentium.[297]

Non fecit taliter omni nationi,[298] said David, in speaking of the Law. But, in speaking of Jesus Christ, we must say: Fecit taliter omni nationi. Parum est ut, etc., Isaiah. So it belongs to Jesus Christ to be universal. Even the Church offers sacrifice only for the faithful. Jesus Christ offered that of the cross for all.

774

There is heresy in always explaining omnes by "all," and heresy in not explaining it sometimes by "all." Bibite ex hoc omnes;[299] the Huguenots are heretics in explaining it by "all." In quo omnes peccaverunt;[300] the Huguenots are heretics in excepting the children of true believers. We must then follow the Fathers and tradition in order to know when to do so, since there is heresy to be feared on both sides.

775

Ne timeas pusillus grex.[301] Timore et tremore.—Quid ergo? Ne timeas [modo] timeas. Fear not, provided you fear; but if you fear not, then fear.

Qui me recipit, non me recipit, sed eum qui me misit.[302]

Nemo scit, neque Filius.

Nubes lucida obumbravit.

Saint John[303] was to turn the hearts of the fathers to the children, and Jesus Christ[304] to plant division. There is not contradiction. [Pg 231]

776

The effects in communi and in particulari. The semi-Pelagians err in saying of in communi what is true only in particulari; and the Calvinists in saying in particulari what is true in communi. (Such is my opinion.)

777

Omnis Judæa regio, et Jerosolomymi universi, et baptizabantur.[305] Because of all the conditions of men who came there. From these stones there can come children unto Abraham.[306]

778

If men knew themselves, God would heal and pardon them. Ne convertantur et sanem eos, et dimittantur eis peccata.[307]

779

Jesus Christ never condemned without hearing. To Judas: Amice, ad quid venisti?[308] To him that had not on the wedding garment, the same.

780

The types of the completeness of the Redemption, as that the sun gives light to all, indicate only completeness; but [the types] of exclusions, as of the Jews elected to the exclusion of the Gentiles, indicate exclusion.

"Jesus Christ the Redeemer of all."—Yes, for He has offered, like a man who has ransomed all those who were willing to come to Him. If any die on the way, it is their misfortune; but, so far as He was concerned, He offered them redemption.—That holds good in this example, where he who ransoms and he who prevents death are two persons, but not of Jesus Christ, who does both these things.—No, for Jesus Christ, in the quality of Redeemer, is not perhaps Master of all; and thus, in so far as it is in Him, He is the Redeemer of all.

When it is said that Jesus Christ did not die for all, you take undue advantage of a fault in men who at once apply this exception to themselves; and this is to favour despair, instead of turning them from it to favour hope. For men thus accustom themselves in inward virtues by outward customs.

781

The victory over death. "What is a man advantaged if he gain the whole world and lose his own soul?[309] Whosoever will save his soul, shall lose it."[Pg 232][310]

"I am not come to destroy the law, but to fulfil."[311]

"Lambs took not away the sins of the world, but I am the lamb which taketh away the sins."[312]

"Moses[313] hath not led you out of captivity, and made you truly free."

782

... Then Jesus Christ comes to tell men that they have no other enemies but themselves; that it is their passions which keep them apart from God; that He comes to destroy these, and give them His grace, so as to make of them all one Holy Church; that He comes to bring back into this Church the heathen and Jews; that He comes to destroy the idols of the former and the superstition of the latter. To this all men are opposed, not only from the natural opposition of lust; but, above all, the kings of the earth, as had been foretold, join together to destroy this religion at its birth. (Proph.: Quare fremuerunt gentes ... reges terræ ... adversus Christum.)[314]

All that is great on earth is united together; the learned, the wise, the kings. The first write; the second condemn; the last kill. And notwithstanding all these oppositions, these men, simple and weak, resist all these powers, subdue even these kings, these learned men and these sages, and remove idolatry from all the earth. And all this is done by the power which had foretold it.

783

Jesus Christ would not have the testimony of devils, nor of those who were not called, but of God and John the Baptist.

784

I consider Jesus Christ in all persons and in ourselves: Jesus Christ as a Father in His Father, Jesus Christ as a Brother in His Brethren, Jesus Christ as poor in the poor, Jesus Christ as rich in the rich, Jesus Christ as Doctor and Priest in priests, Jesus Christ as Sovereign in princes, etc. For by His glory He is all that is great, being God; and by His mortal life He is all that is poor and abject. Therefore He has taken this unhappy condition, so that He could be in all persons, and the model of all conditions.

785

Jesus Christ is an obscurity (according to what the world calls obscurity), such that historians, writing only of important matters of states, have hardly noticed Him.[Pg 233]

786

On the fact that neither Josephus, nor Tacitus, nor other historians have spoken of Jesus Christ.—So far is this from telling against Christianity, that on the contrary it tells for it. For it is certain that Jesus Christ has existed; that His religion has made a great talk; and that these persons were not ignorant of it. Thus it is plain that they purposely concealed it, or that, if they did speak of it, their account has been suppressed or changed.

787

"I have reserved me seven thousand."[315] I love the worshippers unknown to the world and to the very prophets.

788

As Jesus Christ remained unknown among men, so His truth remains among common opinions without external difference. Thus the Eucharist among ordinary bread.

789

Jesus would not be slain without the forms of justice; for it is far more ignominious to die by justice than by an unjust sedition.

790

The false justice of Pilate only serves to make Jesus Christ suffer; for he causes Him to be scourged by his false justice, and afterwards puts Him to death. It would have been better to have put Him to death at once. Thus it is with the falsely just. They do good and evil works to please the world, and to show that they are not altogether of Jesus Christ; for they are ashamed of Him. And at last, under great temptation and on great occasions, they kill Him.

791

What man ever had more renown? The whole Jewish people foretell Him before His coming. The Gentile people worship Him after His coming. The two peoples, Gentile and Jewish, regard Him as their centre.

And yet what man enjoys this renown less? Of thirty-three years, He lives thirty without appearing. For three years He passes as an impostor; the priests and the chief people reject Him; His friends and His nearest relatives despise Him. Finally,[Pg 234] He dies, betrayed by one of His own disciples, denied by another, and abandoned by all.

What part, then, has He in this renown? Never had man so much renown; never had man more ignominy. All that renown has served only for us, to render us capable of recognising Him; and He had none of it for Himself.

792

The infinite distance between body and mind is a symbol of the infinitely more infinite distance between mind and charity; for charity is supernatural.

All the glory of greatness has no lustre for people who are in search of understanding.

The greatness of clever men is invisible to kings, to the rich, to chiefs, and to all the worldly great.

The greatness of wisdom, which is nothing if not of God, is invisible to the carnal-minded and to the clever. These are three orders differing in kind.

Great geniuses have their power, their glory, their greatness, their victory, their lustre, and have no need of worldly greatness, with which they are not in keeping. They are seen, not by the eye, but by the mind; this is sufficient.

The saints have their power, their glory, their victory, their lustre, and need no worldly or intellectual greatness, with which they have no affinity; for these neither add anything to them, nor take away anything from them. They are seen of God and the angels, and not of the body, nor of the curious mind. God is enough for them.

Archimedes,[316] apart from his rank, would have the same veneration. He fought no battles for the eyes to feast upon; but he has given his discoveries to all men. Oh! how brilliant he was to the mind!

Jesus Christ, without riches, and without any external exhibition of knowledge, is in His own order of holiness. He did not invent; He did not reign. But He was humble, patient, holy, holy to God, terrible to devils, without any sin. Oh! in what great pomp, and in what wonderful splendour, He is come to the eyes of the heart, which perceive wisdom!

It would have been useless for Archimedes to have acted the prince in his books on geometry, although he was a prince.

It would have been useless for our Lord Jesus Christ to[Pg 235] come like a king, in order to shine forth in His kingdom of holiness. But He came there appropriately in the glory of His own order.

It is most absurd to take offence at the lowliness of Jesus Christ, as if His lowliness were in the same order as the greatness which He came to manifest. If we consider this greatness in His life, in His passion, in His obscurity, in His death, in the choice of His disciples, in their desertion, in His secret resurrection, and the rest, we shall see it to be so immense, that we shall have no reason for being offended at a lowliness which is not of that order.

But there are some who can only admire worldly greatness, as though there were no intellectual greatness; and others who only admire intellectual greatness, as though there were not infinitely higher things in wisdom.

All bodies, the firmament, the stars, the earth and its kingdoms, are not equal to the lowest mind; for mind knows all these and itself; and these bodies nothing.

All bodies together, and all minds together, and all their products, are not equal to the least feeling of charity. This is of an order infinitely more exalted.

From all bodies together, we cannot obtain one little thought; this is impossible, and of another order. From all bodies and minds, we cannot produce a feeling of true charity; this is impossible, and of another and supernatural order.

793

Why did Jesus Christ not come in a visible manner, instead of obtaining testimony of Himself from preceding prophecies? Why did He cause Himself to be foretold in types?

794

If Jesus Christ had only come to sanctify, all Scripture and all things would tend to that end; and it would be quite easy to convince unbelievers. If Jesus Christ had only come to blind, all His conduct would be confused; and we would have no means of convincing unbelievers. But as He came in sanctificationem et in scandalum, [317] as Isaiah says, we cannot convince unbelievers, and they cannot convince us. But by this very fact we convince them; since we say that in His whole conduct there is no convincing proof on one side or the other.[Pg 236]

795

Jesus Christ does not say that He is not of Nazareth, in order to leave the wicked in their blindness; nor that He is not Joseph's son.

796

Proofs of Jesus Christ.—Jesus Christ said great things so simply, that it seems as though He had not thought them great; and yet so clearly that we easily see what He thought of them. This clearness, joined to this simplicity, is wonderful.

797

The style of the gospel is admirable in so many ways, and among the rest in hurling no invectives against the persecutors and enemies of Jesus Christ. For there is no such invective in any of the historians against Judas, Pilate, or any of the Jews.

If this moderation of the writers of the Gospels had been assumed, as well as many other traits of so beautiful a character, and they had only assumed it to attract notice, even if they had not dared to draw attention to it themselves, they would not have failed to secure friends, who would have made such remarks to their advantage. But as they acted thus without pretence, and from wholly disinterested motives, they did not point it out to any one; and I believe that many such facts have not been noticed till now, which is evidence of the natural disinterestedness with which the thing has been done.

798

An artisan who speaks of wealth, a lawyer who speaks of war, of royalty, etc.; but the rich man rightly speaks of wealth, a king speaks indifferently of a great gift he has just made, and God rightly speaks of God.

799

Who has taught the evangelists the qualities of a perfectly heroic soul, that they paint it so perfectly in Jesus Christ? Why do they make Him weak in His agony? Do they not know how to paint a resolute death? Yes, for the same Saint Luke paints the death of Saint Stephen as braver than that of Jesus Christ.

They make Him therefore capable of fear, before the necessity of dying has come, and then altogether brave.[Pg 237]

But when they make Him so troubled, it is when He afflicts Himself; and when men afflict Him, He is altogether strong.

800

Proof of Jesus Christ.—The supposition that the apostles were impostors is very absurd. Let us think it out. Let us imagine those twelve men, assembled after the death of Jesus Christ, plotting to say that He was risen. By this they attack all the powers. The heart of man is strangely inclined to fickleness, to change, to promises, to gain. However little any of them might have been led astray by all these attractions, nay more, by the fear of prisons, tortures, and death, they were lost. Let us follow up this thought.

801

The apostles were either deceived or deceivers. Either supposition has difficulties; for it is not possible to mistake a man raised from the dead ...

While Jesus Christ was with them, He could sustain them. But, after that, if He did not appear to them, who inspired them to act?

[Pg 238]

SECTION XIII

THE MIRACLES

802

The beginning.—Miracles enable us to judge of doctrine, and doctrine enables us to judge of miracles.

There are false miracles and true. There must be a distinction, in order to know them; otherwise they would be useless. Now they are not useless; on the contrary, they are fundamental. Now the rule which is given to us must be such, that it does not destroy the proof which the true miracles give of the truth, which is the chief end of the miracles.

Moses has given two rules: that the prediction does not come to pass (Deut. xviii), and that they do not lead to idolatry (Deut. xiii); and Jesus Christ[318] one.

If doctrine regulates miracles, miracles are useless for doctrine.

If miracles regulate....

Objection to the rule.—The distinction of the times. One rule during the time of Moses, another at present.

803

Miracle.—It is an effect, which exceeds the natural power of the means which are employed for it; and what is not a miracle is an effect, which does not exceed the natural power of the means which are employed for it. Thus, those who heal by invocation of the devil do not work a miracle; for that does not exceed the natural power of the devil. But ...

804

The two fundamentals; one inward, the other outward; grace and miracles; both supernatural.

805

Miracles and truth are necessary, because it is necessary to convince the entire man, in body and soul.[Pg 239]

806

In all times, either men have spoken of the true God, or the true God has spoken to men.

807

Jesus Christ has verified that He was the Messiah, never in verifying His doctrine by Scripture and the prophecies, but always by His miracles.

He proves by a miracle that He remits sins.

Rejoice not in your miracles, said Jesus Christ, but because your names are written in heaven.[319]

If they believe not Moses, neither will they believe one risen from the dead.

Nicodemus recognises by His miracles that His teaching is of God. Scimus quia venisti a Deo magister; nemo enim potest hæc signa facere quæ tu facis nisi Deus fuerit cum eo.[320] He does not judge of the miracles by the teaching, but of the teaching by the miracles.

The Jews had a doctrine of God as we have one of Jesus Christ, and confirmed by miracles. They were forbidden to believe every worker of miracles; and they were further commanded to have recourse to the chief priests, and to rely on them.

And thus, in regard to their prophets, they had all those reasons which we have for refusing to believe the workers of miracles.

And yet they were very sinful in rejecting the prophets, and Jesus Christ, because of their miracles; and they would not have been culpable, if they had not seen the miracles. Nisi fecissem ... peccatum non haberent.[321] Therefore all belief rests upon miracles.

Prophecy is not called miracle; as Saint John speaks of the first miracle in Cana, and then of what Jesus Christ says to the woman of Samaria, when He reveals to her all her hidden life. Then He heals the centurion's son; and Saint John calls this "the second miracle."[322]

808

The combinations of miracles.

809

The second miracle can suppose the first, but the first cannot suppose the second.[Pg 240]

810

Had it not been for the miracles, there would have been no sin in not believing in Jesus Christ.

811

I should not be a Christian, but for the miracles, said Saint Augustine.

812

Miracles.—How I hate those who make men doubt of miracles! Montaigne[323] speaks of them as he should in two places. In one, we see how careful he is; and yet, in the other, he believes, and makes sport of unbelievers.

However it may be, the Church is without proofs if they are right.

813

Montaigne against miracles.

Montaigne for miracles.

814

It is not possible to have a reasonable belief against miracles.

815

Unbelievers the most credulous. They believe the miracles of Vespasian, in order not to believe those of Moses.

816

Title: How it happens that men believe so many liars, who say that they have seen miracles, and do not believe any of those who say that they have secrets to make men immortal, or restore youth to them.—Having considered how it happens that so great credence is given to so many impostors, who say they have remedies, often to the length of men putting their lives into their hands, it has appeared to me that the true cause is that there are true remedies. For it would not be possible that there should be so many false remedies, and that so much faith should be placed in them, if there were none true. If there had never been any remedy for any ill, and all ills had been incurable, it is impossible that men should have imagined that they could give remedies, and still more impossible that so many others should have believed those who boasted of having remedies; in the same way as did a man boast of preventing[Pg 241] death, no one would believe him, because there is no example of this. But as there were a number of remedies found to be true by the very knowledge of the greatest men, the belief of men is thereby induced; and, this being known to be possible, it has been therefore concluded that it was. For people commonly reason thus: "A thing is possible, therefore it is"; because the thing cannot be denied generally, since there are particular effects which are true, the people, who cannot distinguish which among these particular effects are true, believe them all. In the same way, the reason why so many false effects are credited to the moon, is that there are some true, as the tide.

It is the same with prophecies, miracles, divination by dreams, sorceries, etc. For if there had been nothing true in all this, men would have believed nothing of them; and thus, instead of concluding that there are no true miracles because there are so many false, we must, on the contrary, say that there certainly are true miracles, since there are false, and that there are false miracles only because some are true. We must reason in the same way about religion; for it would not be possible that men should have imagined so many false religions, if there had not been a true one. The objection to this is that savages have a religion; but the answer is that they have heard the true spoken of, as appears by the deluge, circumcision, the cross of Saint Andrew, etc.

817

Having considered how it comes that there are so many false miracles, false revelations, sorceries, etc., it has seemed to me that the true cause is that there are some true; for it would not be possible that there should be so many false miracles, if there were none true, nor so many false revelations, if there were none true, nor so many false religions, if there were not one true. For if there had never been all this, it is almost impossible that men should have imagined it, and still more impossible that so many others should have believed it. But as there have been very great things true, and as they have been believed by great men, this impression has been the cause that nearly everybody is rendered capable of believing also the false. And thus, instead of concluding that there are no true miracles, since there are so many false, it must be said, on the contrary, that there are true miracles, since there are so many false; and that there are false ones only because there are true; and that[Pg 242] in the same way there are false religions because there is one true.—Objection to this: savages have a religion. But this is because they have heard the true spoken of, as appears by the cross of Saint Andrew, the deluge, circumcision, etc.—This arises from the fact that the human mind, finding itself inclined to that side by the truth, becomes thereby susceptible of all the falsehoods of this ...

818

Jeremiah xxiii, 32. The miracles of the false prophets. In the Hebrew and Vatable[324] they are the tricks.

Miracle does not always signify miracle. I Sam. xiv, 15; miracle signifies fear, and is so in the Hebrew. The same evidently in Job xxxiii, 7; and also Isaiah xxi, 4; Jeremiah xliv, 12. Portentum signifies simulacrum, Jeremiah l, 38; and it is so in the Hebrew and Vatable. Isaiah viii, 18. Jesus Christ says that He and His will be in miracles.

819

If the devil favoured the doctrine which destroys him, he would be divided against himself, as Jesus Christ said. If God favoured the doctrine which destroys the Church, He would be divided against Himself. Omne regnum divisum.[325] For Jesus Christ wrought against the devil, and destroyed his power over the heart, of which exorcism is the symbolisation, in order to establish the kingdom of God. And thus He adds, Si in digito Dei ... regnum Dei ad vos.[326]

820

There is a great difference between tempting and leading into error. God tempts, but He does not lead into error. To tempt is to afford opportunities, which impose no necessity; if men do not love God, they will do a certain thing. To lead into error is to place a man under the necessity of inferring and following out what is untrue.

821

Abraham and Gideon are above revelation. The Jews blinded themselves in judging of miracles by the Scripture. God has never abandoned His true worshippers.

I prefer to follow Jesus Christ than any other, because He has miracle, prophecy, doctrine, perpetuity, etc.[Pg 243]

The Donatists. No miracle which obliges them to say it is the devil.

The more we particularise God, Jesus Christ, the Church ...

822

If there were no false miracles, there would be certainty. If there were no rule to judge of them, miracles would be useless, and there would be no reason for believing.

Now there is, humanly speaking, no human certainty, but we have reason.

823

Either God has confounded the false miracles, or He has foretold them; and in both ways He has raised Himself above what is supernatural with respect to us, and has raised us to it.

824

Miracles serve not to convert, but to condemn. (Q. 113, A. 10, Ad. 2.)[327]

825

Reasons why we do not believe.

John xii, 37. Cum autem tanta signa fecisset, non credebant in eum, ut sermo Isayæ impleretur. Excæcavit, etc.

Hæc dixit Isaias, quando vidit gloriam ejus et locutus est de eo.

Judæi signa petunt et Græci sapientiam quærunt, nos autem Jesum crucifixum. Sed plenum signis, sed plenum sapientia; vos autem Christum non crucifixum et religionem sine miraculis et sine sapientia.[328]

What makes us not believe in the true miracles, is want of love. John: Sed vos non creditis, quia non estis ex ovibus.[329] What makes us believe the false is want of love. II Thess. ii.

The foundation of religion. It is the miracles. What then? Does God speak against miracles, against the foundations of the faith which we have in Him?

If there is a God, faith in God must exist on earth. Now the miracles of Jesus Christ are not foretold by Antichrist, but the miracles of Antichrist are foretold by Jesus Christ. And so if Jesus Christ were not the Messiah, He would have indeed led into error. When Jesus Christ foretold the miracles of Antichrist, did He think of destroying faith in His own miracles?

Moses foretold Jesus Christ, and bade to follow Him. Jesus Christ foretold Antichrist, and forbade to follow him.[Pg 244]

It was impossible that in the time of Moses men should keep their faith for Antichrist, who was unknown to them. But it is quite easy, in the time of Antichrist, to believe in Jesus Christ, already known.

There is no reason for believing in Antichrist, which there is not for believing in Jesus Christ. But there are reasons for believing in Jesus Christ, which there are not for believing in the other.

826

Judges xiii, 23: "If the Lord were pleased to kill us, He would not have shewed us all these things."

Hezekiah, Sennacherib.

Jeremiah. Hananiah, the false prophet, dies in seven months.

2 Macc. iii. The temple, ready for pillage, miraculously succoured.—2 Macc. xv.

1 Kings xvii. The widow to Elijah, who had restored her son, "By this I know that thy words are true."

1 Kings xviii. Elijah with the prophets of Baal.

In the dispute concerning the true God and the truth of religion, there has never happened any miracle on the side of error, and not of truth.

827

Opposition.—Abel, Cain; Moses, the Magicians; Elijah, the false prophets: Jeremiah, Hananiah; Micaiah, the false prophets; Jesus Christ, the Pharisees; St. Paul, Bar-jesus; the Apostles, the Exorcists; Christians, unbelievers; Catholics, heretics; Elijah, Enoch, Antichrist.

828

Jesus Christ says that the Scriptures testify of Him. But He does not point out in what respect.

Even the prophecies could not prove Jesus Christ during His life; and so, men would not have been culpable for not believing in Him before His death, had the miracles not sufficed without doctrine. Now those who did not believe in Him, when He was still alive, were sinners, as He said Himself, and without excuse. Therefore they must have had proof beyond doubt, which they resisted. Now, they had not the prophecies, but only the miracles. Therefore the latter suffice, when the doctrine is not inconsistent with them; and they ought to be believed.[Pg 245]

John vii, 40. Dispute among the Jews as among the Christians of to-day. Some believed in Jesus Christ; others believed Him not, because of the prophecies which said that He should be born in Bethlehem. They should have considered more carefully whether He was not. For His miracles being convincing, they should have been quite sure of these supposed contradictions of His teaching to Scripture; and this obscurity did not excuse, but blinded them. Thus those who refuse to believe in the miracles in the present day on account of a supposed contradiction, which is unreal, are not excused.

The Pharisees said to the people, who believed in Him, because of His miracles: "This people who knoweth not the law are cursed. But have any of the rulers or of the Pharisees believed on him? For we know that out of Galilee ariseth no prophet." Nicodemus answered: "Doth our law judge any man before it hear him, [and specially, such a man who works such miracles]?"

829

The prophecies were ambiguous; they are no longer so.

830

The five propositions were ambiguous; they are no longer so.

831

Miracles are no longer necessary, because we have had them already. But when tradition is no longer minded; when the Pope alone is offered to us; when he has been imposed upon; and when the true source of truth, which is tradition, is thus excluded; and the Pope, who is its guardian, is biased; the truth is no longer free to appear. Then, as men speak no longer of truth, truth itself must speak to men. This is what happened in the time of Arius. (Miracles under Diocletian and under Arius.)

832

Miracle.—The people concluded this of themselves; but if the reason of it must be given to you ...

It is unfortunate to be in exception to the rule. The same must be strict, and opposed to exception. But yet, as it is certain that there are exceptions to a rule, our judgment must though strict, be just.[Pg 246]

833

John vi, 26: Non quia vidisti signum, sed quia saturati estis.

Those who follow Jesus Christ because of His miracles honour His power in all the miracles which it produces. But those who, making profession to follow Him because of His miracles, follow Him in fact only because He comforts them and satisfies them with worldly blessings, discredit His miracles, when they are opposed to their own comforts.

John ix: Non est hic homo a Deo, quia sabbatum non custodit. Alii: Quomodo potest homo peccator hæc signa facere?

Which is the most clear?

This house is not of God; for they do not there believe that the five propositions are in Jansenius. Others: This house is of God; for in it there are wrought strange miracles.

Which is the most clear?

Tu quid dicis? Dico quia propheta est. Nisi esset hic a Deo, non poterat facere quidquam.[330]

834

In the Old Testament, when they will turn you from God. In the New, when they will turn you from Jesus Christ. These are the occasions for excluding particular miracles from belief. No others need be excluded.

Does it therefore follow that they would have the right to exclude all the prophets who came to them? No; they would have sinned in not excluding those who denied God, and would have sinned in excluding those who did not deny God.

So soon, then, as we see a miracle, we must either assent to it, or have striking proofs to the contrary. We must see if it denies a God, or Jesus Christ, or the Church.

835

There is a great difference between not being for Jesus Christ and saying so, and not being for Jesus Christ and pretending to be so. The one party can do miracles, not the others. For it is clear of the one party, that they are opposed to the truth, but not of the others; and thus miracles are clearer.

836

That we must love one God only is a thing so evident, that it does not require miracles to prove it.[Pg 247]

837

Jesus Christ performed miracles, then the apostles, and the first saints in great number; because the prophecies not being yet accomplished, but in the process of being accomplished by them, the miracles alone bore witness to them. It was foretold that the Messiah should convert the nations. How could this prophecy be fulfilled without the conversion of the nations? And how could the nations be converted to the Messiah, if they did not see this final effect of the prophecies which prove Him? Therefore, till He had died, risen again, and converted the nations, all was not accomplished; and so miracles were needed during all this time. Now they are no longer needed against the Jews; for the accomplished prophecies constitute a lasting miracle.

838

"Though ye believe not Me, believe at least the works."[331] He refers them, as it were, to the strongest proof.

It had been told to the Jews, as well as to Christians, that they should not always believe the prophets; but yet the Pharisees and Scribes are greatly concerned about His miracles, and try to show that they are false, or wrought by the devil. For they must needs be convinced, if they acknowledge that they are of God.

At the present day we are not troubled to make this distinction. Still it is very easy to do: those who deny neither God nor Jesus Christ do no miracles which are not certain. Nemo facit virtutem in nomine meo, et cito possit de me male loqui.[332]

But we have not to draw this distinction. Here is a sacred relic.[333] Here is a thorn from the crown of the Saviour of the world, over whom the prince of this world has no power, which works miracles by the peculiar power of the blood shed for us. Now God Himself chooses this house in order to display conspiciously therein His power.

These are not men who do miracles by an unknown and doubtful virtue, which makes a decision difficult for us. It is God Himself. It is the instrument of the Passion of His only Son, who, being in many places, chooses this, and makes men come from all quarters there to receive these miraculous alleviations in their weaknesses.[Pg 248]

839

The Church has three kinds of enemies: the Jews, who have never been of her body; the heretics, who have withdrawn from it; and the evil Christians, who rend her from within.

These three kinds of different adversaries usually attack her in different ways. But here they attack her in one and the same way. As they are all without miracles, and as the Church has always had miracles against them, they have all had the same interest in evading them; and they all make use of this excuse, that doctrine must not be judged by miracles, but miracles by doctrine. There were two parties among those who heard Jesus Christ: those who followed His teaching on account of His miracles; others who said.... There were two parties in the time of Calvin.... There are now the Jesuits, etc.

840

Miracles furnish the test in matters of doubt, between Jews and heathens, Jews and Christians, Catholics and heretics, the slandered and slanderers, between the two crosses.

But miracles would be useless to heretics; for the Church, authorised by miracles which have already obtained belief, tells us that they have not the true faith. There is no doubt that they are not in it, since the first miracles of the Church exclude belief of theirs. Thus there is miracle against miracle, both the first and greatest being on the side of the Church.

These nuns,[334] astonished at what is said, that they are in the way of perdition; that their confessors are leading them to Geneva; that they suggest to them that Jesus Christ is not in the Eucharist, nor on the right hand of the Father; know that all this is false, and therefore offer themselves to God in this state. Vide si via iniquitatis in me est.[335] What happens thereupon? This place, which is said to be the temple of the devil, God makes His own temple. It is said that the children must be taken away from it. God heals them there. It is said that it is the arsenal of hell. God makes of it the sanctuary of His grace. Lastly, they are threatened with all the fury and vengeance of heaven; and God overwhelms them with favours. A man would need to have lost his senses to conclude from this that they are therefore in the way of perdition.

(We have without doubt the same signs as Saint Athanasius.)[Pg 249]

841

Si tu es Christus, dic nobis.[336]

Opera quæ ego facio in nomine patris mei, hæc testimonium perhibent de me. Sed vos non creditis quia non estis ex ovibus meis. Oves meœ vocem meam audiunt.[337]

John vi, 30. Quod ergo tu facis signum ut videamus et credamus tibi?—Non dicunt: Quam doctrinam prædicas?

Nemo potest facere signa quæ tu facis nisi Deus.[338]

2 Macc. xiv, 15. Deus qui signis evidentibus suam portionem protegit.

Volumus signum videre de cœlo, tentantes eum. Luke xi, 16.

Generatio prava signum quærit; et non dabitur.[339]

Et ingemiscens ait: Quid generatio ista signum quærit? (Mark viii, 12.) They asked a sign with an evil intention.

Et non poterat facere.[340] And yet he promises them the sign of Jonah, the great and wonderful miracle of his resurrection.

Nisi videritis, non creditis.[341] He does not blame them for not believing unless there are miracles, but for not believing unless they are themselves spectators of them.

Antichrist in signis mendacibus, says Saint Paul, 2 Thess. ii.

Secundum operationem Satanæ, in seductione iis qui pereunt eo quod charitatem veritatis non receperunt ut salvi fierent, ideo mittet illis Deus optationes erroris ut credant mendacio.

As in the passage of Moses: Tentat enim vos Deus, utrum diligatis eum.[342]

Ecce prædixi vobis: vos ergo videte.[343]

842

Here is not the country of truth. She wanders unknown amongst men. God has covered her with a veil, which leaves her unrecognised by those who do not hear her voice. Room is opened for blasphemy, even against the truths that are at least very likely. If the truths of the Gospel are published, the contrary is published too, and the questions are obscured, so that the people cannot distinguish. And they ask, "What have you to make you believed rather than others? What sign do you give? You have only words, and so have we. If you had miracles, good and well." That doctrine ought to be supported by miracles is a truth, which they misuse in order to revile doctrine. And if miracles happen, it is said that miracles are[Pg 250] not enough without doctrine; and this is another truth, which they misuse in order to revile miracles.

Jesus Christ cured the man born blind, and performed a number of miracles on the Sabbath day. In this way He blinded the Pharisees, who said that miracles must be judged by doctrine.

"We have Moses: but, as for this fellow, we know not from whence he is."[344] It is wonderful that you know not whence He is, and yet He does such miracles.

Jesus Christ spoke neither against God, nor against Moses.

Antichrist and the false prophets, foretold by both Testaments, will speak openly against God and against Jesus Christ. Who is not hidden ... God would not allow him, who would be a secret enemy, to do miracles openly.

In a public dispute where the two parties profess to be for God, for Jesus Christ, for the Church, miracles have never been on the side of the false Christians, and the other side has never been without a miracle.

"He hath a devil." John x, 21. And others said, "Can a devil open the eyes of the blind?"

The proofs which Jesus Christ and the apostles draw from Scripture are not conclusive; for they say only that Moses foretold that a prophet should come. But they do not thereby prove that this is He; and that is the whole question. These passages therefore serve only to show that they are not contrary to Scripture, and that there appears no inconsistency, but not that there is agreement. Now this is enough, namely, exclusion of inconsistency, along with miracles.

There is a mutual duty between God and men. We must pardon Him this saying: Quid debui?[345] "Accuse me," said God in Isaiah.

"God must fulfil His promises," etc.

Men owe it to God to accept the religion which He sends. God owes it to men not to lead them into error. Now, they would be led into error, if the workers of miracles announced a doctrine which should not appear evidently false to the light of common sense, and if a greater worker of miracles had not already warned men not to believe them.

Thus, if there were divisions in the Church, and the Arians, for example, who declared themselves founded on Scripture just as the

Catholics, had done miracles, and not the Catholics, men should have been led into error.[Pg 251]

For, as a man, who announces to us the secrets of God, is not worthy to be believed on his private authority, and that is why the ungodly doubt him; so when a man, as a token of the communion which he has with God, raises the dead, foretells the future, removes the seas, heals the sick, there is none so wicked as not to bow to him, and the incredulity of Pharaoh and the Pharisees is the effect of a supernatural obduracy.

When, therefore, we see miracles and a doctrine not suspicious, both on one side, there is no difficulty. But when we see miracles and suspicious doctrine on the same side, we must then see which is the clearest. Jesus Christ was suspected.

Bar-jesus blinded.[346] The power of God surpasses that of His enemies.

The Jewish exorcists[347] beaten by the devils, saying, "Jesus I know, and Paul I know; but who are ye?"

Miracles are for doctrine, and not doctrine for miracles.

If the miracles are true, shall we be able to persuade men of all doctrine? No; for this will not come to pass. Si angelus.[348] ...

Rule: we must judge of doctrine by miracles; we must judge of miracles by doctrine. All this is true, but contains no contradiction.

For we must distinguish the times.

How glad you are to know the general rules, thinking thereby to set up dissension, and render all useless! We shall prevent you, my father; truth is one and constant.

It is impossible, from the duty of God to men, that a man, hiding his evil teaching, and only showing the good, saying that he conforms to God and the Church, should do miracles so as to instil insensibly a false and subtle doctrine. This cannot happen.

And still less, that God, who knows the heart, should perform miracles in favour of such a one.

843

The three marks of religion: perpetuity, a good life, miracles. They destroy perpetuity by their doctrine of probability; a good life by their morals; miracles by destroying either their truth or the conclusions to be drawn from them.

If we believe them, the Church will have nothing to do with perpetuity, holiness, and miracles. The heretics deny them, or deny the conclusions to be drawn from them; they do the[Pg 252] same. But one would need to have no sincerity in order to deny them, or again to lose one's senses in order to deny the conclusions to be drawn from them.

Nobody has ever suffered martyrdom for the miracles which he says he has seen; for the folly of men goes perhaps to the length of martyrdom, for those which the Turks believe by tradition, but not for those which they have seen.

844

The heretics have always attacked these three marks, which they have not.

845

First objection: "An angel from heaven.[349] We must not judge of truth by miracles, but of miracles by truth. Therefore the miracles are useless."

Now they are of use, and they must not be in opposition to the truth. Therefore what Father Lingende[350] has said, that "God will not permit that a miracle may lead into error...."

When there shall be a controversy in the same Church, miracle will decide.

Second objection: "But Antichrist will do miracles."

The magicians of Pharaoh did not entice to error. Thus we cannot say to Jesus respecting Antichrist, "You have led me into error." For Antichrist will do them against Jesus Christ, and so they cannot lead into error. Either God will not permit false miracles, or He will procure greater.

[Jesus Christ has existed since the beginning of the world: this is more impressive than all the miracles of Antichrist.]

If in the same Church there should happen a miracle on the side of those in error, men would be led into error. Schism is visible; a miracle is visible. But schism is more a sign of error than a miracle is a sign of truth. Therefore a miracle cannot lead into error.

But apart from schism, error is not so obvious as a miracle is obvious. Therefore a miracle could lead into error.

Ubi est Deus tuus?[351] Miracles show Him, and are a light.

846

One of the anthems for Vespers at Christmas: Exortum est in tenebris lumen rectis corde.[Pg 253][352]

847

If the compassion of God is so great that He instructs us to our benefit, even when He hides Himself, what light ought we not to expect from Him when He reveals Himself?

848

Will Est et non est be received in faith itself as well as in miracles? And if it is inseparable in the others ...

When Saint Xavier[353] works miracles.—[Saint Hilary. "Ye wretches, who oblige us to speak of miracles."]

Unjust judges, make not your own laws on the moment; judge by those which are established, and by yourselves. Væ qui conditis leges iniquas.[354]

Miracles endless, false.

In order to weaken your adversaries, you disarm the whole Church.

If they say that our salvation depends upon God, they are "heretics." If they say that they are obedient to the Pope, that is "hypocrisy." If they are ready to subscribe to all the articles, that is not enough. If they say that a man must not be killed for an apple, "they attack the morality of Catholics." If miracles are done among them, it is not a sign of holiness, and is, on the contrary, a symptom of heresy.

This way in which the Church has existed is that truth has been without dispute, or, if it has been contested, there has been the Pope, or, failing him, there has been the Church.

849

The five propositions[355] condemned, but no miracle; for the truth was not attacked. But the Sorbonne ... but the bull....

It is impossible that those who love God with all their heart should fail to recognise the Church; so evident is she.—It is impossible that those who do not love God should be convinced of the Church.

Miracles have such influence that it was necessary that God should warn men not to believe in them in opposition to Him, all clear as it is that there is a God. Without this they would have been able to disturb men.

And thus so far from these passages, Deut. xiii, making against the authority of the miracles, nothing more indicates their influence. And the same in respect of Antichrist. "To seduce, if it were possible, even the elect."[Pg 254][356]

850

The history of the man born blind.

What says Saint Paul? Does he continually speak of the evidence of the prophecies? No, but of his own miracle. What says Jesus Christ? Does He speak of the evidence of the prophecies? No; His death had not fulfilled them. But He says, Si non fecissem.[357] Believe the works.

Two supernatural foundations of our wholly supernatural religion; one visible, the other invisible; miracles with grace, miracles without grace.

The synagogue, which had been treated with love as a type of the Church, and with hatred, because it was only the type, has been restored, being on the point of falling when it was well with God, and thus a type.

Miracles prove the power which God has over hearts, by that which He exercises over bodies.

The Church has never approved a miracle among heretics.

Miracles a support of religion: they have been the test of Jews; they have been the test of Christians, saints, innocents, and true believers.

A miracle among schismatics is not so much to be feared; for schism, which is more obvious than a miracle, visibly indicates their error. But when there is no schism, and error is in question, miracle decides.

Si non fecissem quæ alius non fecit. The wretches who have obliged us to speak of miracles.

Abraham and Gideon confirm faith by miracles.

Judith. God speaks at last in their greatest oppression.

If the cooling of love leaves the Church almost without believers, miracles will rouse them. This is one of the last effects of grace.

If one miracle were wrought among the Jesuits!

When a miracle disappoints the expectation of those in whose presence it happens, and there is a disproportion between the state of their faith and the instrument of the miracle, it ought then to induce them to change. But with you it is otherwise. There would be as much reason in saying that, if the Eucharist raised a dead man, it would be necessary for one to turn a Calvinist rather than remain a

Catholic. But when it crowns the expectation, and those, who hoped that God would bless the remedies, see themselves healed without remedies ...[Pg 255]

The ungodly.—No sign has ever happened on the part of the devil without a stronger sign on the part of God, or even without it having been foretold that such would happen.

851

Unjust persecutors of those whom God visibly protects. If they reproach you with your excesses, "they speak as the heretics." If they say that the grace of Jesus Christ distinguishes us, "they are heretics." If they do miracles, "it is the mark of their heresy."

Ezekiel.—They say: These are the people of God who speak thus.

It is said, "Believe in the Church";[358] but it is not said, "Believe in miracles"; because the last is natural, and not the first. The one had need of a precept, not the other. Hezekiah.

The synagogue was only a type, and thus it did not perish; and it was only a type, and so it is decayed. It was a type which contained the truth, and thus it has lasted until it no longer contained the truth.

My reverend father, all this happened in types. Other religions perish; this one perishes not.

Miracles are more important than you think. They have served for the foundation, and will serve for the continuation of the Church till Antichrist, till the end.

The two witnesses.

In the Old Testament and the New, miracles are performed in connection with types. Salvation, or a useless thing, if not to show that we must submit to the Scriptures: type of the sacrament.

852

[We must judge soberly of divine ordinances, my father.

Saint Paul in the isle of Malta.]

853

The hardness of the Jesuits, then, surpasses that of the Jews, since those refused to believe Jesus Christ innocent only because they doubted if His miracles were of God. Whereas the Jesuits, though unable to doubt that the miracles of Port-Royal are of God, do not cease to doubt still the innocence of that house.[Pg 256]

854

I suppose that men believe miracles. You corrupt religion either in favour of your friends, or against your enemies. You arrange it at your will.

855

On the miracle.—As God has made no family more happy, let it also be the case that He find none more thankful.

[Pg 257]

SECTION XIV

APPENDIX: POLEMICAL FRAGMENTS

856

Clearness, obscurity.—There would be too great darkness, if truth had not visible signs. This is a wonderful one, that it has always been preserved in one Church and one visible assembly [of men]. There would be too great clearness, if there were only one opinion in this Church. But in order to recognise what is true, one has only to look at what has always existed; for it is certain that truth has always existed, and that nothing false has always existed.

857

The history of the Church ought properly to be called the history of truth.

858

There is a pleasure in being in a ship beaten about by a storm, when we are sure that it will not founder. The persecutions which harass the Church are of this nature.

859

In addition to so many other signs of piety, they[359] are also persecuted, which is the best sign of piety.

860

The Church is in an excellent state, when it is sustained by God only.

861

The Church has always been attacked by opposite errors, but perhaps never at the same time, as now. And if she suffer more because of the multiplicity of errors, she derives this advantage from it, that they destroy each other.

She complains of both, but far more of the Calvinists, because of the schism.[Pg 258]

It is certain that many of the two opposite sects are deceived. They must be disillusioned.

Faith embraces many truths which seem to contradict each other. There is a time to laugh, and a time to weep,[360] etc. Responde. Ne respondeas,[361] etc.

The source of this is the union of the two natures in Jesus Christ; and also the two worlds (the creation of a new heaven and a new earth; a new life and a new death; all things double, and the same names remaining); and finally the two natures that are in the righteous, (for they are the two worlds, and a member and image of Jesus Christ. And thus all the names suit them: righteous, yet sinners; dead, yet living; living, yet dead; elect, yet outcast, etc.).

There are then a great number of truths, both of faith and of morality, which seem contradictory, and which all hold good together in a wonderful system. The source of all heresies is the exclusion of some of these truths; and the source of all the objections which the heretics make against us is the ignorance of some of our truths. And it generally happens that, unable to conceive the connection of two opposite truths, and believing that the admission of one involves the exclusion of the other, they adhere to the one, exclude the other, and think of us as opposed to them. Now exclusion is the cause of their heresy; and ignorance that we hold the other truth causes their objections.

1st example: Jesus Christ is God and man. The Arians, unable to reconcile these things, which they believe incompatible, say that He is man; in this they are Catholics. But they deny that He is God; in this they are heretics. They allege that we deny His humanity; in this they are ignorant.

2nd example: On the subject of the Holy Sacrament. We believe that, the substance of the bread being changed, and being consubstantial with that of the body of our Lord, Jesus Christ is therein really present. That is one truth. Another is that this Sacrament is also a type of the cross and of glory, and a commemoration of the two. That is the Catholic faith, which comprehends these two truths which seem opposed.

The heresy of to-day, not conceiving that this Sacrament contains at the same time both the presence of Jesus Christ and a type of Him, and that it is a sacrifice and a commemoration of a sacrifice, believes that neither of these truths can be admitted without excluding the other for this reason.

They fasten to this point alone, that this Sacrament is typical;[Pg 259] and in this they are not heretics. They think that we exclude this truth; hence it comes that they raise so many objections to us out of the passages of the Fathers which assert it. Finally, they deny the presence; and in this they are heretics.

3rd example: Indulgences.

The shortest way, therefore, to prevent heresies is to instruct in all truths; and the surest way to refute them is to declare them all. For what will the heretics say?

In order to know whether an opinion is a Father's ...

862

All err the more dangerously, as they each follow a truth. Their fault is not in following a falsehood, but in not following another truth.

863

Truth is so obscure in these times, and falsehood so established, that unless we love the truth, we cannot know it.

864

If there is ever a time in which we must make profession of two opposite truths, it is when we are reproached for omitting one. Therefore the Jesuits and Jansenists are wrong in concealing them, but the Jansenists more so, for the Jesuits have better made profession of the two.

865

Two kinds of people make things equal to one another, as feasts to working days, Christians to priests, all things among them, etc. And hence the one party conclude that what is then bad for priests is also so for Christians, and the other that what is not bad for Christians is lawful for priests.

866

If the ancient Church was in error, the Church is fallen. If she should be in error to-day, it is not the same thing; for she has always the superior maxim of tradition from the hand of the ancient Church; and so this submission and this conformity to the ancient Church prevail and correct all. But the ancient Church did not assume the future Church, and did not consider her, as we assume and consider the ancient.[Pg 260]

867

That which hinders us in comparing what formerly occurred in the Church with what we see there now, is that we generally look upon

Saint Athanasius,[362] Saint Theresa, and the rest, as crowned with glory, and acting towards us as gods. Now that time has cleared up things, it does so appear. But at the time when he was persecuted, this great saint was a man called Athanasius; and Saint Theresa was a nun. "Elias was a man subject to like passions as we are," says Saint James, to disabuse Christians of that false idea which makes us reject the example of the saints, as disproportioned to our state. "They were saints," say we, "they are not like us." What then actually happened? Saint Athanasius was a man called Athanasius, accused of many crimes, condemned by such and such a council for such and such a crime. All the bishops assented to it, and finally the Pope. What said they to those who opposed this? That they disturbed the peace, that they created schism, etc.

Zeal, light. Four kinds of persons: zeal without knowledge; knowledge without zeal; neither knowledge nor zeal; both zeal and knowledge. The first three condemned him. The last acquitted him, were excommunicated by the Church, and yet saved the Church.

868

If Saint Augustine came at the present time, and was as little authorised as his defenders, he would accomplish nothing. God directs His Church well, by having sent him before with authority.

869

God has not wanted to absolve without the Church. As she has part in the offence, He desires her to have part in the pardon. He associates her with this power, as kings their parliaments. But if she absolves or binds without God, she is no longer the Church. For, as in the case of parliament, even if the king have pardoned a man, it must be ratified; but if parliament ratifies without the king, or refuses to ratify on the order of the king, it is no longer the parliament of the king, but a rebellious assembly.[Pg 261]

870

The Church, the Pope. Unity, plurality.—Considering the Church as a unity, the Pope, who is its head, is as the whole. Considering it as a plurality, the Pope is only a part of it. The Fathers have considered the Church now in the one way, now in the other. And thus they have spoken differently of the Pope. (Saint Cyprian: Sacerdos Dei.) But in establishing one of these truths, they have not excluded the other. Plurality which is not reduced to unity is confusion; unity which does not depend on plurality is tyranny. There is scarcely any other country than France in which it is permissible to say that the Council is above the Pope.

871

The Pope is head. Who else is known of all? Who else is recognised by all, having power to insinuate himself into all the body, because he holds the principal shoot, which insinuates itself everywhere? How easy it was to make this degenerate into tyranny! That is why Christ has laid down for them this precept: Vos autem non sic.[363]

872

The Pope hates and fears the learned, who do not submit to him at will.

873

We must not judge of what the Pope is by some words of the Fathers —as the Greeks said in a council, important rules—but by the acts of the Church and the Fathers, and by the canons.

Duo aut tres in unum.[364] Unity and plurality. It is an error to exclude one of the two, as the papists do who exclude plurality, or the Huguenots who exclude unity.

874

Would the Pope be dishonoured by having his knowledge from God and tradition; and is it not dishonouring him to separate him from this holy union?

875

God does not perform miracles in the ordinary conduct of His Church. It would be a strange miracle if infallibility existed in one man. But it appears so natural for it to reside[Pg 262] in a multitude, since the conduct of God is hidden under nature, as in all His other works.

876

Kings dispose of their own power; but the Popes cannot dispose of theirs.

877

Summum jus, summa injuria.

The majority is the best way, because it is visible, and has strength to make itself obeyed. Yet it is the opinion of the least able.

If men could have done it, they would have placed might in the hands of justice. But as might does not allow itself to be managed as men want, because it is a palpable quality, whereas justice is a spiritual quality of which men dispose as they please, they have placed justice in the hands of might. And thus that is called just which men are forced to obey.

Hence comes the right of the sword, for the sword gives a true right. Otherwise we should see violence on one side and justice on the other (end of the twelfth Provincial). Hence comes the injustice of the Fronde,[365] which raises its alleged justice against power. It is not the same in the Church, for there is a true justice and no violence.

878

Injustice.—Jurisdiction is not given for the sake of the judge, but for that of the litigant. It is dangerous to tell this to the people. But the people have too much faith in you; it will not harm them, and may serve you. It should therefore be made known. Pasce oves meas,[366] non tuas. You owe me pasturage.

879

Men like certainty. They like the Pope to be infallible in faith, and grave doctors to be infallible in morals, so as to have certainty.

880

The Church teaches, and God inspires, both infallibly. The work of the Church is of use only as a preparation for grace or condemnation. What it does is enough for condemnation, not for inspiration.[Pg 263]

881

Every time the Jesuits may impose upon the Pope, they will make all Christendom perjured.

The Pope is very easily imposed upon, because of his occupations, and the confidence which he has in the Jesuits; and the Jesuits are very capable of imposing upon him by means of calumny.

882

The wretches who have obliged me to speak of the basis of religion.

883

Sinners purified without penitence; the righteous justified without love; all Christians without the grace of Jesus Christ; God without power over the will of men; a predestination without mystery; a redemption without certitude!

884

Any one is made a priest, who wants to be so, as under Jeroboam.[367]

It is a horrible thing that they propound to us the discipline of the Church of to-day as so good, that it is made a crime to desire to change it. Formerly it was infallibly good, and it was thought that it could be changed without sin; and now, such as it is, we cannot wish it changed! It has indeed been permitted to change the custom of not making priests without such great circumspection, that there were hardly any who were worthy; and it is not allowed to complain of the custom which makes so many who are unworthy!

885

Heretics.—Ezekiel. All the heathen, and also the Prophet, spoke evil of Israel. But the Israelites were so far from having the right to say to him, "You speak like the heathen," that he is most forcible upon this, that the heathen say the same as he.

886

The Jansenists are like the heretics in the reformation of morality; but you are like them in evil.[Pg 264]

887

You are ignorant of the prophecies, if you do not know that all this must happen; princes, prophets, Pope, and even the priests. And yet the Church is to abide. By the grace of God we have not come to that. Woe to these priests! But we hope that God will bestow His mercy upon us that we shall not be of them.

Saint Peter, ii: false prophets in the past, the image of future ones.

888

... So that if it is true, on the one hand, that some lax monks, and some corrupt casuists, who are not members of the hierarchy, are steeped in these corruptions, it is, on the other hand, certain that the true pastors of the Church, who are the true guardians of the Divine Word, have preserved it unchangeably against the efforts of those who have attempted to destroy it.

And thus true believers have no pretext to follow that laxity, which is only offered to them by the strange hands of these casuists, instead of the sound doctrine which is presented to them by the fatherly hands of their own pastors. And the ungodly and heretics have no ground for publishing these abuses as evidence of imperfection in the providence of God over His Church; since, the Church consisting properly in the body of the hierarchy, we are so far from being able to conclude from the present state of matters that God has abandoned her to corruption, that it has never been more apparent than at the present time that God visibly protects her from corruption.

For if some of these men, who, by an extraordinary vocation, have made profession of withdrawing from the world and adopting the monks' dress, in order to live in a more perfect state than ordinary Christians, have fallen into excesses which horrify ordinary Christians, and have become to us what the false prophets were among the Jews; this is a private and personal misfortune, which must indeed be deplored, but from which nothing can be inferred against the care which God takes of His Church; since all these things are so clearly foretold, and it has been so long since announced that these temptations would arise from people of this kind; so that when we are well instructed, we see in this rather evidence of the care of God than of His forgetfulness in regard to us.[Pg 265]

889

Tertullian: Nunquam Ecclesia reformabitur.

890

Heretics, who take advantage of the doctrine of the Jesuits, must be made to know that it is not that of the Church [the doctrine of the Church], and that our divisions do not separate us from the altar.

891

If in differing we condemned, you would be right. Uniformity without diversity is useless to others; diversity without uniformity is ruinous for us. The one is harmful outwardly; the other inwardly.

892

By showing the truth, we cause it to be believed; but by showing the injustice of ministers, we do not correct it. Our mind is assured by a proof of falsehood; our purse is not made secure by proof of injustice.

893

Those who love the Church lament to see the corruption of morals; but laws at least exist. But these corrupt the laws. The model is damaged.

894

Men never do evil so completely and cheerfully as when they do it from religious conviction.

895

It is in vain that the Church has established these words, anathemas, heresies, etc. They are used against her.

896

The servant knoweth not what his lord doeth, for the master tells him only the act and not the intention.[368] And this is why he often obeys slavishly, and defeats the intention. But Jesus Christ has told us the object. And you defeat that object.

897

They cannot have perpetuity, and they seek universality; and therefore they make the whole Church corrupt, that they may be saints.[Pg 266]

898

Against those who misuse passages of Scripture, and who pride themselves in finding one which seems to favour their error.—The chapter for Vespers, Passion Sunday, the prayer for the king.

Explanation of these words: "He that is not with me is against me."[369] And of these others: "He that is not against you is for you."[370] A person who says: "I am neither for nor against", we ought to reply to him ...

899

He who will give the meaning of Scripture, and does not take it from Scripture, is an enemy of Scripture. (Aug., De Doct. Christ.)

900

Humilibus dat gratiam; an ideo non dedit humilitatem?[371]

Sui eum non receperunt; quotquot autem non receperunt an non erant sui?[372]

901

"It must indeed be," says Feuillant, "that this is not so certain; for controversy indicates uncertainty, (Saint Athanasius, Saint Chrysostom, morals, unbelievers)."

The Jesuits have not made the truth uncertain, but they have made their own ungodliness certain.

Contradiction has always been permitted, in order to blind the wicked; for all that offends truth or love is evil. This is the true principle.

902

All religions and sects in the world have had natural reason for a guide. Christians alone have been constrained to take their rules from without themselves, and to acquaint themselves with those which Jesus Christ bequeathed to men of old to be handed down to true believers. This constraint wearies these good Fathers. They desire, like other people, to have liberty to follow their own imaginations. It is in vain that we cry to them, as the prophets said to the Jews of old: "Enter into the Church; acquaint yourselves with the precepts which the men of old left to her, and follow those paths." They have answered like the Jews: "We will not walk in them; but we will follow the thoughts of our hearts"; and they have said, "We will be as the other nations."[Pg 267][373]

903

They make a rule of exception.

Have the men of old given absolution before penance? Do this as exceptional. But of the exception you make a rule without exception, so that you do not even want the rule to be exceptional.

904

On confessions and absolutions without signs of regret.

God regards only the inward; the Church judges only by the outward. God absolves as soon as He sees penitence in the heart; the Church when she sees it in works. God will make a Church pure within, which confounds, by its inward and entirely spiritual holiness, the inward impiety of proud sages and Pharisees; and the Church will make an assembly of men whose external manners are so pure as to confound the manners of the heathen. If there are hypocrites among them, but so well disguised that she does not discover their venom, she tolerates them; for, though they are not accepted of God, whom they cannot deceive, they are of men, whom they do deceive. And thus she is not dishonoured by their conduct, which appears holy. But you want the Church to judge neither of the inward, because that belongs to God alone, nor of the outward, because God dwells only upon the inward; and thus, taking away from her all choice of men, you retain in the Church the most dissolute, and those who dishonour her so greatly, that the synagogues of the Jews and sects of philosophers would have banished them as unworthy, and have abhorred them as impious.

905

The easiest conditions to live in according to the world are the most difficult to live in according to God, and vice versa. Nothing is so difficult according to the world as the religious life; nothing is easier than to live it according to God. Nothing is easier, according to the world, than to live in high office and great wealth; nothing is more difficult than to live in them according to God, and without acquiring an interest in them and a liking for them.

906

The casuists submit the decision to the corrupt reason, and the choice of decisions to the corrupt will, in order that all[Pg 268] that is corrupt in the nature of man may contribute to his conduct.

907

But is it probable that probability gives assurance?

Difference between rest and security of conscience. Nothing gives certainty but truth; nothing gives rest but the sincere search for truth.

908

The whole society itself of their casuists cannot give assurance to a conscience in error, and that is why it is important to choose good guides.

Thus they will be doubly culpable, both in having followed ways which they should not have followed, and in having listened to teachers to whom they should not have listened.

909

Can it be anything but compliance with the world which makes you find things probable? Will you make us believe that it is truth, and that if duelling were not the fashion, you would find it probable that they might fight, considering the matter in itself?

910

Must we kill to prevent there being any wicked? This is to make both parties wicked instead of one. Vince in bono malum.[374] (Saint Augustine.)

911

Universal.—Ethics and language are special, but universal sciences.

912

Probability.—Each one can employ it; no one can take it away.

913

They allow lust to act, and check scruples; whereas they should do the contrary.

914

Montalte.[375]—Lax opinions please men so much, that it is strange that theirs displease. It is because they have exceeded all[Pg 269] bounds. Again, there are many people who see the truth, and who cannot attain to it; but there are few who do not know that the purity of religion is opposed to our corruptions. It is absurd to say that an eternal recompense is offered to the morality of Escobar.

915

Probability.—They have some true principles; but they misuse them. Now, the abuse of truth ought to be as much punished as the introduction of falsehood.

As if there were two hells, one for sins against love, the other for those against justice!

916

Probability.[376]—The earnestness of the saints in seeking the truth was useless, if the probable is trustworthy. The fear of the saints who have always followed the surest way (Saint Theresa having always followed her confessor).

917

Take away probability, and you can no longer please the world; give probability, and you can no longer displease it.

918

These are the effects of the sins of the peoples and of the Jesuits. The great have wished to be flattered. The Jesuits have wished to be loved by the great. They have all been worthy to be abandoned to the spirit of lying, the one party to deceive, the others to be deceived. They have been avaricious, ambitious, voluptuous. Coacervabunt tibi magistros.[377] Worthy disciples of such masters, they have sought flatterers, and have found them.

919

If they do not renounce their doctrine of probability, their good maxims are as little holy as the bad, for they are founded on human authority; and thus, if they are more just, they will be more reasonable, but not more holy. They take after the wild stem on which they are grafted.[Pg 270]

If what I say does not serve to enlighten you, it will be of use to the people.

If these[378] are silent, the stones will speak.

Silence is the greatest persecution; the saints were never silent. It is true that a call is necessary; but it is not from the decrees of the Council that we must learn whether we are called, it is from the necessity of speaking. Now, after Rome has spoken, and we think that she has condemned the truth, and that they have written it, and after the books which have said the contrary are censured; we must cry out so much the louder, the more unjustly we are censured, and the more violently they would stifle speech, until there come a Pope who hears both parties, and who consults antiquity to do justice. So the good Popes will find the Church still in outcry.

The Inquisition and the Society[379] are the two scourges of the truth.

Why do you not accuse them of Arianism? For, though they have said that Jesus Christ is God, perhaps they mean by it not the natural interpretation, but as it is said, Dii estis.

If my Letters are condemned at Rome, that which I condemn in them is condemned in heaven. Ad tuum, Domine Jesu, tribunal appello.

You yourselves are corruptible.

I feared that I had written ill, seeing myself condemned; but the example of so many pious writings makes me believe the contrary. It is no longer allowable to write well, so corrupt or ignorant is the Inquisition!

"It is better to obey God than men."

I fear nothing; I hope for nothing. It is not so with the bishops. Port-Royal fears, and it is bad policy to disperse them; for they will fear no longer and will cause greater fear. I do not even fear your like censures, if they are not founded on those of tradition. Do you censure all? What! even my respect? No. Say then what, or you will do nothing, if you do not point out the evil, and why it is evil. And this is what they will have great difficulty in doing.

Probability.—They have given a ridiculous explanation of certitude; for, after having established that all their ways are sure, they have no longer called that sure which leads to heaven without danger of not arriving there by it, but that which leads there without danger of going out of that road.[Pg 271]

920

... The saints indulge in subtleties in order to think themselves criminals, and impeach their better actions. And these indulge in subtleties in order to excuse the most wicked.

The heathen sages erected a structure equally fine outside, but upon a bad foundation; and the devil deceived men by this apparent resemblance based upon the most different foundation.

Man never had so good a cause as I; and others have never furnished so good a capture as you....

The more they point out weakness in my person, the more they authorise my cause.

You say that I am a heretic. Is that lawful? And if you do not fear that men do justice, do you not fear that God does justice?

You will feel the force of the truth, and you will yield to it ...

There is something supernatural in such a blindness. Digna necessitas. [380] Mentiris impudentissime ...

Doctrina sua noscitur vir ...

False piety, a double sin.

I am alone against thirty thousand. No. Protect, you, the court; protect, you, deception; let me protect the truth. It is all my strength. If I lose it, I am undone. I shall not lack accusations, and persecutions. But I possess the truth, and we shall see who will take it away.

I do not need to defend religion, but you do not need to defend error and injustice. Let God, out of His compassion, having no regard to the evil which is in me, and having regard to the good which is in you, grant us all grace that truth may not be overcome in my hands, and that falsehood ...

921

Probable.—Let us see if we seek God sincerely, by comparison of the things which we love. It is probable that this food will not poison me. It is probable that I shall not lose my action by not prosecuting it ...

922

It is not absolution only which remits sins by the sacrament of penance, but contrition, which is not real if it does not seek the sacrament.[Pg 272]

923

People who do not keep their word, without faith, without honour, without truth, deceitful in heart, deceitful in speech; for which that amphibious animal in fable was once reproached, which held itself in a doubtful position between the fish and the birds ...

It is important to kings and princes to be considered pious; and therefore they must confess themselves to you.

[Pg 273]

NOTES

The following brief notes are mainly based on those of M. Brunschvicg. But those of MM. Faugère, Molinier, and Havet have also been consulted. The biblical references are to the Authorised English Version. Those in the text are to the Vulgate, except where it has seemed advisable to alter the reference to the English Version.

[1] P. 1, l. 1. The difference between the mathematical and the intuitive mind.—Pascal is here distinguishing the logical or discursive type of mind, a good example of which is found in mathematical

reasoning, and what we should call the intuitive type of mind, which sees everything at a glance. A practical man of sound judgment exemplifies the latter; for he is in fact guided by impressions of past experience, and does not consciously reason from general principles.

[2] P. 2, l. 34. There are different kinds, etc.—This is probably a subdivision of the discursive type of mind.

[3] P. 3, l. 31. By rule.—This is an emendation by M. Brunschvicg. The MS. has sans règle.

[4] P. 4, l. 3. I judge by my watch.—Pascal is said to have always carried a watch attached to his left wrist-band.

[5] P. 5, l. 21. Scaramouch.—A traditional character in Italian comedy.

[6] P. 5, l. 22. The doctor.—Also a traditional character in Italian comedy.

[7] P. 5, l. 24. Cleobuline.—Princess, and afterwards Queen of Corinth, figures in the romance of Mademoiselle de Scudéry, entitled Artamène ou le Grand Cyrus. She is enamoured of one of her subjects, Myrinthe. But she "loved him without thinking of love; and remained so long in that error, that this affection was no longer in a state to be overcome, when she became aware of it." The character is supposed to have been drawn from Christina of Sweden.

[8] P. 6, l. 21. Rivers are, etc.—Apparently suggested by a chapter in Rabelais: How we descended in the isle of Odes, in which the roads walk.

[9] P. 6, l. 30. Salomon de Tultie.—A pseudonym adopted by Pascal as the author of the Provincial Letters.

[10] P. 7, l. 7. Abstine et sustine.—A maxim of the Stoics.

[Pg 274]

[11] P. 7, l. 8. Follow nature.—The maxim in which the Stoics summed up their positive ethical teaching.

[12] P. 7, l. 9. As Plato.—Compare Montaigne, Essais, iii, 9.

[13] P. 9, l. 29. We call this jargon poetical beauty.—According to M. Havet, Pascal refers here to Malherbe and his school.

[14] P. 10, l. 23. Ne quid nimis.—Nothing in excess, a celebrated maxim in ancient Greek philosophy.

[15] P. 11, l. 26. That epigram about two one-eyed people.—M. Havet points out that this is not Martial's, but is to be found in Epigrammatum Delectus, published by Port-Royal in 1659.

Lumine Æon dextro, capta est Leonilla sinistro,
Et potis est forma vincere uterque deos.
Blande puer, lumen quod habes concede parenti,
Sic tu cæcus Amor, sic erit ilia Venus.

[16] P. 11, l. 29. Ambitiosa recidet ornamenta.—Horace, De Arte Poetica, 447.

[17] P. 13, l. 2. Cartesian.—One who follows the philosophy of Descartes (1596-1650), "the father of modern philosophy."

[18] P. 13, l. 8. Le Maître.—A famous French advocate in Pascal's time. His Plaidoyers el Harangues appeared in 1657. Plaidoyer VI is entitled Pour un fils mis en religion par force, and on the first page occurs the word répandre: "Dieu qui répand des aveuglements et des ténèbres sur les passions illégitimes." Pascal's reference is probably to this passage.

[19] P. 13, l. 12. The Cardinal.—Mazarin. He was one of those statesmen who do not like condolences.

[20] P. 14, l. 12. Saint Thomas.—Thomas Aquinas (1223-74), one of the greatest scholastic philosophers.

[21] P. 14, l. 16. Charron.—A friend of Montaigne. His Traité de la Sagesse (1601), which is not a large book, contains 117 chapters, each of which is subdivided.

[22] P. 14, l. 17. Of the confusion of Montaigne.—The Essays of Montaigne follow each other without any kind of order.

[23] P. 14, l. 27. Mademoiselle de Gournay.—The adopted daughter of Montaigne. She published in 1595 an edition of his Essais, and, in a Preface (added later), she defends him on this point.

[24] P. 15, l. 1. People without eyes.—Montaigne, Essais, ii, 12.

[25] P. 15, l. 1. Squaring the circle.—Ibid., ii, 14.

[26] P. 15, l. 1. A greater world.—Ibid., ii, 12.

[27] P. 15, l. 2. On suicide and on death.—Ibid., ii, 3.

[28] P. 15, l. 3. Without fear and without repentance.—Ibid., iii., 2.

[29] P. 15, l. 7. (730, 231).—These two references of Pascal are to the edition of the Essais of Montaigne, published in 1636.

[Pg 275]

[30] P. 16, l. 32. The centre which is everywhere, and the circumference nowhere.—M. Havet traces this saying to Empedocles. Pascal must have read it in Mlle de Gournay's preface to her edition of Montaigne's Essais.

[31] P. 18, l. 33. I will speak of the whole.—This saying of Democritus is quoted by Montaigne, Essais, ii, 12.

[32] P. 18, l. 37. Principles of Philosophy.—The title of one of Descartes's philosophical writings, published in 1644. See note on p. 13, l. 8 above.

[33] P. 18, l. 39. De omni scibili.—The title under which Pico della Mirandola announced nine hundred propositions which he proposed to uphold publicly at Rome in 1486.

[34] P. 19, l. 26. Beneficia eo usque læta sunt.—Tacitus, Ann., lib. iv, c. xviii. Compare Montaigne, Essais, iii, 8.

[35] P. 21, l. 35. Modus quo, etc.—St. Augustine, De Civ. Dei, xxi, 10. Montaigne, Essais, ii, 12.

[36] P. 22, l. 8. Felix qui, etc.—Virgil, Georgics, ii, 489, quoted by Montaigne, Essais, iii, 10.

[37] P. 22, l. 10. Nihil admirari, etc.—Horace, Epistles, I. vi. 1. Montaigne, Essais, ii, 10.

[38] P. 22, l. 19. 394.—A reference to Montaigne, Essais, ii, 12.

[39] P. 22, l. 20. 395.—Ibid.

[40] P. 22, l. 22. 399.—Ibid.

[41] P. 22, l. 28. Harum sententiarum.—Cicero, Tusc., i, 11, Montaigne, Essais, ii, 12.

[42] P. 22, l. 39. Felix qui, etc.—See above, notes on p. 22, l. 8 and l. 10.

[43] P. 22, l. 40. 280 kinds of sovereign good in Montaigne.—Essais, ii, 12.

[44] P. 23, l. 1. Part I, 1, 2, c. 1, section 4.—This reference is to Pascal's Traité du vide.

[45] P. 23, l. 25. How comes it, etc.—Montaigne, Essais, iii, 8.

[46] P. 23, l. 29. See Epictetus, Diss., iv, 6. He was a great Roman Stoic in the time of Domitian.

[47] P. 24, l. 9. It is natural, etc.—Compare Montaigne, Essais, i, 4.

[48] P. 24, l. 12. Imagination.—This fragment is suggestive of Montaigne. See Essais, iii, 8.

[49] P. 25, l. 16. If the greatest philosopher, etc. See Raymond Sebond's Apologie, from which Pascal has derived his illustrations.

[50] P. 26, l. 1. Furry cats.—Montaigne, Essais, ii, 8.

[51] P. 26, l. 31. Della opinione, etc.—No work is known under this name. It may refer to a treatise by Carlo Flori, which bears a title like

this. But its date (1690) is after Pascal's death (1662), though there may have been earlier editions.

[52] P. 27, l. 12. Source of error in diseases.—Montaigne, Essais, ii, 12.

[53] P. 27, l. 27. They rival each other, etc.—Ibid.

[54] P. 28, l. 31. Næ iste, etc.—Terence, Heaut., IV, i, 8. Montaigne, Essais, iii, 1.

[55] P. 28, l. 15. Quasi quidquam, etc.—Plin., ii, 7. Montaigne, ibid.

[56] P. 28, l. 29. Quod crebro, etc.—Cicero, De Divin., ii, 49.

[57] P. 29, l. 1. Spongia solis.—The spots on the sun. Pascal sees in[Pg 276] them the beginning of the darkening of the sun, and thinks that there will therefore come a day when there will be no sun.

[58] P. 29, l. 15. Custom is a second nature, etc.—Montaigne, Essais, i, 22.

[59] P. 29, l. 19. Omne animal.—See Genesis vii, 14.

[60] P. 30, l. 22. Hence savages, etc.—Montaigne, Essais, i, 22.

[61] P. 32, l. 3. A great part of Europe, etc.—An allusion to the Reformation.

[62] P. 33, l. 13. Alexander's chastity.—Pascal apparently has in mind Alexander's treatment of Darius's wife and daughters after the battle of Issus.

[63] P. 34, l. 17. Lustravit lampade terras.—Part of Cicero's translation of two lines from Homer, Odyssey, xviii, 136. Montaigne, Essais, ii, 12.

Tales sunt hominum mentes, quali pater ipse
Jupiter auctiferas lustravit lampade terras.

[64] P. 34, l. 32. Nature gives, etc.—Montaigne, Essais, i, 19.

[65] P. 37, l. 23. Our nature consists, etc.—Montaigne, Essais, iii, 13.

[66] P. 38, l. 1. Weariness.—Compare Montaigne, Essais, ii, 12.

[67] P. 38, l. 8. Cæsar was too old, etc.—See Montaigne, Essais, ii, 34.

[68] P. 38, l. 30. A mere trifle, etc.—Montaigne, Essais, iii, 4.

[69] P. 40, l. 21. Advice given to Pyrrhus.—Ibid., i, 42.

[70] P. 41, l. 2. They do not know, etc.—Ibid., i, 19.

[71] P. 44, l. 14. They are, etc.—Compare Montaigne, Essais, i, 38.

[72] P. 46, l. 7. Those who write, etc.—A thought of Cicero in Pro Archia, mentioned by Montaigne, Essais, i, 41.

[73] P. 47, l. 3. Ferox gens.—Livy, xxxiv, 17. Montaigne, Essais, i, 40.

[74] P. 47, l. 5. Every opinion, etc.—Montaigne, ibid.

[75] P. 47, l. 12. 184.—This is a reference to Montaigne, Essais, i, 40. See also ibid., iii, 10.

[76] P. 48, l. 8. I know not what (Corneille).—See Médée, II, vi, and Rodogune, I, v.

[77] P. 48, l. 22. In omnibus requiem quæsivi.—Eccles. xxiv, II, in the Vulgate.

[78] P. 50, l. 5. The future alone is our end.—Montaigne, Essais, i, 3.

[79] P. 50, l. 14. Solomon.—Considered by Pascal as the author of Ecclesiastes.

[80] P. 50, l. 20. Unconscious of approaching fever.—Compare Montaigne, Essais, i, 19.

[81] P. 50, l. 22. Cromwell.—Cromwell died in 1658 of a fever, and not of the gravel. The Restoration took place in 1660, and this fragment was written about that date.

[82] P. 50, l. 28. The three hosts.—Charles I was beheaded in 1649; Queen Christina of Sweden abdicated in 1654; Jean Casimir, King of Poland, was deposed in 1656.[Pg 277]

[83] P. 50, l. 32. Macrobius.—A Latin writer of the fifth century. He was a Neo-Platonist in philosophy. One of his works is entitled Saturnalia.

[84] P. 51, l. 5. The great and the humble, etc.—See Montaigne, Essais, ii, 12.

[85] P. 53, l. 5. Miton.—A man of fashion in Paris known to Pascal.

[86] P. 53, l. 15. Deus absconditus.—Is. xiv, 15.

[87] P. 60, l. 26. Fascinatio nugacitatis.—Book of Wisdom iv, 12.

[88] P. 61, l. 10. Memoria hospitis, etc.—Book of Wisdom v, 15.

[89] P. 62, l. 5. Instability.—Compare Montaigne, Essais, iii, 12.

[90] P. 66, l. 19. Foolishness, stultitium.—I Cor. i, 18.

[91] P. 71, l. 5. To prove Divinity from the works of nature.—A traditional argument of the Stoics like Cicero and Seneca, and of rationalist theologians like Raymond Sebond, Charron, etc. It is the argument from Design in modern philosophy.

[92] P. 71, l. 27. Nemo novit, etc.— Matthew xi, 27. In the Vulgate, it is Neque patrem quis novit, etc. Pascal's biblical quotations are often incorrect. Many seem to have been made from memory.

[93] P. 71, l. 30. Those who seek God find Him.—Matthew vii, 7.

[94] P. 72, l. 3. Vere tu es Deus absconditus.—Is. xiv, 15.

[95] P. 72, l. 22. Ne evacuetur crux Christi.—I Cor. i, 17. In the Vulgate we haveut non instead of ne.

[96] P. 72, l. 25. The machine.—A Cartesian expression. Descartes considered animals as mere automata. According to Pascal, whatever does not proceed in us from reflective thought is a product of a

necessary mechanism, which has its root in the body, and which is continued into the mind in imagination and the passions. It is therefore necessary for man so to alter, and adjust this mechanism, that it will always follow, and not obstruct, the good will.

[97] P. 73, l. 3. Justus ex fide vivit.—Romans i, 17.

[98] P. 73, l. 5. Fides ex auditu.—Romans x, 17.

[99] P. 73, l. 12. The creature.—What is purely natural in us.

[100] P. 74, l. 15. Inclina cor meum, Deus.—Ps. cxix, 36.

[101] P. 75, l. 11. Unus quisque sibi Deum fingit.—See Book of Wisdom xv, 6, 16.

[102] P. 76, l. 34. Eighth beatitude.—Matthew v, 10. It is to the fourth beatitude that the thought directly refers.

[103] P. 77, l. 6. One thousand and twenty-eight.—The number of the stars according to Ptolemy's catalogue.

[104] P. 77, l. 29. Saint Augustine.—Epist. cxx, 3.

[105] P. 78, l. 1. Nisi efficiamini sicut parvuli.—Matthew xviii, 3.

[106] P. 80, l. 20. Inclina cor meum, Deus, in....—Ps. cxix, 36.

[107] P. 80, l. 22. Its establishment.—The constitution of the Christian Church.

[108] P. 81, l. 20. The youths and maidens and children of the Church would prophesy.—Joel ii, 28.[Pg 278]

[109] P. 83, l. 11. On what, etc.—See Montaigne, Essais, ii, 12.

[110] P. 84, l. 16. Nihil amplius ... est.—Ibid. Cicero, De Finibus, v, 21.

[111] P. 84, l. 17. Ex senatus ... exercentur.—Montaigne, Essais, iii, 1. Seneca, Letters, 95.

[112] P. 84, l. 18. Ut olim ... laboramus.—Montaigne, Essais, iii, 13. Tacitus, Ann., iii, 25.

[113] P. 84, l. 20. The interest of the sovereign.—The view of Thrasymachus in Plato's Republic, i, 338.

[114] P. 84, l. 21. Another, present custom.—The doctrine of the Cyrenaics. Montaigne, Essais, iii, 13.

[115] P. 84, l. 24. The mystical foundation of its authority.—Montaigne, Essais, iii, 13. See also ii, 12.

[116] P. 85, l. 2. The wisest of legislators.—Plato. See Republic, ii, 389, and v, 459.

[117] P. 85, l. 4. Cum veritatem, etc.—An inexact quotation from St. Augustine, De Civ. Dei, iv, 27. Montaigne, Essais, ii, 12.

[118] P. 85, l. 17. Veri juris.—Cicero, De Officiis, iii, 17. Montaigne, Essais, iii, I.

[119] P. 86, l. 9. When a strong man, etc.—Luke xi, 21.

[120] P. 86, l. 26. Because he who will, etc.—See Epictetus, Diss., iii, 12.

[121] P. 88, l. 19. Civil wars are the greatest of evils.—Montaigne, Essais, iii, 11.

[122] P. 89, l. 5. Montaigne.—Essais, i, 42.

[123] P. 91, l. 8. Savages laugh at an infant king.—An allusion to a visit of some savages to Europe. They were greatly astonished to see grown men obey the child king, Charles IX. Montaigne, Essais, i, 30.

[124] P. 92, l. 8. Man's true state.—See Montaigne, Essais, i, 54.

[125] P. 95, l. 3. Omnis ... vanitati.—Eccles. iii, 19.

[126] P. 95, l. 4. Liberabitur.—Romans viii, 20-21.

[127] P. 95, l. 4. Saint Thomas.—In his Commentary on the Epistle of St. James. James ii, 1.

[128] P. 96, l. 9. The account of the pike and frog of Liancourt.—The story is unknown. The Duc de Liancourt led a vicious life in youth, but was converted by his wife. He became one of the firmest supporters of Port-Royal.

[129] P. 97, l. 18. Philosophers.—The Stoics.

[130] P. 97, l. 24. Epictetus.—Diss., iv, 7.

[131] P. 97, l. 26. Those great spiritual efforts, etc.—On this, and the following fragment, see Montaigne, Essais, ii, 29.

[132] P. 98, l. 3. Epaminondas.—Praised by Montaigne, Essais, ii, 36. See also iii, 1.

[133] P. 98, l. 17. Plerumque gratæ principibus vices.—Horace, Odes, III, xxix, 13, cited by Montaigne, Essais, i, 42. Horace has divitibus instead of principibus.[Pg 279]

[134] P. 99, l. 4. Man is neither angel nor brute, etc.—Montaigne, Essais, iii, 13.

[135] P. 99, l. 14. Ut sis contentus, etc.—A quotation from Seneca. See Montaigne, Essais, ii, 3.

[136] P. 99, l. 21. Sen. 588.—Seneca, Letter to Lucilius, xv. Montaigne, Essais, iii, I.

[137] P. 99, l. 23. Divin.—Cicero, De Divin., ii, 58.

[138] P. 99, l. 25. Cic.—Cicero, Tusc, ii, 2. The quotation is inaccurate. Montaigne, Essais, ii, 12.

[139] P. 99, l. 27. Senec.—Seneca, Epist., 106.

[140] P. 99, l. 28. Id maxime, etc.—Cicero, De Off., i, 31.

[141] P. 99, l. 29. Hos natura, etc.—Virgil, Georgics, ii, 20.

[142] P. 99, l. 30. Paucis opus, etc.—Seneca, Epist., 106.

[143] P. 100, l. 3. Mihi sic usus, etc.—Terence, Heaut., I, i, 28.

[144] P. 100, l. 4. Rarum est, etc.—Quintilian, x, 7.

[145] P. 100, l. 5. Tot circa, etc.—M. Seneca, Suasoriæ, i, 4.

[146] P. 100, l. 6. Cic.—Cicero, Acad., i, 45.

[147] P. 100, l. 7. Nec me pudet, etc.—Cicero, Tusc., i, 25.

[148] P. 100, l. 8. Melius non incipiet.—The rest of the quotation is quam desinet. Seneca, Epist., 72.

[149] P. 100, l. 25. They win battles.—Montaigne, in his Essais, ii, 12, relates that the Portuguese were compelled to raise the siege of Tamly on account of the number of flies.

[150] P. 100, l. 27. When it is said, etc.—By Descartes.

[151] P. 102, l. 20. Arcesilaus.—A follower of Pyrrho, the sceptic. He lived in the third century before Christ.

[152] P. 105, l. 20. Ecclesiastes.—Eccles. viii, 17.

[153] P. 106, l. 16. The academicians.—Dogmatic sceptics, as opposed to sceptics who doubt their own doubt.

[154] P. 107, l. 10. Ego vir videns.—Lamentations iii, I.

[155] P. 108, l. 26. Evil is easy, etc.—The Pythagoreans considered the good as certain and finite, and evil as uncertain and infinite. Montaigne, Essais, i, 9.

[156] P. 109, l. 7. Paulus Æmilius.—Montaigne, Essais, i, 19. Cicero, Tusc., v, 40.

[157] P. 109, l. 30. Des Barreaux.—Author of a licentious love song. He was born in 1602, and died in 1673. Balzac call him "the new Bacchus."

[158] P. 110, l. 16. For Port-Royal.—The letters, A. P. R., occur in several places, and are generally thought to indicate what will be afterwards treated in lectures or conferences at Port-Royal, the famous Cistercian abbey, situated about eighteen miles from Paris. Founded early in the thirteenth century, it acquired its greatest fame in its closing years. Louis XIV was induced to believe it heretical; and the monastery was finally demolished in 1711. Its downfall was no doubt brought about by the Jesuits.[Pg 280]

[159] P. 113, l. 4. They all tend to this end.—Montaigne, Essais, i, 19.

[160] P. 119, l. 15. Quod ergo, etc.—Acts xvii, 23.

[161] P. 119, l. 26. Wicked demon.—Descartes had suggested the possibility of the existence of an evil genius to justify his method of universal doubt. See his First Meditation. The argument is quite Cartesian.

[162] P. 122, l. 18. Deliciæ meæ, etc.—Proverbs viii, 31.

[163] P. 122, l. 18. Effundam spiritum, etc.—Is. xliv, 3; Joel ii, 28.

[164] P. 122, l. 19. Dii estis.—Ps. lxxxii, 6.

[165] P. 122, l. 20. Omnis caro fænum.—Is. xl, 6.

[166] P. 122, l. 20. Homo assimilatus, etc.—Ps. xlix, 20.

[167] P. 124, l. 24. Sapientius est hominibus.—1 Cor. i, 25.

[168] P. 125, l. 1. Of original sin.—The citations from the Rabbis in this fragment are borrowed from a work of the Middle Ages, entitled Pugio christianorum ad impiorum perfidiam jugulandam et maxime judæorum. It was written in the thirteenth century by Raymond Martin, a Catalonian monk. An edition of it appeared in 1651, edited by Bosquet, Bishop of Lodève.

[169] P. 125, l. 24. Better is a poor and wise child, etc.—Eccles. iv, 13.

[170] P. 126, l. 17. Nemo ante, etc.—See Ovid, Met., iii, 137, and Montaigne, Essais, i, 18.

[171] P. 127, l. 10. Figmentum.—Borrowed from the Vulgate, Ps. ciii, 14.

[172] P. 128. l. 5. All that is in the world, etc.—First Epistle of St. John, ii, 16.

[173] P. 128, l. 7. Wretched is, etc.—M. Faugère thinks this thought is taken from St. Augustine's Commentary on Ps. cxxxvii, Super flumina Babylonis.

[174] P. 129, l. 6. Qui gloriatur, etc.—1 Cor. i, 31.

[175] P. 130, l. 13. Via, veritas.—John xiv, 6.

[176] P. 130, l. 14. Zeno.—The original founder of Stoicism.

[177] P. 130, l. 15. Epictetus.—Diss., iv, 6, 7.

[178] P. 131, l. 32. A body full of thinking members.—See I Cor. xii.

[179] P. 133, l. 5. Book of Wisdom.—ii, 6.

[180] P. 134, l. 28. Qui adhæret, etc.—1 Cor. vi, 17.

[181] P. 134, l. 36. Two laws.—Matthew xxii, 35-40; Mark xii, 28-31.

[182] P. 135, l. 6. The kingdom of God is within us.—Luke xvii, 29.

[183] P. 137, l. 1. Et non, etc.—Ps. cxliii, 2.

[184] P. 137, l. 3. The goodness of God leadeth to repentance.—Romans ii, 4.

[185] P. 137, l. 5. Let us do penance, etc.—See Jonah iii, 8, 9.

[186] P. 137, l. 27. I came to send war.—Matthew x, 34.

[187] P. 137, l. 28. I came to bring fire and the sword.—Luke xii, 49.

[188] P. 138, l. 2. Pharisee and the Publican.—Parable in Luke xviii, 9-14.

[189] P. 138, l. 13. Abraham.—Genesis xiv, 22-24.[Pg 281]

[190] P. 138, l. 17. Sub te erit appetitus tuus.—Genesis iv, 7.

[191] P. 140, l. 1. It is, etc.—A discussion on the Eucharist.

[192] P. 140, l. 34. Non sum dignus.—Luke vii, 6.

[193] P. 140, l. 35. Qui manducat indignus.—I Cor. xi, 29.

[194] P. 140, l. 36. Dignus est accipere.—Apoc. iv, II.

[195] P. 141. In the French edition on which this translation is based there was inserted the following fragment after No. 513:

"Work out your own salvation with fear."

Proofs of prayer. Petenti dabitur.

Therefore it is in our power to ask. On the other hand, there is God. So it is not in our power, since the obtaining of (the grace) to pray to Him is not in our power. For since salvation is not in us, and the obtaining of such grace is from Him, prayer is not in our power.

The righteous man should then hope no more in God, for he ought not to hope, but to strive to obtain what he wants.

Let us conclude then that, since man is now unrighteous since the first sin, and God is unwilling that he should thereby not be estranged from Him, it is only by a first effect that he is not estranged.

Therefore, those who depart from God have not this first effect without which they are not estranged from God, and those who do not depart from God have this first effect. Therefore, those whom we have seen possessed for some time of grace by this first effect, cease to pray, for want of this first effect.

Then God abandons the first in this sense.

It is doubtful, however that this fragment should be included in the Pensées, and it has seemed best to separate it from the text. It has only once before appeared—in the edition of Michaut (1896). The first half of it has been freely translated in order to give an interpretation in accordance with a suggestion from M. Emile Boutroux, the eminent authority on Pascal. The meaning seems to be this. In one sense it is in our power to ask from God, who promises to give us what we ask. But, in another sense, it is not in our power to ask; for it is not in our power to obtain the grace which is necessary in asking. We know that salvation is not in our power. Therefore some condition of salvation is not in our power. Now the conditions of salvation are two: (1) The asking for it, and (2) the obtaining it. But God promises to give us what we ask. Hence the obtaining is in our power. Therefore the condition which is not in our power must be the first, namely, the asking. Prayer presupposes a grace which it is not within our power to obtain.

After giving the utmost consideration to the second half of this obscure fragment, and seeking assistance from some eminent scholars, the translator has been compelled to give a strictly literal translation of it, without attempting to make sense.

[196] P. 141, l. 14. Lord, when saw we, etc.—Matthew xxv, 37.

[197] P. 143, l. 19. Qui justus est, justificetur adhuc.—Apoc. xxii, II.

[198] P. 144, l. 2. Corneille.—See his Horace, II, iii.[Pg 282]

[199] P. 144, l. 15. Corrumpunt mores, etc.—I Cor. xv, 33.

[200] P. 145. l. 25. Quod curiositate, etc.—St. Augustine, Sermon CXLI.

[201] P. 146, l. 34. Quia ... facere.—I Cor. i, 21.

[202] P. 148, l. 7. Turbare semetipsum.—John xi, 33. The text is turbavit seipsum.

[203] P. 148, l. 25. My soul is sorrowful even unto death.—Mark xiv, 34.

[204] P. 149, l. 3. Eamus. Processit.—John xviii, 4. But eamus does not occur. See, however, Matthew xxvi, 46.

[205] P. 150, l. 36. Eritis sicut, etc.—Genesis iv, 5.

[206] P. 151, l. 2. Noli me tangere.—John xx, 17.

[207] P. 156, l. 14. Vere discipuli, etc.—Allusions to John viii, 31, i, 47; viii, 36; vi, 32.

[208] P. 158, l. 41. Signa legem in electis meis.—Is. viii, 16. The text of the Vulgate is in discipulis meis.

[209] P. 159, l. 2. Hosea.—xiv, 9.

[210] P. 159, l. 13. Saint John.—xii, 39.

[211] P. 160, l. 17. Tamar.—Genesis xxxviii, 24-30.

[212] P. 160, l. 17. Ruth.—Ruth iv, 17-22.

[213] P. 163, l. 13. History of China.—A History of China in Latin had been published in 1658.

[214] P. 164, l. I. The five suns, etc.—Montaigne, Essais, iii, 6.

[215] P. 164, l. 9. Jesus Christ.—John v, 31.

[216] P. 164, l. 17. The Koran says, etc.—There is no mention of Saint Matthew in the Koran; but it speaks of the Apostles generally.

[217] P. 165, l. 35. Moses.—Deut. xxxi, 11.

[218] P. 166, l. 23. Carnal Christians.—Jesuits and Molinists.

[219] P. 170, l. 14. Whom he welcomed from afar.—John viii, 56.

[220] P. 170, l. 19. Salutare, etc.—Genesis xdix, 18.

[221] P. 173, l. 33. The Twelve Tables at Athens.—There were no such tables. About 450 B.C. a commission is said to have been

appointed in Rome to visit Greece and collect information to frame a code of law. This is now doubted, if not entirely discredited.

[222] P. 173, l. 35. Josephus.—Reply to Apion, ii, 16. Josephus, the Jewish historian, gained the favour of Titus, and accompanied him to the siege of Jerusalem. He defended the Jews against a contemporary grammarian, named Apion, who had written a violent satire on the Jews.

[223] P. 174, l. 27. Against Apion.—ii, 39. See preceding note.

[224] P. 174, l. 28. Philo.—A Jewish philosopher, who lived in the first century of the Christian era. He was one of the founders of the Alexandrian school of thought. He sought to reconcile Jewish tradition with Greek thought.

[225] P. 175, l. 20. Prefers the younger.—See No. 710.

[226] P. 176, l. 32. The books of the Sibyls and Trismegistus.—The Sibyls[Pg 283] were the old Roman prophetesses. Their predictions were preserved in three books at Rome, which Tarquinius Superbus had bought from the Sibyl of Erythræ. Trismegistus was the Greek name of the Egyptian god Thoth, who was regarded as the originator of Egyptian culture, the god of religion, of writing, and of the arts and sciences. Under his name there existed forty-two sacred books, kept by the Egyptian priests.

[227] P. 177, l. 3. Quis mihi, etc.—Numbers xi, 29. Quis tribuat ut omnis populus prophetet?

[228] P. 177, l. 25. Maccabees.—2 Macc. xi, 2.

[229] P. 177, l. 7. This book, etc.—Is. xxx, 8.

[230] P. 178, l. 9. Tertullian.—A Christian writer in the second century after Christ. The quotation is from his De Cultu Femin., ii, 3.

[231] P. 178, l. 16. (Θεὸς), etc.—Eusebius, Hist., lib. v, c. 8.

[232] P. 178, l. 22. And he took that from Saint Irenæus.—Hist., lib. x, c 25.

[233] P. 179, l. 5. The story in Esdras.—2 Esdras xiv. God appears to Esdras in a bush, and orders him to assemble the people and deliver the message. Esdras replies that the law is burnt. Then God commands him to take five scribes to whom for forty days He dictates the ancient law. This story conflicted with many passages in the prophets, and was therefore rejected from the Canon at the Council of Trent.

[234] P. 181, l. 14. The Kabbala.—The fantastic secret doctrine of interpretation of Scripture, held by a number of Jewish rabbis.

[235] P. 181, l. 26. Ut sciatis, etc.—Mark ii, 10, 11.

[236] P. 183, l. 29. This generation, etc.—Matthew xxiv, 34.

[237] P. 184, l. 11. Difference between dinner and supper.—Luke xiv, 12.

[238] P. 184, l. 28. The six ages, etc.—M. Havet has traced this to a chapter in St. Augustine, De Genesi contra Manichæos, i, 23.

[239] P. 184, l. 31. Forma futuri.—Romans v, 14.

[240] P. 186, l. 13. The Messiah, etc.—John xii, 34.

[241] P. 186, l. 30. If the light, etc.—Matthew vi, 23.

[242] P. 187, l. 1. Somnum suum.—Ps. lxxvi, 5.

[243] P. 187, l. 1. Figura hujus mundi.—1 Cor. vii, 31.

[244] P. 187, l. 2. Comedes panem tuum.—Deut. viii, 9. Panem nostrum, Luke xi, 3.

[245] P. 187, l. 3. Inimici Dei terram lingent.—Ps. lxxii, 9.

[246] P. 187, l. 8. Cum amaritudinibus.—Exodus xii, 8. The Vulgate has cum lacticibus agrestibus.

[247] P. 187, l. 9. Singularis sum ego donec transeam.—Ps. cxli, 10.

[248] P. 188, l. 19. Saint Paul.—Galatians iv, 24; I Cor. iii, 16, 17; Hebrews ix, 24; Romans ii, 28, 29.

[249] P. 188, l. 25. That Moses, etc.—John vi, 32.

[250] P. 189, l. 3. For one thing alone is needful.—Luke x, 42.

[251] P. 189, l. 9. The breasts of the Spouse.—Song of Solomon iv, 5. [Pg 284]

[252] P. 189, l. 15. And the Christians, etc.—Romans vi, 20; viii, 14, 15.

[253] P. 189, l. 17. When Saint Peter, etc.—Acts xv. See Genesis xvii, 10; Leviticus xii, 3.

[254] P. 189, l. 27. Fac secundum, etc.—Exodus xxv, 40.

[255] P. 190, l. 1. Saint Paul.—1 Tim. iv, 3; 1 Cor. vii.

[256] P. 190, l. 7. The Jews, etc.—Hebrews viii, 5.

[257] P. 192, l. 15. That He should destroy death through death.—Hebrews ii, 14.

[258] P. 192, l. 30. Veri adoratores.—John iv, 23.

[259] P. 192, l. 30. Ecce agnus, etc.—John i, 29.

[260] P. 193, l. 15. Ye shall be free indeed.—John viii, 36.

[261] P. 193, l. 17. I am the true bread from heaven.—Ibid., vi, 32.

[262] P. 194, l. 27. Agnus occisus, etc.—Apoc. xiii, 8.

[263] P. 194, l. 34. Sede a dextris meis.—Ps. cx, 1.

[264] P. 195, l. 12. A jealous God.—Exodus xx, 5.

[265] P. 195, l. 14. Quia confortavit seras.—Ps. cxlvii, 13.

[266] P. 195, l. 17. The closed mem.—The allusions here are to certain peculiarities in Jewish writing. There are some letters written in two ways, closed or open, as the mem.

[267] P. 199, l. 1. Great Pan is dead.—Plutarch, De Defect. Orac., xvii.

[268] P. 199, l. 2. Susceperunt verbum, etc.—Acts xvii, 11.

[269] P. 199, l. 20. The ruler taken from the thigh.—Genesis xlix, 10.

[270] P. 208, l. 6. Make their heart fat.—Is. vi, 10; John xii, 40.

[271] P. 209, l. 1. Non habemus regem nisi Cæsarem.—John xix, 15.

[272] P. 218, l. 17. In Horeb, etc.—Deut. xviii, 16-19.

[273] P. 220, l. 34. Then they shall teach, etc.—Jeremiah xxxi, 34.

[274] P. 221, l. 1. Your sons shall prophesy.—Joel ii, 28.

[275] P. 221, l. 20. Populum, etc.—Is. lxv, 2; Romans x, 21.

[276] P. 222, l. 25. Eris palpans in meridie.—Deut. xxviii, 29.

[277] P. 222, l. 26. Dabitur liber, etc.—Is. xxix, 12. The quotation is inaccurate.

[278] P. 223, l. 24. Quis mihi, etc.—Job xix, 23-25.

[279] P. 224, l. 1. Pray, etc.—The fragments here are Pascal's notes on Luke. See chaps. xxii and xxiii.

[280] P. 225, l. 20. Excæca.—Is. vi, 10.

[281] P, 226, l. 9. Lazarus dormit, etc.—John xi, 11, 14.

[282] P. 226, l. 10. The apparent discrepancy of the Gospels.—To reconcile the apparent discrepancies in the Gospels, Pascal wrote a short life of Christ.

[283] P. 227, l. 13. Gladium tuum, potentissime.—Ps. xlv, 3.

[284] P. 228, l. 25. Ingrediens mundum.—Hebrews x, 5.

[285] P. 228, l. 26. Stone upon stone.—Mark xiii, 2.

[286] P. 229, l. 20. Jesus Christ at last, etc.—See Mark xii.

[287] P. 230, l. 1. Effundam spiritum meum.—Joel ii, 28.[Pg 285]

[288] P. 230, l. 6. Omnes gentes ... eum.—Ps. xxii, 27.

[289] P. 230, l. 7. Parum est ut, etc.—Is. xlix, 6.

[290] P. 230, l. 7. Postula a me.—Ps. ii, 8.

[291] P. 230, l. 8. Adorabunt ... reges.—Ps. lxxii, 11.

[292] P. 230, l. 8. Testes iniqui.—Ps. xxv, 11.

[293] P. 230, l. 8. Dabit maxillam percutienti.—Lamentations iii, 30.

[294] P. 230, l. 9. Dederunt fel in escam.—Ps. lxix, 21.

[295] P. 230, l. 11. I will bless them that bless thee.—Genesis xii, 3.

[296] P. 230, l. 12. All nations blessed in his seed.—Ibid., xxii, 18.

[297] P. 230, l. 13. Lumen ad revelationem gentium.—Luke ii, 32.

[298] P. 230, l. 14. Non fecit taliter, etc.—Ps. cxlvii, 20.

[299] P. 230, l. 20. Bibite ex hoc omnes.—Matthew xxvi, 27.

[300] P. 230, l. 22. In quo omnes peccaverunt.—Romans v, 12.

[301] P. 230, l. 26. Ne timeas pusillus grex.—Luke xii, 32.

[302] P. 230, l. 29. Qui me, etc.—Matthew x, 40.

[303] P. 230, l. 32. Saint John.—Luke i, 17.

[304] P. 230, l. 33. Jesus Christ.—Ibid., xii, 51.

[305] P. 231, l. 5. Omnis Judæa, etc.—Mark i, 5.

[306] P. 231, l. 7. From these stones, etc.—Matthew iii, 9.

[307] P. 231, l. 9. Ne convertantur, etc.—Mark iv, 12.

[308] P. 231, l. 11. Amice, ad quid venisti?—Matthew xxvi, 50.

[309] P. 231, l. 31. What is a man, etc.—Luke ix, 25.

[310] P. 231, l. 32. Whosoever will, etc.—Ibid., 24.

[311] P. 232, l. 1. I am not come, etc.—Matthew v, 17.

[312] P. 232, l. 2. Lambs took not, etc.—See John i, 29.

[313] P. 232, l. 4. Moses.—Ibid., vi, 32; viii, 36.

[314] P. 232, l. 15. Quare, etc.—Ps. ii, 1, 2.

[315] P. 233, l. 8. I have reserved me seven thousand.—1 Kings xix, 18.

[316] P. 234, l. 27. Archimedes.—The founder of statics and hydrostatics. He was born at Syracuse in 287 B.C., and was killed in 212 B.C. He was not a prince, though a relative of a king. M. Havet points out that Cicero talks of him as an obscure man (Tusc, v, 23).

[317] P. 235, l. 33. In sanctificationem et in scandalum.—Is. viii, 14.

[318] P. 238, l. 11. Jesus Christ.—Mark ix, 39.

[319] P. 239, l. 7. Rejoice not, etc.—Luke x, 20.

[320] P. 239, l. 12. Scimus, etc.—John iii, 2.

[321] P. 239, l. 25. Nisi fecissem ... haberent.—Ibid., xv, 24.

[322] P. 239, l. 32. The second miracle.—Ibid., iv, 54.

[323] P. 240, l. 6. Montaigne.—Essais, ii, 26, and iii, 11.

[324] P. 242, l. 9. Vatable.—Professor of Hebrew at the Collège Royal, founded by Francis I. An edition of the Bible with notes under his name, which were not his, was published in 1539.

[325] P. 242, l. 19. Omne regnum divisum.—Matthew xii, 25; Luke xi, 17.[Pg 286]

[326] P. 242, l. 23. Si in digito ... vos.—Luke xi, 20.

[327] P. 243, l. 12. Q. 113, A. 10, Ad. 2.—Thomas Aquinas's Summa, Pt. I, Question 113, Article 10, Reply to the Second Objection.

[328] P. 243, l. 18. Judæi signa petunt, etc.—I Cor. i, 22.

[329] P. 243, l. 23. Sed vos, etc.—John x, 26.

[330] P. 246, l. 15. Tu quid dicis? etc.—John ix, 17, 33.

[331] P. 247, l. 14. Though ye believe not, etc.—John x, 38.

[332] P. 247, l. 25. Nemo facit, etc.—Mark ix, 39.

[333] P. 247, l. 27. A sacred relic.—This is a reference to the miracle of the Holy Thorn. Marguerite Périer, Pascal's niece, was cured of a fistula lachrymalis on 24 March, 1656, after her eye was touched with this sacred relic, supposed to be a thorn from the crown of Christ. This miracle made a great impression upon Pascal.

[334] P. 248, l. 23. These nuns.—Of Port-Royal, as to which, see note on page 110, line 16, above. They were accused of Calvinism.

[335] P. 248, l. 28. Vide si, etc.—Ps. cxxxix, 24.

[336] P. 249, l. 1. Si tu, etc.—Luke xxii, 67.

[337] P. 249, l. 2. Opera quæ, etc.—John v, 36; x, 26-27.

[338] P. 249, l. 7. Nemo potest, etc.—John iii, 2.

[339] P. 249, l. 11. Generatio prava, etc.—Matthew xii, 39.

[340] P. 249, l. 14. Et non poterat facere.—Mark vi, 5.

[341] P. 249, l. 16. Nisi videritis, non creditis.—John iv, 8, 48.

[342] P. 249, l. 23. Tentat enim, etc.—Deut. xiii, 3.

[343] P. 249, l. 25. Ecce prædixi vobis: vos ergo videte.—Matthew xxiv, 25, 26.

[344] P. 250, l. 7. We have Moses, etc.—John ix, 29.

[345] P. 250, l. 30. Quid debui.—Is. v, 3, 4. The Vulgate is Quis est quod debui ultra facere vineæ meæ, et non feci ei.

[346] P. 251, l. 12. Bar-jesus blinded.—Acts xiii, 6-11.

[347] P. 251, l. 14. The Jewish exorcists.—Ibid., xix, 13-16.

[348] P. 251, l. 18. Si angelus.—Galatians i, 8.

[349] P. 252, l. 10. An angel from heaven.—See previous note.

[350] P. 252, l. 14. Father Lingende.—Claude de Lingendes, an eloquent Jesuit preacher, who died in 1660.

[351] P. 252, l. 33. Ubi est Deus tuus?—Ps. xiii, 3.

[352] P. 252, l. 34. Exortum est, etc.—Ps. cxii, 4.

[353] P. 253, l. 6. Saint Xavier.—Saint François Xavier, the friend of Ignatius Loyola, became a Jesuit.

[354] P. 253, l. 9. Væ qui, etc.—Is. x, I.

[355] P. 253, l. 24. The five propositions.—See Preface.

[356] P. 253, l. 36. To seduce, etc.—Mark xiii, 22.

[357] P. 254, l. 6. Si non fecissem.—John xv, 24.

[358] P. 255, l. 11. Believe in the Church.—Matthew xviii, 17-20.

[359] P. 257, l. 14. They.—The Jansenists, who believed in the system[Pg 287] of evangelical doctrine deduced from Augustine by Cornelius Jansen (1585-1638), the Bishop of Ypres. They held that interior grace is irresistible, and that Christ died for all, in reaction against the ordinary Catholic dogma of the freedom of the will, and merely sufficient grace.

[360] P. 258, l. 4. A time to laugh, etc.—Eccles. iii, 4.

[361] P. 258, l. 4. Responde. Ne respondeas.—Prov. xxvi, 4, 5.

[362] P. 260, l. 3. Saint Athanasius.—Patriarch of Alexandria, accused of rape, of murder, and of sacrilege. He was condemned by the Councils of Tyre, Aries, and Milan. Pope Liberius is said to have finally ratified the condemnation in A.D. 357. Athanasius here stands for Jansenius, Saint Thersea for Mother Angélique, and Liberius for Clement IX.

[363] P. 261, l. 17. Vos autem non sic.—Luke xxii, 26.

[364] P. 261, l. 23. Duo aut tres in unum.—John x, 30; First Epistle of St. John, V, 8.

[365] P. 262, l. 18. The Fronde.—The party which rose against Mazarin and the Court during the minority of Louis XIV. They led to civil war.

[366] P. 262, l. 25. Pasce oves meas.—John xxi, 17.

[367] P. 263, l. 14. Jeroboam.—I Kings xii, 31.

[368] P. 265, l. 21. The servant, etc.—John xv, 15.

[369] P. 266, l. 4. He that is not, etc.—Matthew xii, 30.

[370] P. 266, l. 5. He that is not, etc.—Mark ix, 40.

[371] P. 266, l. 11. Humilibus dot gratiam.—James iv, 6.

[372] P. 266, l. 12. Sui eum non, etc.—John i, 11, 12.

[373] P. 266, l. 33. We will be as the other nations.—I Sam. viii, 20.

[374] P. 268, l. 19. Vince in bono malum.—Romans xii, 21.

[375] P. 268, l. 26. Montalte.—See note on page 6, line 30, above.

[376] P. 269, l. 11. Probability.—The doctrine in casuistry that of two probable views, both reasonable, one may follow his own inclinations, as a doubtful law cannot impose a certain obligation. It was held by the Jesuits, the famous religious order founded in 1534 by Ignatius Loyola. This section of the Pensées is directed chiefly against them.

[377] P. 269, l. 22. Coacervabunt sibi magistros.—2 Tim. iv, 3.

[378] P. 270, l. 3. These.—The writers of Port-Royal.

[379] P. 270, l. 15. The Society.—The Society of Jesus.

[380] P. 271, l. 15. Digna necessitas.—Book of Wisdom xix, 4.

[Pg 291]

14341224R00192

Printed in Poland
by Amazon Fulfillment
Poland Sp. z o.o., Wrocław